A Union of Diversity

The European Union's motto, 'United in Diversity', contrasts with the cultural standardization entailed in the formation of nation-states and the forging of political identities in Europe. So what does being 'united in diversity' mean? Focusing on language politics and policies, this book offers a thorough assessment of the implications of cultural and linguistic diversity for the process of constructing a European polity. It sheds light on some of the most pressing problems associated with contemporary identity politics. It is often claimed that the recurrent celebration of diversity in Europe's programmatic declarations has an effective political impact. Kraus offers a critical analysis of how the European Union has responded to the normative challenge of creating an institutional frame for integration, which allows cultural differences to be transcended without ignoring them.

PETER A. KRAUS is Professor at the Faculty of Social Sciences and Chair of Ethnic Relations at the University of Helsinki. He has previously been an associate professor of political science at Humboldt University in Berlin, Acting Chair of Political Science and Political Sociology at the University of Frankfurt, a John F. Kennedy Memorial Fellow at the Center of European Studies at Harvard University and a Theodor Heuss Visiting Lecturer at the New School in New York. He has published widely and in several languages on problems of democratic transition and consolidation; politics in Southern Europe; ethnicity, nationalism and identity politics; and the present dilemmas of European integration. Among his publications in German are the monographs *Nationalismus und Demokratie: Politik im spanischen Staat der Autonomen Gemeinschaften* (*Nationalism and Democracy: Politics in the Spanish State of the Autonomous Communities*, 1996) and *Eine kleine Geschichte Kataloniens* (*A Little History of Catalonia*, 2007, with W. L. Bernecker and T. Eßer).

Themes in European Governance

Series Editor
Andreas Føllesdal

Editorial Board

The evolving European systems of governance, in particular the European Union, challenge and transform the state, the most important locus of governance and political identity and loyalty over the past 200 years. The series *Themes in European Governance* aims to publish the best theoretical and analytical scholarship on the impact of European governance on the core institutions, policies and identities of nation-states. It focuses upon the implications for issues such as citizenship, welfare, political decision-making and economic, monetary and fiscal policies. An initiative of Cambridge University Press and the Programme on Advanced Research on the Europeanisation of the Nation-State (ARENA), Norway, the series aims to provide theoretically informed studies analysing key issues at the European level and within European states. Volumes in the series will be of interest to scholars and students of Europe both within Europe and worldwide. They will be of particular relevance to those interested in the development of sovereignty and governance of European states and in the issues raised by multilevel governance and multinational integration throughout the world.

Other books in the series:

Continued after the Index

A Union of Diversity

Language, Identity and Polity-Building in Europe

Peter A. Kraus

University of Helsinki

CAMBRIDGE
UNIVERSITY PRESS

CAMBRIDGE UNIVERSITY PRESS
Cambridge, New York, Melbourne, Madrid, Cape Town, Singapore,
São Paulo, Delhi

Cambridge University Press
32 Avenue of the Americas, New York, NY 10013-2473, USA

www.cambridge.org
Information on this title: www.cambridge.org/9780521676724

First published 2008

Printed in the United States of America

A catalog record for this publication is available from the British Library.

Library of Congress Cataloging in Publication Data

Kraus, Peter A.
    A Union of diversity: language, identity and polity-building in Europe/
    Peter A. Kraus.
        p. cm. – (Themes in european governance)
    Includes bibliographical references and index.
    ISBN 978-0-521-85939-4 (hardback) – ISBN 978-0-521-67672-4 (pbk.)
    1. Language and culture – European Union countries. 2. Politics and culture –
    European Union countries. 3. European Union countries – Languages –
    Political aspects. I. Title. II. Series.

    P35.5.E85K83   2008
    306.4′49094–dc22   2007037504

ISBN   978-0-521-85939-4 hardback
ISBN   978-0-521-67672-4 paperback

Contents

List of Tables and Figure

Tables

Figure

Preface

Language politics and language policies played a crucial role in the historical processes of nation-state formation. Cultural and political integration in modern societies is largely based upon language. Thus, the making of nation-states went hand in hand with political attempts to introduce and maintain standardized communication codes. At later stages of political development, language policy was frequently associated with the goal of establishing a comprehensive and democratic public sphere. In multilingual settings, however, the political definition of a common language regime often became a matter of conflict. These general observations hold particularly true in the context of European history. It is in Europe where the idea of the national language originated and where it became inextricably connected with the dynamics of nation- and state-building. All over Europe, the forging of modern political identities entailed introducing communicative practices based on shared linguistic standards.

Against this background, it is quite obvious that the language issue bears extraordinary relevance if we want to assess to what extent the former logic of political integration has undergone substantial changes. We are experiencing the emergence of 'postnational' patterns of identification, which will ultimately reduce the salience of our 'national' attachments. The European Union has often been characterized as a regional harbinger of a coming global age of postnationalism. Accordingly, analyzing the role of language in the process of building Europe should improve our knowledge on the actual scope of the transition from 'national' to 'postnational' forms of political association in this part of the world.

At the same time, focusing on the role language and languages play in creating a 'union of diversity' will allow us to discuss some of the most demanding normative challenges related to present-day identity politics in a thorough way: Language can be considered a 'hard' evidence for how *cultural* elements play a role in the construction of our *civic* identities. In Europe (as elsewhere), the contemporary discourse on citizens' rights tends to accept the intrinsic value of linguistic bonds, thereby conceding that members of smaller language groups deserve to be protected against assimilationist pressures. Yet the complex setting of the European Union reveals that there may be a potential trade-off between recognizing the value of linguistic pluralism and creating an institutional context that allows for smooth and functional communication. At any rate, it should not be taken for granted that the recurrent celebration of diversity in the Union's programmatic declarations of intent has an effective impact on the often rather harsh realm of European *realpolitik*.

Acknowledgments

There were many people who helped me to move on with this study, and there were quite a few occasions on which I had the chance to present and discuss my ideas. All lists of gratitude are bound to be incomplete, but I would still like to point out a few people and a few places that played an important role on the long trajectory leading to this monograph. My stay as a Kennedy Fellow at the Center for European Studies at Harvard University in 2000–2001 gave me an exceptional opportunity to gain momentum on the project. In the context of that stay, my gratitude goes to Karen Alter, Lars-Erik Cederman, Abby Collins, Pratap Mehta, Andy Moravcsik, Glyn Morgan, Andrea Sangiovanni and Judith Vichniak. Looking back at the long and rewarding period I spent in Berlin at Humboldt University, I thank Henri Band, Harald Bluhm, Klaus Eder, Michael Kreile, Ulrich K. Preuß, Stefan Solleder and Christina Wendt; in different ways, they all helped me to keep momentum. Claus Offe definitely deserves special mention for his constructive criticisms and his continuous encouragement. I also thank those who offered me a forum for discussing European identity politics at the University of Frankfurt, in particular Rainer Forst, Christian Lammert, Hans-Jürgen Puhle and Martin Saar.

My research in Brussels would not have been possible without the support of Johan De Deken, Renée Haferkamp and Barbara Rhode. Among the numerous experts I met at the headquarters of the European Commission as well as at the General Secretariat of the Council of the European Union in Brussels, let me specifically mention Ian Andersen, Hans Brunmayr and Paul Nemitz. Without their help, it would have been much more difficult for me to proceed with my agenda in the 'capital' of Europe.

Moreover, my thanks go to Ulrich Ammon (Duisburg), Thomas Faist (Toronto/Bielefeld), Wolfgang Merkel (Social Science Research Center Berlin), Nadine Berenguier (University of New Hampshire), Isabelle de Courtivron and Bernd Widdig (Massachusetts Institute of Technology), Juan Linz (Yale), Gary Marks (University of North Carolina at Chapel Hill), Jan-Werner Müller (Oxford/Princeton), Ari Zolberg (New School for Social Research), Ronald Beiner and Phil Triadafilopoulos (Toronto), Yolande Cohen, Alain Gagnon and Laurence McFalls (Montréal), Oliver Schmidtke and James Tully (Victoria), Richard Bellamy (London), Dario Castiglione and Chris Longman (Exeter), Lynn Dobson (Edinburgh), Philippe Van Parijs (Brussels), Jürgen Nagel and Ferran Requejo (Universitat Pompeu Fabra, Barcelona), Kari Palonen (Jyväskylä) as well as Erik Allardt, Maria Kreander and Heikki Patomäki (Helsinki).

A previous version of this book was published in German in 2004 (*Europäische Öffentlichkeit und Sprachpolitik*, Frankfurt: Campus). The English edition includes substantial revisions and updates. Several former sections disappeared; other sections were largely modified to take into account recent political developments and additional sources; new sections were added. Eventually, therefore, we cannot speak of the same book anymore, and I very much hope that the changes have contributed to improving the argumentation. Ciaran Cronin was an invaluable support in making this volume possible, translating parts of the German manuscript and editing those chapters that I chose to (re)write in English myself.

Material in Chapter 2 has been included in 'Cultural Pluralism and European Polity-Building: Neither Westphalia nor Cosmopolis', published in the *Journal of Common Market Studies*, 41 (2003), 665–86. Parts of Chapter 3 have appeared as 'A Union of Peoples? Diversity and the Predicaments of a Multinational Polity', in *Political Theory and the European Constitution*, edited by Lynn Dobson and Andreas Føllesdal (2004). Chapter 4 incorporates parts of 'Intercultural Recognition and Linguistic Diversity in Europe', in *The Language Question in Europe and Diverse Societies*, edited by Dario Castiglione and Chris Longman (2007). In Section 6.4 of Chapter 6, I drew on some material that was also used for 'Transnational Communication and the European Demos' (with Lars-Erik Cederman), in *Digital Formations*, edited by Robert Latham and Saskia Sassen (2005).

I express my gratitude to Andreas Føllesdal as series editor and John Haslam at Cambridge University Press for their patience and for their support in the publication of this project.

Finally, I dedicate this to my (multilingual) family, to Reetta, Aura and Pau.

A Union of Diversity

1 Introduction: The dynamics of European integration

The 'European question', namely, the question concerning the foundations of the political unification of Europe and its prospects of success, has by now become primarily a question of democracy. It touches, on the one hand, upon the impacts of processes of Europeanization on democratic will-formation in the member states of the European Union (EU) and, on the other, upon the possibilities of a democratization of the Union itself. Both aspects of the question have become objects of heated controversies that have long since spread beyond the boundaries of academic circles and have secured a fixed and prominent place on the political agenda. As the debates on the unfortunate European constitution have revealed, the fronts in these controversies are quite intricate, depending on ideological preference and national background. Nevertheless, one can discern a rough polarization between those who sceptically regard integration as a progressive hollowing out of the sovereignty of the democratic nation-state and those who embrace it instead as an opportunity to disclose new democratic options beyond the nation-state.

However, there appears to be widespread agreement, notwithstanding numerous other conflicts, that the technocratic approach of the initial decades of integration is no longer viable. Since the adoption and ratification of the Treaty on European Union at the beginning of the 1990s, the situation has been marked by continuing – and some would say, increasingly acute – problems of legitimation of policy-making at the European level and by a more and more contentious treatment of European issues in the domestic affairs of the nation-states. The desire to strengthen the basis of legitimation of transnational governance in substantial ways and to circumscribe clearly the competences of the Union in relation to the member states found expression in Europe's constitutional experiment. However, an EU constitution – should it eventually come into force – would not overcome the dilemma which seems to be a necessary concomitant of the construction of a comprehensive transnational institutional framework: The creation of a constitutional system of governance at the European level is subject from the beginning to the

1

expectation that political power must derive its justification from a collective context that is, in the final analysis, coextensive with the contours of a political community that cannot be defined exclusively in institutional terms. Yet in contrast with the classical nation-states, the EU cannot be regarded as the political form of organization of an already existing 'European nation' nor is it in a position, let alone authorized, to undertake the project of constituting such a nation 'from above'. In the most general sense, the resulting dilemma is the topic of this study.

On the other hand, the political challenges associated with this dilemma, viewed from the perspective of an up-to-date theory of democracy, are also the source of possibly the principal normative appeal of the EU. For the legitimation of political authority in the Union must of necessity take place simultaneously at the levels of the political institutional order *and* that of the political community. In other words, the agent with the task of founding a community and serving as the symbol of European rule is from the beginning an emperor without clothes and is destined to remain such. A major expression of this 'imperial nakedness' is the requirement that the project of integration must be realized in a way that accords the greatest possible respect to the political–cultural 'distinctiveness' of the member states and the substate constitutional entities of the EU. The aspiration to create 'an ever closer union among the peoples of Europe', as enunciated in the Maastricht Treaty, should on no account – at least according to the official doctrine of integration – entail that specific, for example, linguistically based, cultural identities are impaired.

In this introductory chapter I first want to trace succinctly the main lines of political development in the process of European unification since the foundation of the European Economic Community (EEC) and to outline the changes in the situation after Maastricht. I will then sketch the interrelation between constitutional politics and cultural diversity in the EU, identify the essential features of the problem I want to address and explain the plan of the present study.

1.1   The Transnational Political Space of the European Union

The first phase in the process of European integration reached its conclusion with the coming into force of the Treaty of Rome in January 1958. The EEC created by the Treaty proved to be the interim high point of a development to which the federalist advocates of the idea of Europe after the Second World War had initially attached far higher expectations.[1] In place of the 'United States of Europe', there arose a community of six composed of Italy, France, Germany and the Benelux countries which implied, in addition to a customs union and the integration of markets in particular sectors, the harmonization of regulations in such policy areas as agriculture, transport and competition. Hence only a fraction of the federalists' hopes was initially realized. On the other hand, the formation of the EEC unleashed a dynamic that would fundamentally alter the overall political countenance of Europe.

This is not the place for a detailed examination of the causes and background conditions which shaped the initial course of European integration.[2] Summarizing in a very rough way a complex mixture of political parameters and impulses, one can highlight three factors in particular in the constellation which decisively shaped the concrete course of the project of unification between 1945 and 1960:

- Important in the first place was the desire for a stable European peace which substantially characterized the first generation of 'architects' of Europe's institutional framework, among whom must be numbered such figures as Jean Monnet, Robert Schuman, Alcide de Gasperi and Walter Hallstein. This desire played a major role in the immediate influence of the consequences of the Second World War; for the construction of the EEC was seen as a major contribution to erecting a European security community. The specific concern was to bind Germany into a system of reciprocal controls and guarantees. In this respect at least, the doctrine of European federalism attained a relatively concrete influence on politics. In the years following 1945, the newly formed European Movement was tireless in its calls to surmount the age-old conflicts between nation-states. Among Christian Democrats and Social Democrats in France, Germany and Italy, there were numerous points of personal contact between the Eurofederalists and the newly emerging political elites.
- The project of integration, however, was soon restricted exclusively to the western half of the continent on account of the Cold War. In fact, the East–West conflict developed into a moment from which the EEC and later also the European Community (EC) derived important impulses. Plans to construct a European Defence Community (EDC) supported primarily by France and Germany were quickly

---

[1] On the ideas of the Eurofederalists in the post-war period see Niess (2001).
[2] Of the copious literature devoted to this topic, I would mention here the following selection of studies reflecting in part different and in part complementary perspectives: Dedman (1996), Loth (1996), Milward (1992), O'Neill (1996) and Schneider (1997).

shelved in the 1950s. The security policy concerns of the EDC were subsumed into the North Atlantic Treaty Organization (NATO) under the hegemonic influence of the USA. Nonetheless, the establishment of the state socialist alternative on European territory had consequences beyond the level of military strategy. The competition between the systems remains an important key for understanding the peculiar mixture of market-oriented economics and moderate dirigisme that marked the EEC its constitutive phase.

- Therefore, the final driving force behind European unification was the convergence of national economic priorities in the six member states of the EEC. The decrease in the costs of economic transactions associated with the institutionalization of the Common Market was an option clearly favoured by a large majority of the dominant interest groups in the member states. Market integration corresponded with phases of growth that undoubtedly played a major role in the consolidation of a Western European 'welfare model' between 1950 and 1970. As the successive enlargements of the original circle of EEC members show, participation in the project of integration became for an increasing number of European states a recipe for success that seemed to combine the preservation of a sufficient degree of political autonomy with economic prosperity and access to a transnational level of problem-solving.

The dynamic early years were followed by a period of political stagnation after 1960. France under de Gaulle blocked efforts aimed at reinforcing the organs of the Community. Thus for many years the consolidation of the Common Market had no noteworthy effects in the area of political integration. Only with the accession of Denmark, Ireland and the United Kingdom in 1973 did the European institutional framework slowly begin to get in motion again. After 1980 there were new major breakthroughs. In 1986, the Single European Act brought a revision of the Treaty of Rome and the transition to qualified majority voting for important areas of regulation of the Common Market. With Maastricht a further high point on the road to a political union was reached.[3] The institutional reforms during the one and a half decades between 1981 and 1995 leading up to the Maastricht Treaty were book-ended by the southern and northern enlargements.

---

[3] For an assessment of the negotiations that culminated in the Treaty on European Union, see Keohane and Hoffmann (1991), Kreile (1992), Sbragia (1992), Weiler (1991) and Wildenmann (1991).

What were the essential characteristics of the development of the EEC/EC[4] as a political project up to Maastricht? The division of the continent continued to operate as a powerful external incentive for integration in the west even after the period leading to the foundation of the EEC. Political affiliation to the community of Europe was shaped above all by three components: commitment to liberal democracy, to anticommunism and to a model of capitalism cushioned by the welfare state (Wallace 1999: 293–4). Otherwise, the political programme of (Western) European unification remained relatively diffuse. Integration occurred primarily under the banner of shared economic imperatives. Ultimately, the domain of market integration must be regarded to this day as the primary pillar of the EC/EU. It is also certainly important in this context that the unification process can be attributed only to a very limited degree to the successes of a transnational movement that inscribed 'Europeanism' on its banner. After the EEC had been established, the Eurofederalists and their aims rarely occupied a prominent place on the stage of European *realpolitik*. Accordingly, for many years positions on integration did not play a central role in political controversies among the influential political parties in the member states either. 'Europe' was rather the result of an understanding among elites who could count on the 'permissive consensus'[5] of the affected populations of the nation-states. When it came to implementing the integration agenda, the *méthode Monnet* held sway: political-administrative action at a supranational level was often presented as a matter of following supposed factual constraints. Consequently, European will-formation exhibited pronounced technocratic features. Politics in the EC/EU appeared to be merely a matter for expert specialists. It is no accident that law served as the preferred medium of integration. In this context the *acquis communautaire* stood not for decisions of political principle but rather for an 'incrementalistically' expanding catalogue of rules.

The 1990s brought a lasting change in the situation described, as the European question turned into a subject of often heated debates in virtually all of the member states. The unification process became politicized at a completely new level. The epochal watershed of 1989 played a primary role in this regard. The end of the East–West conflict meant that an often implicit yet highly significant external impulse for integration in the west of the European continent was removed. At the same time,

---

[4] The EC was formed in 1967 through the fusion of the EEC with the institutions of the European Coal and Steel Community and Euratom.

[5] The application of the concept of *permissive consensus* to the context of European integration goes back to Lindbergh and Scheingold (1970); see also Hix (1999: 134–5).

the collapse of the state socialist system in Eastern Europe produced a close interconnection between the problems of deepening and enlarging the Union. It posed unexpected and extremely difficult problems for the political actors on the European stage. The escalating crisis in the Balkans into the wake of 1989 and the problems of achieving an effective crisis management on the borders of the Union within the framework of the European institutions elevated the Common Foreign and Security Policy to a central topic on the European political agenda. In this way, integration became centred once again on a key political domain which had been neglected since the failure of the EDC or had been entrusted to the US-dominated decision-making framework of NATO.

An additional prominent factor driving change was clearly Maastricht itself. The signal sent out by the Treaty on European Union directed the political spotlight onto the project of integration in all member states. Even though the introduction of citizenship of the Union in the EU Treaty had a largely symbolic character, it had the effect of placing the question of the relation between the European institutions and the European citizenry on the agenda. Finally, over and above Maastricht, the transition to the Economic and Monetary Union meant that the 'European dimension' acquired an enormously increased visibility and concrete practical content for the citizens. The increase in political importance of Europe is also clearly apparent from the dynamic development of the system of transnational institutions. The EC/EU has steadily increased its competences vis-à-vis the nation-states. In a considerable number of areas of political regulation, the member states only implement what has been decided upon in the transnational arena. Thus the institutional activities unfolding at the European level have multiplied steadily over the course of the past decades (Wessels 1997).

Against the background sketched, it is hardly surprising that the need for legitimation of the EU has increased dramatically since Maastricht. Europe has become a highly controversial topic in several member states.[6] The permissive consensus which for many years facilitated the advance of the project of integration seems in the meantime to have given way to much more suspicious attitudes on the issue of European polity-building. The efforts to define a new mode of consensus found expression, on the one hand, in the fact that Europe's 'finality' is again a topic of lively debate. On the other hand, these efforts have led to a series of more or

---

[6] The Eurobarometer surveys commissioned at regular intervals by the European Commission are informative in this regard. The findings of the decade following Maastricht can be summarized in the formula 'Europe divides' (on this see also Section 3.3 of Chapter 3).

less controversial proposals for democratizing the EU as well as in the drafting of a European constitution.

1.2   Integration and Legitimation in a Diverse Polity

What are the bases required for building a political community beyond the realm of the nation-states? A question that had been prominent in the initial stage of the integration process has come to the fore again in the debates revolving around the European constitution. Pioneers of unification such as Jean Monnet believed that Europe should be the product of a politics of small steps. The strengthening of the supranational dimension would be a quasi-automatic consequence of the successive agreements adopted to regulate specific policy areas. Thus the progress of integration depended essentially on intensifying the interaction of elites and functional groups rather than on obtaining the strong normative commitment of the 'peoples of Europe'. The purpose of an 'enlightened technocracy' was ultimately to pave the way for a European federation. The advantages of pooling expertise and resources at the European level would soon become unquestionable enough to provide Community institutions with a high level of a legitimacy of their own, which would give them greater political weight vis-à-vis the national governments.

The developments since Maastricht are a striking evidence of how limited the success of the strategy to count on functional imperatives for securing political loyalties has been. After 1990 the former 'permissive consensus' seems to have turned into a 'diffuse scepticism'. Ultimately, the rejection of the Treaty establishing a Constitution for Europe in the referenda held in France and the Netherlands in spring of 2005 and the ensuing political turbulences may well be interpreted as the symptoms of a crisis of legitimation that had been latent for a longer time. When the uniting of Europe was still an incipient phenomenon, Karl Deutsch emphasized that the political dynamics of processes of integration cannot be properly understood without taking into account their social embeddedness.[7] Europe's constitutional impasse has reconfirmed this view quite dramatically. Hence, departing from approaches that have focused primarily on institutional design in a narrow sense and devoted much space to discussing issues such as the appropriate number of Commissioners in an enlarged Union, the technicalities of qualified majority voting or the division of competences between the European Parliament and the

---

[7] Deutsch et al. (1957); for a more recent assessment of the socio-cultural aspects of integration see Cerutti and Rudolph (2001), Dewandre and Lenoble (1994), García (1993), Howe (1995), Laffan (1996) and Wallace (1997).

European Council, our analysis should be more sensitive of the societal factors involved in legitimizing a European polity. The precarious character of the structures that could sustain a transnational civic space in the EU reflects the shortcomings of a constitutional politics that has neglected the 'Europe of the citizens'. More than ever before, a substantial discussion of the perspectives of European constitution-making seems to require a thorough reflection on how Europe's institutional framework relates to the identity of the political subjects of the Union.

This takes us directly to the topic of the present study. Both for the identity of Europe as a political community and for the identity of a European civil society cultural diversity bears a crucial significance. Europe is a mosaic composed of different ethnic, regional or national patterns of identification, manifold historical traditions and a variegated set of languages and cultural standards. These should not be conceived of as static 'primordial' ties. The mosaic rather gives expression to a plurality of interpretive contexts that form specific political cultures. Such a plurality of cultures stands in no tension with democratic norms; it represents a repertoire of equally legitimate ways of connecting general political principles to particular life-worlds. Accordingly, Europe's constitutional discourse[8] establishes a close link between the affirmation of common civic ties and the protection of diversity. Thus, characteristically, the Treaty establishing a Constitution for Europe defines European identity along two main axes: on the one hand, a set of common political values demarcates the normative framework of unity; on the other hand, the constitution assigns cultural diversity a pivotal role within this framework. As stated in the constitutional text, the EU's motto reads 'united in diversity', and there are several paragraphs in the constitution which stress the high normative status diversity has for the construction of a European polity.

At first sight, such declarations of good intent may sound quite uncontroversial. Nonetheless, things begin to look more complicated as soon as we assess the meaning of diversity against the background experience of political integration in modern times. In the political order that emerged in Europe after the Peace of Westphalia, to strive for making discrete territorial units culturally homogeneous was to become the general rule. All over the continent, the processes of building modern polities – nation-states – and of creating a body of citizens were quite hostile to diversity.

---

[8] By constitutional discourse I do not only mean the contents of the European constitution in the strict sense; as I use it here, the term also refers to the main treaties and to other documents which point out the normative guidelines of integration, such as the Treaty of Rome, the Treaty on European Union or the Charter of Rights of the European Union.

To a significant extent, the historical legacy of state-building continues to permeate the mainstream of European constitutionalism up to our times. From the corresponding perspective, the argument is often made that the very lack of strong identity ties, of a feeling of 'peoplehood' at the European level, considerably hampers the chances to provide the EU with a proper constitutional framework. This view has increasingly come under the fire of the advocates of postnational and cosmopolitan approaches to political integration. They would hold that the European project's normative appeal lies precisely in not pretending to push for cultural homogeneity. The cosmopolitans' point that our understanding of integration today must not be governed by a one-sided fixation on previous national models is well taken. However, to accept the point does not relieve us from showing how diversity should be and is dealt with within the new kind of political community the EU is supposed to represent. While nationalists experience diversity as a problem, in the first place, cosmopolitans tend to underestimate the actual political effort involved in finding legitimate and effective ways of institutionalizing diversity.

From the angle adopted in this study, to make for unity in diversity is by no means a trivial endeavour. Rather, the question of how to constitute political unity – be it in terms of an integrated democratic collectivity or in terms of a common public sphere – under conditions of entrenched cultural diversity has to be one of the main challenges involved in the making of a citizens' Europe. The experience since Maastricht indicates that a political community of Europeans who are 'united in diversity' will not come into being as a simple by-product of constitution-making. After the rejection of the constitution in France and the Netherlands, the Union is facing an institutional crisis that has made it impossible to ignore that the bases of a common European identity cannot be established one-sidedly 'from above', in a top-down process. By now, it seems obvious that to be 'united in diversity' requires more than the combination of political good will and skilful constitutional engineering, if the motto is not supposed to be taken as mere rhetorical formula. After a protracted period of nationalist strife, during which the contending parties typically articulated their political goals in the name of mutually excluding cultural identities, the project of European integration was meant to entail an entirely new approach towards achieving political unity, an approach that would refrain from all attempts at creating a culturally homogeneous space, as they were characteristic of the history of state-making and nation-building in Europe. Yet, for reasons which will be put under closer scrutiny in the following chapters, the EU has thus far not been able to live up to its normative potential and to set up a truly innovative frame for responding to the challenges of diversity. Although Europe's constitutional discourse celebrates diversity in general and abstract terms, the diversity-related elements in the process of European polity-building remain blurred.

How the Union meets the challenge of diversity will have a great significance not only for the overall orientation of Europe's institutional politics in the coming decades. It is hardly an exaggeration to affirm that the question of diversity occupies a central place in all attempts at elaborating a theory of democracy that is up to our times. Few other issues have attracted as much attention in the current normative debates. One strand of these debates, which has been highly influential for my argumentation, regards recognition as a key category for reconciling cultural diversity and democratic citizenship. However, political philosophers and theorists have discussed the politics of recognition at a high level of abstraction. The constellation that we face in the EU at present offers an excellent opportunity to develop the concept in the context of the empirical analysis of an emerging institutional order.

To find a straightforward way to address the dilemmas posed by diversity in the Union, this study places its focus on the area of language policy. In the vast and sometimes diffuse realm of 'identity politics', language occupies a rather concrete and clear-cut territory. Thus the regulation of linguistic pluralism in Europe has evident practical consequences for the citizens of the Union. Europe's multilingualism is a very important factor when it comes to defining the terms of communication in a transnational political space. In the analyses of European language policy, there is often a tendency to concentrate upon 'utilitarian' criteria, which relate to the actual distribution of linguistic communication potentials and to communicative efficiency. I do certainly not pretend to deny that the instrumental aspects of language have to be fully taken into account when we reflect on the rules that should regulate transnational communication in Europe. In multilingual settings, it is typically the function of a lingua franca to facilitate a matter-of-fact and 'neutral' communication across language groups. Still, I think we have to choose a different approach to understand the linkage of diversity and recognition: a *political* theory of language must devote particular attention to the expressive aspects of linguistic identities and linguistic repertoires. From the expressive angle, language has a great bearing on how a community and its members understand 'themselves'. By endorsing in the institutional realm the connections that exist between language as a social bond and language as a source of self-esteem, the recognition of linguistic identities contributes substantially to the protection of individual freedoms. At this point, it should be emphasized that the sharp contrasting of an instrumental and of an expressive dimension of language that underlies the second part of this study is primarily motivated by heuristic intentions. In many situations of real communication, we will hardly be able to distinguish neatly between the two dimensions. Nonetheless, 'expressivity' retains its central importance for any attempt at grasping the specifically political aspects of linguistic attachments.

The present study has an explorative character. It moves along the borderlines of political theory, political sociology and comparative politics. While focusing on the dynamics of Europeanization, its aim is to shed light on normative key questions concerning the relationship between cultural diversity, language policy and democratic integration. The structure of the argumentation is as follows:

The second chapter summarizes contrasting views of Europe's potential for becoming a constitutional community. The differing assessments of the Union's constitutional momentum derive largely from differing positions regarding the socio-cultural foundations needed and available for constructing a democratic transnational polity. The constitutional debate thus takes us directly to examining to what extent and how political and cultural identities are intertwined in the European context.

In Chapter 3 my starting point is to show that in modern societies cultural identities must be conceived of as a result of the political institutionalization of cultural practices. Against this background, the interplay of culture and politics at the level of European institutions leads to particular 'identity dilemmas'. A peculiar and tension-ridden confluence of both 'thin' nationalism and of tendencies to 'transcend' the model of the nation-state seems to have a strong impact on the political development of the EC/EU. If it is to open up new paths on the terrain of constitutional politics, the Union needs to tackle the challenges posed by the 'multinational constellation' in present-day Europe.

Chapter 4 begins with an assessment of the relevance language has for the politics of recognition. Societal multilingualism has far-reaching implications for the constitution of a democratic polity. They become patent when we look at the institutional strategies adopted by Western European democracies in their dealing with language issues, as well as in the conflicts related to these strategies. The chapter concludes with a discussion of recent initiatives which aim at firmly anchoring the protection of linguistic identities in a catalogue of European civil rights.

The fifth chapter is devoted to examining the language regime that is at work *within* the EU's institutional framework. After scrutinizing the political logic underlying institutional multilingualism, I turn to the problems which are characteristic of the present situation. At the end of the chapter, I suggest a possible way to overcome the impasse in which the EU seems to have manoeuvred itself due to the contradictions built into its internal language regime.

Chapter 6 focuses on how the language issue connects with the problematic character of a European public sphere. The chapter offers a critical analysis of the parameters which have governed EU language policy in the field of *external* communication. In recent times, these parameters have included plans to enhance processes of political communication on a European scale by making massive use of new information technologies. Neither information technology nor the linguistic market alone, however, is a sufficient basis for finding language regulations that could bolster a dynamic of democratic political communication in Europe. Hence, I put forward a perspective that links the making of a European public sphere to the option of a converging multilingualism.

The final chapter reassesses the main results of the study in the light of the challenges of constitutional politics in Europe. On the one hand, I explore to what extent the principle of subsidiarity may serve as a normative support for an institutional politics of recognition in the EU. On the other hand, I reinterpret the concept of democratic self-determination in the context of European polity-building. The study concludes with a defence of politics as the appropriate medium for defining what it means to become a citizen in a union of diversity.

2   The European Union's democratic deficit and the search for a European demos

After Maastricht, there was increasing evidence that the permissive consensus which formerly sustained the European project had become fragile. Those who advocated a deepening of the Union faced considerable resistance. This was due in the first place to the successful mobilization of Euro-sceptical or anti-European political forces. The European Union (EU) became a preferred target of right-wing populist groups in several member states. It had to confront a growing antipathy on the part of important sectors of the established right as well, who considered that existential national interests would be endangered in the European polity. At the same time, parts of the socialist and social-democratic European left felt more and more uncomfortable in view of the dominant position that untamed market liberalism had attained in the formation of the Economic and Monetary Union. The manifestations of discontent towards the EU appeared to be particularly strong within the political spectrum of recent adherents such as Austria and Sweden. In the first case, they were concentrated on the right; in the second, on the left.

Moreover, the situation after Maastricht was marked by a silent crumbling of the diffuse support which the bulk of the public in almost all member states had shown for the EU over a long period of time. According to the Eurobarometer surveys regularly conducted for the European Commission, it seemed that, with the increasing politicization of European affairs, the proportion of Euro-sceptical citizens was increasing too. Yet rather than giving rise to active protest, the scepticism turned the previous diffuse support into an equally diffuse distrust or into indifference. Regarding citizens' involvement in European politics, the elections to the European Parliament held in 1999 and 2004 were successive low points in political participation.

Finally, the changes in Europe's political constellation became manifest in a lively debate on the legitimacy of the Union that reached well beyond academic circles. The starting point of this broad and still ongoing debate was the question of whether the EU suffers from a substantial democratic deficit. All over Europe, the issue generated a continuous flow of

13

controversial assessments.[1] Quite often, the conclusion drawn was that the EU would not be entitled to join its own institutional domain: should it apply for membership, the Union itself would not be admitted, as it failed to meet the democratic criteria which all of its members have to observe. The debate was an important factor in the dynamics which ultimately led to the drafting of a European constitution. Its advocates consider the document to be a decisive step along the route towards reinforcing the Union's political legitimacy.[2] Their view is that the constitution is not only necessary to assure Europe a higher level of democratic legitimacy; it is also held to be an indispensable instrument for dealing with the challenges posed by the eastern enlargement.[3] In this regard, the central argument is that a Union with 27 to 30 members will not be able to function without major institutional reforms.

This chapter will show that the problems related to the democratic deficit cannot be separated from the questions concerning the quality and the role of a European demos in the process of transnational polity-building. To assess these questions, I will focus on the social and cultural bases available for strengthening the EU as a political community and try to elaborate a suitable approach for understanding the intricate interplay of identity, culture and democracy in Europe today.

2.1   The Challenge of Democracy in the European Union

The constitutional debate has, once again, highlighted the novel political character of the EU. A main aspect of this novelty is that the European level of political rule does not reflect the typical structures of established statehood: Europe's prospective frontiers continue to be an open question, and the institutional form of a polity that is increasingly subject to the dynamics of differentiated integration can't but remain blurred. Thus, neither can a European democracy be linked to a clearly defined frame of territorial statehood[4], nor can democratic sovereignty in the Union be conceived of in the traditional terms of national sovereignty.

---

[1] See Schmitter (2000: 2–10) for an overview.

[2] For contrasting positions on the constitutional document see Bellamy (2005), Castiglione (2004), De Witte (2003), Dobson and Follesdal (2004) and Walker (2004).

[3] On the dialectics of deepening and enlarging the Union see Amato and Batt (1999) and Deubner (2003).

[4] In comparative research on democracy, the lack of such a link is frequently considered to be a factor that seriously hampers the prospects of democratization; cf. Linz and Stepan (1996: 16–37) or Przeworski et al. (1995: 19–33). In recent years, the experiences with failed states in different areas of the world seem to have led to a general renaissance of approaches which make democratization contingent upon successful nation- and state-building (cf. Fukuyama 2004, Ignatieff 2003, Krasner and Pascual 2005).

The EU may be regarded as the paradigmatic exponent of a sweeping transformation giving rise to transnational systems that severely limit the political, economic, social and cultural autonomy of nation-states (Dahl 1994: 26). While the supposed certainties enshrined in modern political thought become dubious, the fundamental elements of a proper theory of 'postnational government' (or rather, 'governance') are still to be laid down. Apparently, thus far the nation-states continue to be the essential points of reference in normative assessments of the European project. For some observers, the task is to unite them in a federation[5]; for others, priority must be given to safeguarding national sovereignty in the expanding net of trans-European relations. It remains to be seen whether the tendency to keep focusing on the classical model of the nation-state is not ultimately an obstacle to a closer understanding of the current problems of political integration in Europe.

Politics in the EU is politics in a multilevel system in which supranational, national and subnational actors, as well as functional interest groups, participate in political decision-making to varying degrees and according to varying rules. In this system, the institutional dispersion of regulatory competences eludes the traditional patterns of the division of political powers; at some point, the functions of constitutionally authorized *government* even seem to dissipate in the networks of transnational *governance*.[6] From the beginning, the constitutionalization of the Union was intended to create more transparent and legitimate forms of European governance and to delimit the different levels of decision-making in the transnational polity more clearly. In the same context, new sources of political legitimation were to be activated in order to overcome Europe's democracy deficit.

The debate on integration and democracy in Europe has two main dimensions. They are closely interconnected, yet analytically distinct. The *first dimension* relates to the delimitation of competences between the EU, the nation-states and – in countries with a federal state structure, such as Germany, Belgium or Spain – the subnational level. This delimitation would not only have to take into account criteria of functional efficiency; it should also make a substantial contribution to rendering multilevel politics more transparent and to securing the political competences of the member states and the regions vis-à-vis Brussels. The basic issue at stake here is the *compatibility of European polity-building*

---

[5] This is the idea of a federation of nation-states, which will be discussed at the end of this chapter.

[6] There is a vast literature which focuses on the EU as a multilevel system; see, among many others, Hooghe and Marks (2001), Jachtenfuchs and Kohler-Koch (1996) and Marks et al. (1996).

with the established realms of democratic rule in Europe. The application
of the principle of subsidiarity, which was introduced by the Treaty on
European Union and reaffirmed in the Treaty establishing a Constitution
for Europe, should make for good European governance and protect the
spaces of democratic self-rule embedded in the member states. From this
perspective, the legitimation of the EU as a new political order requires
that the democratic structures which evolved historically below the supranational level are not put at risk by the progress of integration.

However, the developments since Maastricht have shown that the
subsidiarity principle was never much more than the symbol of a dilatory
intergovernmental compromise; to the present, it lacks a specific meaning
in the Union's institutional framework. Ultimately, the principle was the
expression of a diffuse minimal consensus reflecting the fact that, when it
came to defining the political role of the supranational level, the member
states differed greatly in their propensities for integration. Subsidiarity
was embraced as a convenient mechanism for avoiding conflicts and
continuing the European project on the basis of differentiated integration
(Ebbinghaus and Kraus 1997). The potential subsidiarity might have
for lending bottom-up dynamics greater weight in Europe and reducing
the top-heaviness of EU politics has been relegated to a subordinate
role. Indeed, regarding the EU's democratic compatibility, the argument
is often made that the quality of democracy in the member states has
already been altered dramatically by the shift of political decision-making
to the European level. Even observers who are certainly not suspicious of
Euro-scepticism think that such a dynamic involves the danger of a
creeping erosion of the valuable stock of historically rooted democratic
practices.[7]

The area of economic and social policies offers one of the most characteristic examples of such a trend. When the Economic and Monetary Union was established, the dominance of rigidly market-oriented
liberal strategies implied that the nation-states lost significant leeway
for autonomous policy-making. This can be shown by the budgetary
and distributional restrictions which reflected the efforts of governments
throughout Europe to meet the convergence criteria set up for the introduction of the Euro. As important areas of decision-making are shifted
to the EU level, discussions of the agenda of democratic politics in the
member states seem to become an increasingly symbolic exercise. Since
the nation-state remains their environment for organizing and mobilizing, the conflicting parties are scarcely able to settle central political issues any longer (Scharpf 1996, Streeck 1996). Regarding these

---

[7] See, for example, Abromeit (2002) or Kohler-Koch (1998).

developments, we must keep in mind the historical symbiosis of liberal democracy and the welfare state in Western Europe after the Second World War, a symbiosis in which the old European Economic Community/European Community (EC) played a functional role. Over several decades, the Europeanization of markets was absolutely compatible with the extension of country-specific welfare provisions. However, the situation changed drastically with the transition from the EC to the EU. Market integration was accomplished well before the contours that an in any case diffuse social dimension should assume on a transnational scale were defined.[8] At the same time, the heightened competition between member states committed to meet the convergence criteria required by the Monetary Union led to a growing pressure to reduce national welfare entitlements (Wallace 1997: 227).

Against the sceptical assessments of Europe's democratic compatibility it can be argued, though, that the loss of policy-making autonomy on the side of the nation-states should not simply be understood as an inescapable structural consequence of integration; rather, it should be seen as a widely accepted, if not deliberately intended, effect of intergovernmental arrangements. In times of increasing global pressure for economic competitiveness, the European governments, regardless of their ideological orientation, might well have taken the opportunity to point to rigid external constraints imposed by 'Europe' in order to justify unpopular cuts in social spending and other measures aimed at consolidating the state finances. European policy priorities could be changed in the Council if the democratically elected governments of the member states opted to do so. In that case, the EU would offer these governments a suitable institutional environment to regain capacities for political control by pooling sovereignty and resources.

This kind of reasoning immediately raises an additional objection that can be made against the thesis of an ineluctable trade-off between Europeanization and democracy. It can be summarized as follows: the weak democratic compatibility of the EU relates to transitional phenomena, which will cease to have a serious impact as soon as a sufficient degree of democratic legitimacy is produced on a transnational scale. At any rate, the problem of the EU's democratic compatibility would have to be seriously qualified if economic, social and political integration were better synchronized and the EU constituted as a genuinely democratic community. In such a scenario, the European 'general will' would ultimately have to prevail against the sum of the particular preferences of the

---

[8] The EU's withdrawal from the social dimension is analyzed in Offe (1998a) and Scharpf (1997).

nation-states in those domains falling under the political competence of the Union.

Hence, the *second dimension* of the debate over how to legitimize the emerging European polity concerns the possibilities of fully implanting democratic principles within the Union's institutional structures. Under the aspect of democratic compatibility, the European constitution should primarily respect the member states' autonomy. When the focus is placed on overcoming the democracy deficit in the proper sense, by contrast, the issue becomes the EU's own democratic potential. What is then at stake might be called the *democratic capability* of the EU.

Modern Western democracies derive the legitimacy of political rule from the principle of popular sovereignty. In differentiated societies, the principle can rarely be applied in a direct way. Sovereignty, therefore, becomes manifest in the institutionally mediated control of the rulers by the ruled. In the first place, this implies regular and general elections in which the citizens choose their representatives. It is one of the key aspects of Europe's democratic deficit that this representative relationship has no equivalent in the EU's institutional system (Kielmansegg 1996: 53). The primary legislative organ is the Council, which is not directly accountable to the European electorate. Nor does the Commission, which is expected to serve 'the cause of the Community', enjoy a direct electoral mandate when it performs its executive tasks or makes use of its initiative powers in the procedure of legislation. The European Parliament, on the other hand, which is elected by Europe's citizens, has only restricted legislative competences. Unsurprisingly, then, most of the publicly aired proposals for democratizing the EU aim at reforming its institutional system.

The main thrust of the recommendations made in recent years is to give the Union a stronger parliamentary character, providing the European Parliament with the classical functions of a legislative power. Proposals to strengthen the parliamentary component are often combined with a preference for installing a bicameral system, which would accentuate the federative moment in the Union. In this scenario, a chamber representing the 'Europe of the nation-states' would be placed alongside the chamber representing the 'Europe of the citizens'.[9] Other proposals aim at strengthening the Commission's democratic legitimacy. To mention only one example, in May 2001, Lionel Jospin, at the time Prime Minister of France, delivered a general policy statement on Europe

---

[9] As Germany's former Minister of Foreign Affairs Joschka Fischer (2000: 11–12) suggested in a speech delivered at the Humboldt University in Berlin as the constitutional debate was getting under way.

in which he argued that, in the future, the President of the Commission should be nominated from the ranks of the parliamentary group which obtained the largest number of votes in the European elections.[10] In a similar vein, the former German head of state, Johannes Rau, suggested in an appearance before the European Parliament in Strasbourg that the President as well as the members of the Commission should be directly elected by the citizens.[11] More audacious seems to be an idea that has thus far been debated among political science experts rather than in day-to-day politics: Essentially, it aims at fostering the Union's democratization by plebiscitary means, convoking Europe-wide referenda on political questions of major transnational relevance.[12] Several of the reform proposals summarized here are often seen as complementary options and bundled into a 'democracy package' for the EU.[13] It has to be said that the Treaty establishing a Constitution for Europe has taken up such ideas only to a very limited extent. All in all, the constitutional document does not break with the intergovernmental bias which characterizes decision-making in the European polity.

In the discussions on how to democratize Europe through institutional reforms, different political proposals reflect preferences for different degrees of integration and models of democracy. Nonetheless, the proposals share an important common feature: ultimately, they regard the making of a European democracy as an objective to be realized primarily through a reform of political institutions. The constitutional process is supposed to make a crucial contribution to a thorough remodelling of Europe's institutional framework. The initiatives put forward are frequently driven by the apparent conviction that the birth of a democratic collective subject at the European level can be induced by relying on appropriate institutional measures. This becomes particularly patent when Europe-wide referenda are seen as tools not only for enhancing institutional transparency in European decision-making, but also for creating a political community of Europeans. Here, the assumptions underlying those models of democracy according to which democratic legitimacy results from collective self-determination are virtually inverted. Such models highlight the dimension of democratic politics which Scharpf (1999: 7) calls 'input-oriented legitimacy'; the concept of input refers to the dynamics of government *by* the people. In normative political analysis, Scharpf (1999: 10–11) argues, the

---

[10] The complete statement was published in the online edition of *Le Monde* (Jospin 2001).

[11] Spiegel Online, 4 March 2001 [www.spiegel.de/politik/europa/0,1518,126525,00.html].

[12] See, for example, Grande (2000a: 130–2) and Zürn (2000: 104–7).

[13] A detailed critical overview of the manifold suggestions made for a democratic reform of the EU can be found in Abromeit (1998: 25–51).

input-oriented perspective has to be distinguished from an output-oriented approach to democratic rule. The latter views democracy essentially as rule *for* the people whose quality ultimately hinges on its problem-solving effectiveness.

Input-oriented models of legitimacy assume that the people, as the collective subject of politics, share a comprehensive identity, which provides the basis for the articulation of conflicting interests within the channels of institutional decision-making. In some proposals aiming at a democratic renewal of the EU by institutional reforms, this approach is all but turned on its head, as democratic will-formation ultimately appears to be primarily the result of appropriate institutional techniques. The arguments put forward by the supporters of Europe-wide referenda are a case in point. Thus Zürn (2000: 105) writes: 'In Europe, the aim must therefore be to introduce majoritarian procedures that function in the absence of a fully developed political community while at the same time fostering its development, and that contain a safety valve against bargaining blockades and non-transparent situations. Within the context of the European multi-level system, European referenda on more general issues could be a useful instrument.' The assumption here is that referenda could make a substantial contribution to the formation of a transnational community of Europeans. Plebiscites are seen as an instrument that ultimately generates the very subject whose political voice they supposedly manifest. Such a view, however, still begs the question of whose will is ultimately to be reflected in the political process, as the collectivity expected to articulate its sovereign voice has still to come into being. How should the 'people' decide when there is as yet no 'people'?

Hence, defining a shared identity space (Taylor 2003, 2004) involves serious challenges for those who speculate on the possibilities of 'inducing' a European demos primarily by institutional means. What does democratization mean, if its subject remains blurred? How will a transnational union bound together exclusively by institutional arrangements maintain its cohesion if it is ridden by severe internal conflicts? Democratic capability essentially implies capability for conflict. Can the bases of a Europe which is able to deal with intense conflicts be laid down by relying on sophisticated strategies of institutional design? The project of consolidating a community that lacks collective ties which its members experience as 'authentic' runs the risk of overestimating the possibilities of an elite-driven constitution-making and neglecting the dilemmas of 'hyperrationality' (Offe 1998b: 217), thereby creating a hollow framework of political institutions that remain disconnected from social realities. To a great extent, Europe's constitutional setbacks can be considered a consequence of this kind of strategy.

Focusing on the institutional aspects of the EU's democratic compatibility and democratic capability ultimately leads us back to a substantial problem. In terms of compatibility, the question is to what extent the project of European integration collides with the sovereignty of previously constituted *demoi*. Does the subsidiarity principle offer sufficient protection against the erosion of local, regional and national structures of democracy which may be caused by the Europeanization of political decision-making? Regarding the Union's democratic capability, the matter to be discussed concerns the prospects of constituting a genuinely transnational demos in the EU. How can Europe come into being as a political community that represents more than the sum of institutional arrangements adopted to sustain a complex system of multilevel governance? All in all, against the background sketched out thus far, Europe's democracy deficit seems to overlap to a significant extent with the problems of what we might call a 'demos deficit'.

2.2   The Democracy Deficit: A 'Demos Deficit'?

Since the German Constitutional Court handed down its Maastricht judgment in October 1993, the thesis that there is no European demos has become a recurrent topic in the discussions on the political future of Europe. On the one hand, the Court's judgment rejected constitutional objections which argued that the institutional system of the EU violated democratic standards. On the other hand, however, the *Bundesverfassungsgericht* adopted the position that the Treaty on European Union was in conformity with democratic principles because, instead of a European state, it only established a union of states. According to its view, the member states were to be considered the basic bearers of democratic legitimacy in the EU, as the Union could not base itself upon a European people (*Staatsvolk*).[14]

With its decision, the German Federal Constitutional Court adopted the position that the non-existence of a European people set clear limits to the foundations of the political legitimacy which a European polity could claim to possess on its own account, while the nation-states retained a crucial role in legitimizing the EU. As a consequence, the Court held that – in the terminology introduced in the previous section of this chapter – the deepening of the Union had to respect the criteria of democratic compatibility in the context of transnational decision-making.

---

[14] For a summary of the *Maastricht-Urteil* see Thiel (1998: 59–62); MacCormick (1995) and Weiler (1995) analyze the sentence critically.

In Germany, the 'no demos' thesis became a vigorously debated issue in the realms of politics, social science and constitutional law. The historical situation the country was going through in the 1990s may have contributed a good deal to the interest inspired by the topic. In the whirl of the events of 1989, an important segment of the protest movement in the GDR had modified its political priorities. The change was succinctly reflected by a change of slogans: the initial 'We are *the* people'[15] became 'We are *one* people'.[16] It seems reasonable to assume that many German observers who were facing the new dynamics of European integration used the process of unification in their country as an immediate point of reference. Thus, when looking at the EU, they raised the question of whether *the* people can exist where there is no *one* people.

The expert in constitutional law and former member of the Federal Constitutional Court, Dieter Grimm, joined the debate concerning possibilities for alleviating the tension between integration and democracy in Europe through a constitutional process with a particularly noteworthy and widely discussed contribution. Although a member of the Court at the time it pronounced its Maastricht judgment, Grimm was not involved in drafting the decision. In his reflections on Europe's political future after Maastricht, Grimm (1995) takes the lack of democratic legitimacy in the political construction of Europe as his point of departure for an analysis aimed at clarifying the options available for overcoming the EU's democratic impasse. In this respect, he is not too optimistic. From his perspective, the prospects of establishing a foundational political consensus in Europe that transcends the nation-state level are contingent upon preconditions beyond the reach of constitutional deliberations. Grimm (1995: 293–4) doubts whether these prerequisites are available for the EU at its present stage of political development:

It is well known that the mediation process essential to democracy is not running satisfactorily even at nation-state level, partly because of the growing self-absorption of the political parties, partly because of asymmetries in interest representation, partly because of deficits in communication systems, which are often oriented more to economic imperatives than to opinion formation. At European level, though, even the prerequisites are largely lacking. Mediatory structures have hardly even been formed yet . . . This makes the European Union fall short not just of ideal conceptions of a model democracy but even of the already deficient situation in Member States.

According to Grimm, plans elaborated with the intention of enhancing the democratic integration of the EU are bound to remain irrelevant

---

[15] 'Wir sind *das* Volk.'
[16] 'Wir sind *ein* Volk.'

as long as there are no real opportunities for cultural integration across national borders. The constitutional lawyer is particularly sceptical about the chances of establishing a European community of participation without first creating a European community of communication. He uses a straightforward line of argument to stress this point: there can be no European democracy because there is no European public sphere; there can be no European public sphere because there is no European people (in the sense of a demos possessing a collective identity that would serve as a frame for political unity); and there can be no European people because there is no common European language (Grimm 1995: 295). From Grimm's point of view, linguistic differentiation appears as one of the main features of cultural pluralism in Europe. He considers the latter to be a factor that hinders the formation of intermediary political structures so seriously that, at present, any attempt to delimit the proper institutional space for a truly European democracy seems doomed to failure. Providing the idea of a European demos with a meaningful content would require a socio-cultural underpinning not at present in sight. From such an angle, attempts at democratizing the EU which concentrate primarily on the institutional domain might even be counterproductive, as Grimm (1995: 296–7) argues, adducing the example of a stronger parliamentarization of the Euro-polity:

The European Parliament does not meet with any European mediatory structure in being; still less does it constitute a representative body, since there is as yet no European people. This is not an argument against any expansion of Parliament's powers . . . Its objective ought not, however, to be full parliamentarization on the national model, since political decisions would otherwise move away to where they can only be inadequately democratically accountable.

Grimm's target is ultimately an understanding of democracy that focuses exclusively on political institutions, as he considers the articulation of conflicts and intermediation of interests in the realm of society to be crucial components of democratic will-formation. Thus the weakness of intermediary structures is the main factor restricting the EU's constitutional and democratic capability. Grimm's reasoning must not be misinterpreted as a symptom of the long-lasting influence of ethnocultural traditions on political thought in Germany. Leaning on such traditions might indeed entail an exaggeration of the problems which heterogeneity implies for the establishment of democratic rule. But this is not Grimm's point. The reflections just summarized do not emphasize the weight of ethnic ties; rather they highlight the importance of the 'capacity for transnational discourse' (Grimm 1995: 297) for the construction of a politically meaningful collective identity among Union citizens.

The thesis that the lack of a European demos implies a major structural problem for all initiatives devoted to democratizing the institutional system of the EU may have had a special significance in German political debates.[17] However, it would be a mistake to think that we are dealing with a peculiarly German phenomenon. In different versions, the thesis has been put forward in other member states of the EU as well.[18] In addition to the points highlighted by Grimm, the literature that tends to give a sceptical account of the Union's potential for deeper political integration typically points out the following five aspects of the 'demos problem':

1. The existence of a democratic community requires, as an often-made assumption holds, clearly demarcated territorial boundaries. If the identity of the demos is to be stabilized, democratic processes must be located within a fixed territorial framework. To the extent that this is not the case, the criteria for political inclusion become diffuse, and the citizens lose their capacity to determine the common good (Offe 1998a: 101–3). As the EU is the institutional expression of an unfinished and basically open process of integration, its scope for giving an unambiguous definition of its population and its territory remains limited (Manent 1997). The collective subject of the political process of Europeanization appears to be highly fragmented internally and to lack clear external boundaries.

2. A shared historical experience is a central feature in the democratic self-understanding of modern societies. According to Ernst-Wolfgang Böckenförde, another former member of Germany's Federal Constitutional Court – who, as it happens, did participate in the deliberations leading to the Maastricht judgment – it is this historical embeddedness which makes for a significant part of the political relevance we continue to attribute to the category of the 'people'. Böckenförde (1999: 92) argues that a collective memory and consciousness transmitted from generation to generation are pivotal factors for constituting a people and sustaining national allegiances. If one adopts such a view, to weaken the political framework of the nation-state implies the risk of devaluing the capital a specific culture has for reproducing a democratic order. Collective learning processes, which are an indispensable element of democratic politics, are contingent upon the continuity in time and space provided by a national community.

---

[17] See, apart from Grimm, Böckenförde (1999), Greven (1997), Kielmansegg (1996), Scharpf (1999) or Streeck (1998).

[18] See, among other examples, Manent (1997) for France, Siedentop (2000) for the United Kingdom or Zetterholm (1994) for Denmark.

3. As a societal resource, solidarity in Europe remains closely bound up with national patterns of identification. To the extent that shared political identities become disconnected from loyalties towards a state, the foundations of economic solidarity that were characteristic of post-war Western European societies crumble. In comparison to the nation-state, the EU constitutes an institutional domain with a feeble identity basis. Hence, its potential for building up a system of mutual socio-political obligations seems reduced. From this perspective, the Europeanization of distributional policies would lead to a further dismantling of social rights and to a substantial decrease in the quality of democratic citizenship (Streeck 1999).

4. For minorities to respect the legitimacy of democratic majority decisions there must be a minimum of reciprocal loyalty among the members of a particular political community; but it is uncertain whether such a minimum is available beyond national borders (Scharpf 1999). Even if one assumes that a majority of Europeans is convinced of the advantages of a closer political union, the question remains whether this makes for a sufficiently stable basis of collective consent in a European democracy. At any rate, the democratic institutionalization of conflicts in the transnational realm would call for levels of affective support that the project of European integration has thus far failed to mobilize.

5. The very 'comprehensibility' of political discourses – not to mention their deliberative quality – is linked to the medium of language. Lacking the possibility of immediate linguistic exchange, democratic politics loses a great deal of its persuasive and integrative potential. Democracies are communities of communication constituted in an encompassing public space. For such a space to emerge, the EU would need a linguistic infrastructure which is not yet in sight. Thus the nation-states must still be considered the primary sites of political communication and public deliberation in Europe (Greven 2000, Kielmansegg 1996).

Regardless of their particular points of concern, the different positions roughly summarized in the preceding paragraphs seem to share one important argumentative feature: the question of a European demos is scrutinized against the standards defined by the political form of organization represented by the nation-state. That the EU is unable to constitute a proper demos is thus the consequence of its lacking substantial attributes of nation-statehood. It must be said that, in this respect, Grimm (1995: 297–8) takes a fairly moderate stance. In his approach, the nation-state is not to be preserved for its own sake; rather, functional considerations dictate that, for the time being, it should be considered the main arena of democratic politics in relation to the EU. However, the discussions of the potential role of a European demos also tend to establish a close equation between democratic capability and nation-statehood. Democratic theory then becomes amalgamated to a specific view of the modern state. This has far-reaching implications for the political analysis of European integration which will be critically assessed in the following sections.

2.3   Between Westphalia and Cosmopolis

To a considerable extent, the current discussions devoted to the political future of Europe seem to be influenced in essence by two opposite positions.[19] On one side, there are those who are not willing to put at risk the safety net of 'democracy in one country' by trying to develop a democratic frame for the EU. For the sake of clarity, I will call them the 'Westphalians', although the label probably oversimplifies their positions.[20] The designation is meant to pay tribute to the importance of the Peace of Westphalia in the formation of a system of sovereign states in Europe. In Westphalian approaches to the EU, one of the major concerns is that the process of European integration devalues democratic decision-making in the nation-states without creating new options for transnational political control.

The arguments put forward by observers adopting such a view were already exposed at the beginning of this chapter. Let us recapitulate them briefly. Important decisions that affect a growing number of social and economic policy issues are made at the European level. Thereby, some of the central links between liberal democracy and the welfare state are being weakened. Market integration is accomplished without corresponding efforts aimed at achieving social and political integration as well. Westphalians question the EU's compatibility with existing forms of democracy, as Europeanization is contributing to the erosion of effectiveness and legitimacy of democratic rule by the nation-state. At the same time – and for my purposes, this is the more interesting part of the arguments presented – they are very sceptical concerning the possibility that the EU will become a distinctive kind of democracy and foster the birth of a system of transnational democratic governance, thus counterbalancing the loss of nation-state sovereignty. Here, the crucial problem

---

[19] This section draws on Kraus (2003: 668–70).
[20] See the contributions made by Greven (1997), Judt (1996), Kielmansegg (1996), Manent (1997) and Streeck (1999).

is that there are no socio-cultural foundations which seem solid enough to provide a European democracy with the legitimation it will need: politically relevant collective identities are still deeply embedded in the structures of nation-states, and patterns of support transcending their boundaries are scarcely in sight. In brief, the project of enhancing democratic integration in the EU is bound to fail as long as there is no breakthrough in cultural integration across national borders. Cultural pluralism and, especially, the linguistic differentiation it entails are regarded, for the time being, as insurmountable obstacles in any attempt at creating the intermediary political structures and the public sphere which a European democracy that deserves this name would require. Cultural heterogeneity and the weight of those cultural attachments that are characteristic of the well-entrenched European state system inhibit the formation and the articulation of a common political identity among Europeans.

The validity of such claims is challenged by the advocates of postnationalism. In view of the inhospitality of Westphalia, they praise the virtues of 'Cosmopolis'.[21] New political institutions based on the principle of 'postnational identity' are expected to overcome the normative and functional constraints of 'democracy in one country'. Cosmopolitans want to overcome the idea of the homogeneous nation-state by deliberately refraining from any attempt to establish a congruent relationship between culture and polity. In the light of postnationalism, one of the EU's most fascinating aspects is the historically unprecedented possibility of grounding political rule on a 'pure' civic community, a community exempt from any kind of primordial substratum. That European citizens lack a common cultural identity is interpreted as a unique opportunity to constitute a novel and truly 'civic' type of demos, a demos which transcends culture and reflects nothing other than the collective consent emanating from shared moral values. Thus the integration of Europe would neither lead to the invention of an encompassing community of fate conceived of in the spirit of past traditions nor set the official cultural standards for a shared public space yet to be created, but rather rely on a strict separation between cultural and political identities (Ferry 1994: 46). From such a point of view, the EU's normative attractiveness is ultimately grounded in the very lack of a common culture. In consequence, creating a democratic polity in Europe becomes a crucial test case for the more ambitious transition to cosmopolitan democracy on a global scale that is envisaged in the long run.

---

[21] A cosmopolitan mood permeates the work of Archibugi (1995), Beck (1998), Ferry (1994), Habermas (2001) and Held (1995).

It seems that both the Westphalian and the cosmopolitan positions have serious difficulties in developing convincing approaches to cultural identity and its role in modern democracies. Westphalians view nation-states as political units containing uncontested and homogeneous cultures. At least implicitly, their assumption is that democratic self-government is contingent upon the loyalty of citizens who have common ties rooted in their basic identity patterns, as symbolized by language and culture. The overlaps between this position and the more or less official French versions of republicanism are evident. As democratic sovereignty is assumed to be embodied in the nation-state, a close connection is made between state theory and democratic theory. Democratic deliberation and decision-making are coextensive with the socio-cultural domains defined by national rule. Political theories influenced by the Westphalian tradition usually take it for granted that states possess an indivisible source of sovereignty, which is the expression of a uniform collective identity, and presuppose societies that are culturally homogeneous (Parekh 1997: 192). Taking an abstract, reifying and to a great extent even idealizing model of the nation-state as their point of departure for political analysis, they can hardly avoid giving a categorical and one-sided account of the effects of cultural diversity and the multiplicity of identities for sustaining democratic government.

Cosmopolitan democrats, on the other hand, seem to be inclined to throw out the baby with the bath water by simply ignoring the political implications of cultural diversity. In modern societies, culture and politics have become inextricably intertwined.[22] Institutions offering a culturally 'antiseptic' ground for liberal-democratic politics are still to be invented. Even if one is prepared to give up the rigid links established between democracy and the nation-state, one has to admit that political integration can't work without cultural mediation. Civic commitments are not developed in a cultural vacuum. An abstract universalism that ignores the specific cultural context in which political interactions take place may end up turning cosmopolitan hopes into mere wishful thinking. Or even worse, it may confuse cultural neutrality or 'benign neglect' with the tacit support of dominant cultures and the suppression of justified minority claims; thus 'benign neglect' may easily turn into 'malevolent ignorance'. Moreover, keeping the present-day European context in mind, in the end it is not easy to understand why people should feel committed to the construction of a polity that is expected to pay no attention to their cultural identity at all.

---

[22] This is why nationalism is to be considered a constitutive feature of modernity, as was emphatically shown by authors like Gellner (1997) or Deutsch (1966).

To dissect the Westphalian and the cosmopolitan positions is more than merely an academic exercise, as the two perspectives largely sustain the continuing controversies between 'sovereigntists' and 'Euro-federalists'. Thus it is important to point out their analytical weaknesses. Both positions frequently omit to clarify to what extent the diagnosis presented has more a normative or more an empirical status. The problem seems to transpire in inverse ways in each approach. In the Westphalian view, empirical evidence is tacitly turned into a normative justification of the nation-state, whereas cosmopolitans are inclined to take their normative preferences as empirical realities. In the first case, nation-stateness attains an absolute character as the sole legitimate ground of democratic integration; here, the questionable assumption is that patterns of cultural identification that are politically relevant must be congruent with the identity framework offered by the nation-state. In the second case, by contrast, the availability of 'strong' integration resources above the nation-state level may be overrated, and the political weight of the nationalist moment underestimated.

If we are to develop a better understanding of the challenges of political integration in present-day Europe, we must become aware of the shortcomings of both positions in how they deal with the relationship between cultural identities and democratic integration. For Westphalians, the political relevance of a collective identity depends essentially on its being represented by the institutional structure of a nation-state, and a democratic polity must be based on just *one* common cultural identity. From the cosmopolitan perspective, culture and cultural diversity are of secondary importance when it comes to determine the conflict potentials inherent in processes of political integration. Thus, in the context of transnational democracy, cultural identity becomes a blank. Ultimately, the implications of diversity for European integration are ignored by each approach, as neither cosmopolitans nor 'Westphalians' are prepared to offer a critical assessment of the uneasy relationship between cultural heterogeneity and the democratic nation-state.

2.4   Sovereignty as Homogeneity

In an exhaustive volume devoted to a sad and unpleasant subject, the British social theorist and political sociologist Michael Mann puts forward the thesis that ethnic cleansing has not been an anomaly in the process of modernization and state-building, but must rather be understood as *'the dark side of democracy'*.[23] This may sound provocative;

---

[23] Mann (2005: 2); italics in the original.

nevertheless, Mann offers rich empirical evidence to corroborate his argument, which is developed against a historical background that includes both the European and the North American experience. According to Mann, a large majority of EU countries are today over 80 percent culturally homogeneous.[24] An important aspect of this homogeneity, however, is that it is not a 'natural' outcome of quasi-evolutionary processes but in large part reflects the deliberate use of political power by majority elites. Imposed assimilation and enforced migration, not to mention more dramatic steps, played a significant role in the making of democratic statehood all over Europe. Speaking in broad and general terms, one can indeed discern a long-term historical trend toward creating uniformity *within* the units that form the European state system. This is true even if the *overall* picture of the Continent shows a marked and institutionally entrenched cultural diversity.[25] After all, one of the characteristic and somewhat paradoxical elements of the Westphalian legacy in Europe was that it fostered homogeneity within the units comprising the state system, although the system itself was the result of an attempt at institutionalizing heterogeneity after a period of religious wars. Thus the consolidation of national forms of rule became one of the most salient features of Europe's path to modernity. At the same time, national integration often had the explicit meaning of cultural homogenization.

As the exponents of the institutional logics of a Westphalian world, democratic nation-states have tended to create a close link between two distinct normative principles: the particularist principle of sovereignty and the universalist principle of citizenship. The connection becomes most evident in the concept of the 'sovereign people', a central concept in the discourse of those for whom democracy requires the fusion of nationhood and statehood (Giddens 1985). In practice, people or nation has nowhere been the exclusive product of a voluntary contract negotiated by autonomous individuals, but always the expression of the dissemination of a hegemonic cultural identity among the population of a given territory (Schöpflin 1999). The political cement needed to maintain democratic consent was cultural affinity (or ethnic proximity). Where such an affinity was not 'organically' pre-established or had not been imposed by predemocratic rulers, state policies sought to turn the population into a homogeneous people. A case in point is France under the Third Republic, where standard French was a foreign language for

---

[24] Mann (2005: 507) uses the category 'mono-ethnic'.
[25] At least when Europe is compared with America. For this reason, Colin Crouch (1999) takes the Dutch concept of *verzuiling* – pillarization – as a pars pro toto image that sets the European model against traditional views of the USA as a cultural 'melting pot'.

approximately one half of the population, according to the estimates put forward by historians; Eugen Weber (1976) has offered an instructive picture of how the French central state, after 1870, put great efforts into turning 'peasants' into 'Frenchmen', its major assets for accomplishing this task being the republican school system and conscription. Rarely did popular sovereignty emanate directly from the spontaneous articulation of a collective will; to a considerable extent, it was an institutionally manufactured sovereignty, a sovereignty delivered 'from above'. All in all, the people had often already been 'made' before it could become sovereign. As J. H. H. Weiler (2001: 56) puts it, the language of modern constitutionalism has tended to disguise this situation behind a great fallacy, which invites us 'to confuse the juridical presupposition of a constitutional *demos* with political and social reality'.

The exercise of democratic sovereignty presupposes the existence of a collective identity sustaining the polity conceived of as sovereign. However, from the viewpoint of democratic theory, the problem with this identity is that it can hardly be postulated to be an outcome of democratic decision-making. Democracies do not come into being in a historical void, and there is no democracy before democracy. Hence, the roots of a sovereign people's identity are inextricably interwoven with a predemocratic past, and the collective subject in whose name a democracy is established – the demos, democracy's 'we' – enters the democratic scene without democratic credentials.

Establishing a democratic polity implies relying on resources which lack democratic legitimacy themselves; this has been called the paradox of sovereignty or Rousseau's paradox.[26] The substantial asymmetries in the distribution of power, which are inevitably still at work in the very process of establishing democratic rule, can be neutralized effectively only *after* democratic procedures have been introduced. The formation of a sovereign collective will rest upon political grounds which are external to democracy. Such grounds extend deep into the realm of culture. It hardly seems possible to create a democratic framework for public communication if there was no previous system of communication, a system obviously not governed by democratic – but by hegemonic – imperatives. Thus the hegemonic definition of the identity of the demos – a definition in which cultural elements such as collective memories, myths, conventions as well as religion and language often play a substantial role – precedes the dynamics of democratization in the nation-state. It is in this

---

[26] An early discussion of the paradox can be found in the work of Rousseau (1998: 87–9). For more recent approaches to the issue see Connolly (1993: 51–2) and Tully (2000: 475–6).

context that a common cultural identity among the citizens is typically regarded as a prerequisite of integration in a modern polity. Ultimately, the paradox of sovereignty is one of the major blind spots in democratic theory. But the paradox not only involves a great theoretical challenge. Its practical impact is obvious as well, especially in those democracies in which the identity of the nation as the embodiment of popular sovereignty is a contested political issue. More relevant for our concerns is that the paradox can also be perceived in the ongoing debates on the bases available for creating a European democracy.

Two major qualifications must be made, however, against the general background outlined here. First, some states, generally located in Europe's medieval city belt area, offer an important counterbalance to the mainstream trend towards internal uniformity.[27] They institutionalized the pluralism of groups and territories by setting up consociational or federal arrangements, thus facilitating the persistence of diverse identity patterns.[28] Second, the recurrent mobilization of subnational identities even in those states that had made great efforts in the past to safeguard their political sovereignty by combining territorial integration with cultural homogenization demonstrates the limits of national integration. Great Britain and Spain are among the oldest nation-states in Europe. Nonetheless, the political authority of the centre has not remained unchallenged at their peripheries, if we look at Scotland and Wales, in one case, and at the Basque Country and Catalonia, in the other. Even the one and indivisible French Republic faces serious difficulties when it comes to maintaining its hegemony over a territory such as Corsica. Seen in the light of Michael Mann's thesis, the unexpected growth of minority movements in recent times may be interpreted as a belated response to the 'original sin' of democracy regarding culture.

2.5   Assessing the European Union Against the National Model

What conclusions can be drawn from the analysis of the problematic relationship between cultural diversity and democracy in the nation-state with regard to the project of European polity-building? In the first place, it should have become evident that the appeal of the 'mainstream'

---

[27] The impact of the city belt on the formation of nation-states in Western Europe has been masterfully analyzed by Rokkan (1999).

[28] Belgium may at present be seen as the paradigmatic case of a 'consociational federalism' for better and for worse. This makes the country an interesting point of reference for the EU and has given rise to insightful speculations about the desirability of a 'Belgian' Europe (Van Parijs 2000a).

nation-state model of political integration is highly questionable from a normative perspective, if one wants to take issues of 'cultural justice' seriously. Moreover, and this is perhaps the more relevant point for my concerns here, we must assume that the cultural dynamics of European integration will differ sharply from the dominant nation-state pattern. The increasing acceptance of 'diversity-sensitive' approaches to social and political reality has led to a generalization of the view that cultural differences do matter and are to be respected. During the past decades, the discourse of 'multiculturalism' has been shaping to a considerable extent the official approach to diversity all over the Western world. Simultaneously, the protection of minorities has re-emerged as a paramount component of a transnational European human rights regime to degrees unparalleled since the interwar period.[29] Finally, groups that have already experienced mobilizations stressing their specific cultural identity are unlikely to be 'integrated' into a hegemonic domain reproducing the experiences that were typical of the 'high' period of nation-state formation. To put it bluntly, there are no 'peasants' left on the continent who might be happily waiting to be turned into some kind of 'Europeanmen' by institutional means.[30] Whatever the EU will look like in the future, it will certainly differ from the dominant nation-state patterns. If one wants to find possible historical analogies, some instructive evidence might be offered by the more complex federal and consociational variants of state-building.

In his comparative political sociology of modern Europe, Stein Rokkan (1975) attempted to sketch a synthetic view of a complex and differentiated set of historical tendencies by distinguishing four sequences in the political foundation and consolidation of nation-states in the western half of the continent: (1) penetration of a territory by a political centre (state-building); (2) cultural standardization of this territory (nation-building); (3) extension of citizens' rights to political participation (democratization); and (4) political redistribution of economic resources (creation of welfare state systems). Western European nation-states were typically constructed in a situation of latent or manifest conflict between the units of an emerging state system. Quite often, therefore, the drive for cultural uniformity within state borders was supposed to contribute to securing the loyalty of the population, a loyalty needed to defend or expand a territorial sovereignty constantly

---

[29] One may even argue that the situation for minorities today has considerably improved in comparison with the period after the First World War, as there are far fewer restrictions for groups to claim a minority status (Toivanen 2005).

[30] To paraphrase the title of the well-known book by Eugen Weber on the process of nation-building in France (*Peasants into Frenchmen*, 1976).

threatened by neighbouring sovereign entities. State-building and war-making were closely interrelated processes.

European integration, to the contrary, received its initial impulses, which indeed reflected a 'supranational' moment, from an explicit agreement on ending entrenched interstate conflicts over geopolitical hegemony in the region once and for all. At the same time, however, the member states of the EC/EU have never been overly enthusiastic about sacrificing real or supposed portions of their sovereignty for Europe's sake. From the beginning, therefore, the European project seems to have been detached from visible political power in a peculiar way. Political decision-making often remained more or less hidden behind inconspicuous technocratic routines. Whatever Euro-sceptics afraid of an excessive centralization of competences and resources in Brussels may think, it does not seem to be a coincidence that the place where the headquarters of the European Commission is located is not exactly a centre characterized by military glory or a will to an expansive cultural *grandeur*. Consequently, the symbolic presentation of Europe's supranational dimension has remained fairly modest. As the Norwegian social anthropologist Thomas Hylland Eriksen (1997: 249–50) observes ironically:

When walking through the gray corridors of Brussels, meeting with one bureaucrat after another to learn about trade with the Third World, environmental policies, unemployment benefits and language policies – all the time being offered tepid instant coffee while obediently respecting the smoking ban – it seems all but ludicrous to hate the institution. It may be boring, it may be gray and inefficient – but malevolent? In its stiff and awkward friendliness it lacks even a hint of the late Habsburg-Kafkaesque. The European Union, seen from its insides in Brussels, has more in common with Habermas' philosophy. It is an extremely thorough and slowly grinding machine, it can be deadly boring, but it is honest in its own way and important to those whom it concerns.

Measured against the model of the nation-state, the EU appears to be a new kind of polity, whose novelty would reside in the creation of an institutional order that lacks a hegemonic internal force and that has a culturally open or 'undetermined' constitutional structure. This order continues to be characterized, in the first place, by the confluence of two contradictory principles within its institutional framework: intergovernmentalism and supranationalism. Since the beginning of the integration process, the respective weight of these two principles in European politics has regularly been the subject of intense debates.[31] In the European system of multilevel governance (Hooghe and Marks 2001), the logics of

---

[31] Haas (1958) may be considered a classic representative of the 'functionalist' supranational view. For a recent approach to the EU written from the perspective of a 'liberal'

political decision-making vary substantially in different policy areas. The member states do delegate significant portions of the sovereign competences they formerly enjoyed to the level of the Union. At the same time, they take every precaution against tendencies that might provide the EU with state-like powers as far as the interconnection between political and cultural identities is concerned.

Thus the EU offers an overall image that is far less coherent than the ideal type concept we have of the modern nation-state. It is hardly surprising that the interplay of the competing political rationales underlying its institutional development reverberates in Europe's politics of identity. The dialectic of European integration has largely exemplified this, often developing into sheer schizophrenia when the political medication prescribed by a 'supranationally' minded Dr. Jekyll invigorates the spirit of a ferociously 'nation-statist' Mr. Hyde. The tension inherent in the dynamics of the European process is nicely captured in an interview with Jacques Delors published in *Le Monde* in the initial period of the constitutional debate. In the interview, the former president of the European Commission manifested his preference for constructing a European federation of nation-states. An astute journalist immediately reacted to this statement by asking whether this was not an oxymoronic concept. Obviously, the institutional fusion of state and nation is based on the assumption that the resulting nation-state should be able to act as an entity enjoying undivided and indivisible sovereignty. Federations, on the contrary, presuppose the division of sovereignty between different levels of political decision-making.[32]

Confronted with a multilayered and contradictory institutional setting, analyses of the problems experienced when the strengthening of Europe's political dimension is at stake often point to the weak cultural foundations available for constructing a European 'state'. From such a perspective, cultural heterogeneity, embedded in a system of entrenched nation-states, is seen as a major force inhibiting the formation and articulation of a common political will among Europeans. Indeed, what makes for a good deal of the major political interest of the current developments in Europe is the circumstance that normative presuppositions become inextricably intermingled with the sociological realities of democratic politics. In the context of the EU, therefore, the fallacy of modern constitutionalism has lost all of its credibility. In the process of European polity-building, the

---

intergovernmentalism see Moravcsik (1998). See Schmitter (1996a) for a compact overview.

[32] See the interview with Delors published in *Le Monde*, 19 January 2000. Since that date, the concept has been taken up by several high-ranking European politicians, such as Joschka Fischer or Lionel Jospin.

paradox of sovereignty is experienced by a mass public as a palpable social and political reality. Accordingly, the safety nets that were still in place during most of the history of European nation-building have become porous. Without a fixed territorial realm, without a shared past, without an unchallenged cultural identity and without a common language, the foundations of political unity in the EU look precarious. In view of the precariousness of the 'taken for granted' socio-cultural resources sustaining political rule, the emperor has never been as naked as he appears to be in the headquarters of the European institutions in Brussels.

Ultimately, the question of the European demos must be related to the contradictory interplay of political forces that underlies the EU's institutional development. Whenever it is at work, intergovernmentalism places the emphasis exclusively on the importance of the member states' national cultures in the Union. In contrast, the weight of the supranational factor in Europe's institutional framework may encourage the articulation of cultural identities below and beyond the nation-state level and contribute to a new political configuration of identity options.

3 The identity of a multinational polity

European identity has become an all-pervasive concept. In the debate on integration it is used so frequently that to call its currency inflationary would be an understatement. Thus there is an evident risk of the concept turning into a catchall formula whose possible meanings vary arbitrarily from one context to another. Typically, those who tend to evoke it with emphatic intentions are also inclined to amalgamate what they take to be the 'objective' attributes of a European identity, as they may be derived from the realms of geography, history, culture and politics, with normative proposals for what should placed at the core of this identity, be it the canon of 'occidental values' or the idea of a 'social' Europe. All in all, adding the adjective 'European' to the identity concept does not seem to help very much in clarifying terms in a discursive field which is in any case permeated by all kinds of semantic ambiguities.

In this chapter, I do not intend to give a systematic inventory of the manifold 'identity issues' discussed so intensely in different social science disciplines over the last two to three decades. As is to be expected, the steady multiplication of scholarly uses of the category has already triggered the first massive counter-reactions. Brubaker and Cooper (2000: 2–3), for example, speak of an '"identity" crisis' in the social sciences, a crisis they relate to the devaluation of meaning caused by overproduction. In a wide-ranging polemic, they put forward the argument that 'identity' should be completely abandoned as a category of social and political analysis.[1] Although I understand the reasons for the uneasiness Brubaker and Cooper express regarding 'identity inflation', I will not follow their radical advice. My view is that it is all but impossible to elude the identity concept, at least as long as one does not want to engage in long and complicated paraphrasing exercises. To be sure, the concept has to be used in a disciplined and coherent way if we are to avoid depriving it of a coherent

---

[1] For our purposes, it may be left open whether the conceptual catalogue elaborated by Brubaker and Cooper (2001: 14–21), in which 'identity' is replaced by terms such as 'identification', 'self-understanding' and 'commonality', would have the desired effect of making the debate more transparent.

meaning. The ubiquity which the concept has attained in the social sciences and humanities today may well have dubious consequences; however, these are not only bound up with the internal dynamics of academic discourse. To a considerable extent, the 'identity syndrome' seems rather to be a reflection of the profound changes we are experiencing in the realms of politics and society. Behind all navel-gazing tendencies, which are more or less inherent to the general discourse on identity, behind all the attempts to establish links between the individual and the collective dimensions of the human condition, lies a widely shared feeling that, under the pressure of a sweeping transformation, much of what seemed solid is once again melting into thin air.

The intermingling of identity change and identity quest is particularly evident in the European context. In the controversies over the European Union's (EU's) political perspectives, 'European identity' is both considered to be a desideratum and questioned as a chimera. The salience of the identity issue is especially remarkable in the discussion that revolves around Europe's democratic capability. On the one hand, only few observers would challenge the view that a politically resilient European identity is urgently needed for strengthening the legitimation basis of the EU. On the other hand, many would doubt that such an identity currently exists to the required extent. At times one even hears voices arguing that, for structural reasons, it will not come into being at all. Our previous reflections on the question of the European demos have shown that assessments of this type focus primarily on the cultural dimensions of the collective identity of Europeans, their general conclusion being that the cultural supports available for the political articulation of a collective will that could transcend the nation-states are, at best, precarious.

This leads me to the concept of identity on which the argumentation in the following sections will rely. I understand cultural identity as the manifest expression of politically institutionalized cultural practices. After introducing the concept, I will turn to the 'identity dilemmas' generated by the interplay of culture and politics in the institutional framework of the EU. As will be shown, in order to analyze these dilemmas in the appropriate way it is important to conceive of the EU as a multinational polity. At the end of the chapter, I discuss the consequences which a 'multinational constellation' of a new kind entails for the EU's political development.

3.1   Cultural Identity and Political Integration

Where identity matters are debated, culture tends to jump quickly on the stage as well. This seems to be especially the case when the identity of such a highly complex entity as Europe becomes the focus. Since Coudenhove-Kalergi founded the pan-European movement in the interwar period, pointing out the common basic elements of a European culture has been a recurrent strategy used to justify attempts at the political unification of the continent. There are certainly significant degrees of variation in the manifold proposals put forward to specify the core components of a common European culture, but the Judeo-Christian tradition, Hellenism and the Enlightenment are still the most frequently named candidates when it comes to defining the cultural roots of European identity. However, those who delve into the past in search of the origins of European culture can hardly avoid encountering a general dilemma: by trying to find substance, they essentialize particular cultural features and discard alternative identity patterns. Thus, to emphasize the Judeo-Christian legacy implies neglecting the contributions to European history made by Islam; to underline the role of Hellenism means to ignore the 'Barbarians'; and, finally, to concentrate on the Enlightenment may involve the risk of downplaying the significance of Romanticism in the formation of modern European consciousness. In spite of its wide historical scope, the cultural triad in question stands for deliberate choices, thereby excluding other possible options for collective identification from the European project.[2] At the same time and somewhat paradoxically, the selection has an excessively general character, as the elements it embraces are markers not only of the Old Continent but of the whole Western world, which stretches far beyond European territory, wherever one may want to draw Europe's borders.

As we see in the European case, to define cultural identity in terms of a substantial canon of values which appear to be 'inscribed' in a given historical process leads to problematic results. Therefore, I will adopt a different approach when dealing with the concept and focus primarily on those patterns of collective identification located in the realm of culture which have attained instrumental significance for the dynamics of political integration in modern societies. This implies concentrating on such denominators of group membership as collective memories, codified everyday knowledge, ethnicity, language or religion. A normatively rather modest view of cultural identity underlies this approach. Moreover, this approach is deliberately more selective than the perspective that guides social anthropology and related disciplines which aim at a 'deep' analysis of culture. For the purposes of this study, the most interesting aspects of culture are at the same time perhaps the most obvious ones.

---

[2] For a critical account of the long series of attempts to provide the European idea with cultural foundations, see Delanty (1995).

Accordingly, I understand culture as a set of collective practices which are strongly institutionalized, where institutionalization refers basically to *political* institutionalization. While delineating a specific frame of analysis, the approach still includes a broad range of phenomena. Typical examples of cultural identities institutionalized by political means in modern societies are 'national' histories or myths and their public visualization (in monuments, museums, street names, on postage stamps, coins and bank notes), educational curricula, patterns of religious identification that receive some form of official protection (as most ostensibly state churches do), public creeds which may rather have a secular character, or officially recognized and 'standardized' languages (Kraus 2003: 666–7). Under modern conditions, cultural identity ultimately serves as an institutionally entrenched cognitive and normative template for political communication; it can be regarded as the reified or 'structural' communicative framework which makes for the mutual intelligibility of the interactions of the members of a political community.

Regardless of its structural aspects, however, the communicative space generated by an encompassing cultural identity does not delineate a closed system of meaning. Sharing a culture does not imply that there has to be a substantial consensus on shared values. Communication includes the option of articulating dissent. A culture structures areas of common knowledge, but it does not rule out conflict over the contents and interpretation of this knowledge (Eder 1999: 149). Cultural identities do not simply display prefabricated answers to questions which are normatively relevant; rather they offer a changing repertoire of orientations for coming to grips with such questions. Nevertheless, the cultural repertoire has an almost 'taken-for-granted' dimension. It comprehends the 'basics' that the members of a political community learn in the course of being socialized into this community. Precisely because of their taken-for-grantedness, these basics play a crucial role in reproducing a political order. They are the source of the 'diffuse support' (Easton 1965) required if social conflicts are to be institutionalized in democratic ways.

The very intertwining of the dynamics of cultural and political integration paved the way for the spread of nationalism in modern societies. In a nutshell, nationalism's main goal is to make political and cultural borders congruent. With the emergence of national forms of rule, cultural homogeneity became a principle which played an important functional role and, moreover, had great relevance for legitimating a polity (Gellner 1983). The functional aspect results from the increased need for regulating processes of social communication in modern states, as compared to traditional forms of political organization. Industrialism and bureaucracy are well-known motors of cultural standardization. The legitimizing aspect of culture is even more significant for our concerns. In the overlapping areas of cultural reproduction and the democratic exercise of power, cultural identity becomes 'national' identity. Once again, we find ourselves on the terrain of the demos issue, although this time moving in the opposite direction: not from demos to culture, but from culture to demos. In implicit or explicit ways, the extension of citizenship rights in the course of political modernization was based on the definition of a cultural profile common to all citizens. In contrast with a machinery of authoritarian control, democratic institutions are contingent upon high levels of political loyalty and trust within the population. Hence, in the process of democratization at the level of nation-states, cultural homogeneity was regarded as a precondition for political differentiation and the control of the conflict potentials it generates. It showed how the paradox of sovereignty could be circumvented, as described earlier.[3] Common attachments to a political community were typically held to be a reflection of cultural affinities; the identity they configured defined the terms of the basic consensus that was considered to be necessary to provide the processes of democratic will-formation with durable foundations.

It is evident that the identities which played an instrumental role in the making of modern political communities are constructed identities. As a matter of fact, it has become all but a sociological commonplace to point out that all identities are constructs. An identity is not the result of a simple addition of cultural raw materials; it is constituted through the symbolic 'processing' of cultural 'ingredients' in the context of social interaction. The relevant question, then, is not *if*, but how, from what and by whom an identity has been constructed (Castells 1997: 7, 29). New forms of polity-building foster the development of new patterns of collective identity. Yet it would be both empirically false and normatively questionable to assume that these new patterns bear no relationship at all to the universe of former identities, as if there were a zero point of political integration. Therefore, to interpret the construction of cultural identities as an *exclusively* strategic process[4] is to follow a one-sided approach. Cultural identity is produced at the intersections of system and life-world; notwithstanding its instrumental aspects, it can rarely be properly understood without taking into account expressive motives.

---

[3] See Chapter 2, Section 2.4.

[4] In some contributions to the study of nationalism written from a constructivist angle, there is the tendency to interpret national identities as purely ideological devices shaped and used by elites with manipulative intentions (cf. Hobsbawm 1990). In a similar vein, Gellner (1983) radically questions the authenticity of the cultural roots of nationalist movements, while emphasizing the great functional power of nationalism.

To the extent that it is used as a basis for political integration, cultural identity ultimately becomes a matter of politics on its own right. As Robert Dahl (1989: 207) cogently indicates, there can be no democratic decision-making if there is no unit that allows the correct application of democratic procedures. The correctness of the unit itself, however, can't be determined just by making use of procedures that are derived from democratic criteria. Cultural identity has been so relevant for processes of democratic integration because it is an apparently 'prepolitical' and unquestionable resource for democratic politics; as such, it can't be easily called into question. Where a democracy lacks the 'natural' support of a shared cultural identity, political conflicts threaten to tear apart the civic community, evoking the spectre of secession. Yet the contribution cultural identity has typically made to circumventing the paradox of sovereignty is not a politically innocent one. The cultural elements at work when a democratic polity is constructed tend not to have a 'neutral' origin but are manifestations of cultural hegemony. Inasmuch as this is the case, they bear an aspect of domination that makes them politically contestable. Thus, the paradox of sovereignty ultimately reappears as the dilemma of cultural identity for democratic politics.

Which effects cultural heterogeneity and protracted conflicts over the definition of common patterns of identification have on processes of political integration that take place in democratic institutional settings has for a long time been a highly controversial issue both in political theory and in political sociology. Within the tradition of liberal democratic theory, the contrasting basic positions can be traced back to John Stuart Mill and Lord Acton.[5] With a focus on the topic of multiculturalism, the dispute has experienced an ongoing revival since the 1990s.[6] Until today, there has been little agreement on the consequences diversity has for democratic governance. In the meanwhile, as the debates on the question of a transnational demos show, the controversy has reached the realm of European integration too. Critical accounts of the EU's capacity for political deepening have often turned on the problematic character of a European identity. To insist on the important role multiple identities – which are usually split into three categories, namely, regional, national and European – have to play in building Europe as a polity[7] is only of limited help in this context. On the one hand, it remains unclear how these different layers of collective identification relate to each other. One should not take

---

[5] Compare Mill (1972 [1861]), Acton (1922 [1862]).
[6] The Canadian contributions to the debate deserve special mention (cf. Carens 2000, Ignatieff 2000, Kymlicka 1995, Tully 1995).
[7] Reese-Schäfer (1999: 264–5) is a case in point.

for granted that they interact in a complementary way. To cite just one example, the identity combination 'Scottish–British' can be as tension-ridden as the combination 'British–European'. We cannot assume that an equilibrium between identities will always be reached smoothly; often it will not be much more than the precarious expression of a politically contested status quo. On the other hand, the concept of multiple identities leaves open what holds the 'multiplicity' together.

In the post-Maastricht period, it has been widely maintained that, if the project of European polity-building is to materialize, the Union can't but confront the challenge of working towards an overarching cultural identity. The French historian Jacques Le Goff offers a succinct version of this position: 'Europe must become aware that it needs a common culture, which in large part is yet to be created.'[8] It is symptomatic that Jean Monnet is regularly quoted both in the press and in the academic literature as the source of the following statement on how Europe should be rearranged, though this attribution is apparently apocryphal in spite of its popularity: 'If we had to do it again, I would begin with culture.'[9] In view of such categorical declarations, the question must be raised how the European institutions tackle the identity issue.

3.2   European Identity Strategies

The European Community (EC)/EU may claim to have been actively engaged in 'identity politics' well before the latter became a subject of major concern for the humanities and the social sciences. In the domain of European institutions, the career of the identity concept dates back to the early 1970s. More precisely, it begins in December 1973 at the EC summit held in Copenhagen where a Declaration on European Identity was adopted. The declaration listed the principles of representative democracy, the rule of law, social justice and respect for human rights as the main pillars of European identity; in addition, it emphasized the will of the – at that time, nine – member states to preserve the rich diversity of their national cultures. At the same time, European identity was envisioned as something dynamic, both as a starting point and as a product of an open political process. The European 'discovery' of the identity concept reflected the disruptive changes in the global order experienced at the beginning of the 1970s. The breakdown of the Bretton Woods system

---

[8] Cited from an interview with Jacques Le Goff published in the German weekly *Die Zeit* (50/2000), 7 December 2000 (own translation).

[9] Quoted after Berting (1997: 49). In reality, the correct reference for this sentence seems to be the historian Helène Ahrweiler.

and the first oil crisis marked the end of the long period of post-war prosperity. Apparently, while confronting the first dramatic economic setback since the constitution of the European Coal and Steel Community, the participants in the summit sought to redefine the legitimation bases of the process of European unification, finding a new focal point in the concept of 'European identity'. The political attempt at launching the idea of a European identity in that context may well be interpreted as evidence of the weak bases of a common identity that the integration process had generated until that point (Stråth 2000a: 19, 2000b: 403).

The principal ingredients of Europe's 'official' identity discourse have remained surprisingly constant since 1973. On the one hand, the framework for unity is delineated by a common set of political values. On the other hand, cultural diversity is accorded a central normative status for the process of integration. Thus, the Millennium Declaration adopted by the European Council in Helsinki in December 1999, more than 25 years after Copenhagen, reads as follows:

The European Union is based on democracy and the rule of law. The Union's citizens are bound together by common values such as freedom, tolerance, equality, solidarity and cultural diversity.

The European Union is a unique venture, with no model in history. Only together, through the Union, can we and our countries meet tomorrow's challenges.[10]

From Copenhagen through Helsinki, the EC/EU's official approach to the question of cultural identity remained very cautious. In the meanwhile, the recurrent pledge to respect and protect the diversity of cultures seems to have developed almost into a ritual. Obviously, culture is a highly sensitive matter in European politics. It continues to be a competence held by the member states, which are eager to take care of their own 'identity affairs'. Nonetheless, from 1973 onwards, the cultural dimension has attained an increasingly prominent role in the institutional efforts to define Europe's identity, as a look at treaties, declarations and related documents quickly reveals. The evidence is particularly striking when we examine the dynamics of integration in the interval that spans from the signing of the Treaty on European Union in 1992 to the submission of the draft of the European constitution in 2003.

In the preamble of the Maastricht Treaty the member states expressed their desire 'to deepen the solidarity between their peoples while

---

[10] Helsinki European Council, Millennium Declaration, Bulletin EU 12–1999, Annexes to the Presidency conclusions (2/7), Annex I (http://europa.eu.int/abc/doc/off/bull/en/9912/p000030.htm).

respecting their history, their culture and their traditions'.[11] The announcement of a Common Foreign and Security and Policy was linked to the intention of 'reinforcing European identity and its independence'. Article 6 of the Treaty says:

1. The Union is founded on the principles of liberty, democracy, respect for human rights and fundamental freedoms, and the rule of law, principles which are common to the Member States.
. . .
3. The Union shall respect the national identities of its Member States.

Moreover, the treaties of Maastricht and Amsterdam (1997) included an amendment of the Treaty establishing the European Communities, originally signed in Rome in 1957. The modified version of the Treaty of Rome contains a specific title for culture, which was later also incorporated in the constitutional draft.[12] As the corresponding paragraphs affirm:

1. The Union shall contribute to the flowering of the cultures of the Member States, while respecting their national and regional diversity and at the same time bringing the common cultural heritage to the fore.
2. Action by the Union shall be aimed at encouraging cooperation between Member States and, if necessary, supporting and supplementing their action in the following areas:
(a) improvement of the knowledge and dissemination of the culture and history of the European peoples;
(b) conservation and safeguarding of cultural heritage of European significance;
(c) non-commercial cultural exchanges;
(d) artistic and literary creation, including in the audiovisual sector.
. . .
4. The Union shall take cultural aspects into account in its action under other provisions of this Constitution, in particular in order to respect and to promote the diversity of its cultures.
. . .

All in all, one can justly assert that Maastricht and Amsterdam already showed a tendency that ultimately evolved into a fairly stable pattern, as could be seen in the course of the drafting of the Charter of Fundamental

---

[11] Treaty on European Union (signed in Maastricht on 7 February 1992), consolidated version incorporating the changes made by the Treaty of Amsterdam amending the Treaty on European Union, the Treaties establishing the European Communities and certain related acts, signed at Amsterdam on 2 October 1997 (European Union 1999: 11–68).

[12] See Part III of the Treaty establishing a Constitution for Europe (The Policies and Functioning of the Union), Title III, Chapter V, Section 3, Culture, Article III-280 (*Official Journal of the European Union*, C 310, Volume 47, 16 December 2004, pp. 125–6).

Rights and of the Constitutional Treaty. The goals of establishing 'an ever closer union' based on common values and of preserving the diversity of cultures – a diversity understood in essence as the diversity of the cultures of nation-states – are accorded equal status; yet no major efforts are undertaken to reconcile their potentially conflicting logics. The Charter of Fundamental Rights of the European Union, solemnly proclaimed by the European Parliament, the Council and the Commission in Nice in December 2000, may be read as summarizing the main developments in the Union's official doctrine on diversity. As a result of the Convention's deliberations, the Charter was incorporated in the Treaty establishing a Constitution for Europe (as Part II of the document).[13] The following paragraphs are taken from the Charter's Preamble[14]:

The peoples of Europe, in creating an ever closer union among them, are resolved to share a peaceful future based on common values.
  Conscious of its spiritual and moral heritage, the Union is founded on the indivisible, universal values of human dignity, freedom, equality and solidarity; it is based on the principles of democracy and the rule of law. It places the individual at the heart of its activities, by establishing the citizenship of the Union and by creating an area of freedom, security and justice.
  The Union contributes to the preservation and to the development of these common values while respecting the diversity of the cultures and traditions of the peoples of Europe as well as the national identities of the Member States and the organization of their public authorities at national, regional and local levels; it seeks to promote balanced and sustainable development and ensures free movement of persons, goods, services and capital, and the freedom of establishment.

Article 22 of the Charter of Rights (Article II-82 of the Constitutional Treaty) consists of one short sentence that puts additional stress on the political significance of cultural diversity in the EU: 'The Union shall respect cultural, religious and linguistic diversity'.[15] It should be noted that, as this article is included in Title III of the Charter ('Equality'), respect for diversity is directly connected to the purpose of promoting the principle of equality for all European citizens.

Finally, diversity also features as an important concept in the text that represents the principal substantive outcome of the debates held in the Convention, (i.e., in Part One of the Constitutional Treaty). A direct reference to the Union's official motto is already given in the Constitution's Preamble, which invokes a Europe '[u]nited in diversity'.[16] Article I-3

---

[13] The Charter itself is not a legally binding text. Hence, the observance of its provisions by the member states depends on the final ratification of the Constitutional Treaty.
[14] *Official Journal of the European Union*, C 310, Volume 47, 16 December 2004, p. 41.
[15] *Official Journal of the European Union*, C 310, Volume 47, 16 December 2004, p. 46.
[16] *Official Journal of the European Union*, C 310, Volume 47, 16 December 2004, p. 3.

of the Constitution then lists the Union's objectives. In subsection 3 of this Article, two paragraphs may be understood as a specific reference to what it means to be 'united in diversity':

It [i.e., the Union] shall promote economic, social and territorial cohesion, and solidarity among Member States.

It shall respect its rich cultural and linguistic diversity, and shall ensure that Europe's cultural heritage is safeguarded and enhanced.[17]

While trying to consolidate Europe as an 'identity project', the official actors in the EC/EU have not been limiting their efforts to the level of programmatic declarations and grand treaties. This is especially true for the Commission during the period of the Delors presidency (1985–1994), a period that produced important outcomes in terms of both political symbols and political contents.[18] Delors has remained a firm advocate of the idea that the Union should be deliberately involved in 'identity politics'. In a newspaper article written in 2000, he defends the view that referring to Europe's cultural dimension means raising the question of European identity. According to the former president of the Commission, the search for a European identity must not be abandoned. After mentioning different possibilities for grounding this identity, such as the Judeo-Christian tradition, Greek democracy, Roman law and the Enlightenment, Delors concludes that Europe should be seen as a place of eternal self-doubt. He thinks that the Continent's self-doubt will prove to be an advantage in the era of globalization (Delors 2000).

In which ways has Europe's 'identity search', an endeavour in which Delors himself was a prominent participant for over a decade, brought about material results so far? Where is the concrete evidence of the 'identity strategies' adopted by EU institutions?

1. *Citizenship of the European Union* may be adduced as a particularly relevant example in this respect. In modern societies, individual identity finds its foremost legal and political expression in the principle of citizenship. The citizenship status constitutes the elementary bond between a person and the political community to which he or she belongs. Traditionally, the individual rights and obligations which derive from being a citizen are connected to membership in a nation-state. Depending on the specific historical context, the citizenship status has reflected a variable combination of civil, political and social elements (Marshall 1950). With increasing frequency, cultural rights are being added as a fourth essential element to the classical triad (Turner 1994: 158–60).

---

[17] *Official Journal of the European Union*, C 310, Volume 47, 16 December 2004, pp. 11–12.
[18] A detailed analysis of the paper played by Delors in the process of integration is presented in Ross (1995).

EU citizenship was introduced in 1992 with the Treaty on European Union. It did not entail a radical change in established standards: in order to be a European citizen, a person has to be a national of one of the member states of the EU. As Article 17 (1) of the Consolidated Version of the Treaty Establishing the European Community reads: 'Every person holding the nationality of a Member State shall be a citizen of the Union. Citizenship of the Union shall complement and not replace national citizenship.' The list of rights attached to EU citizenship includes the right to move and reside freely within the territory of the member states, the right to vote and to stand as a candidate in local elections as well as in elections to the European Parliament in the member state in which a Union citizen resides and the right to petition the European Parliament.[19] More than 10 years have passed since European citizenship was established, but it is still hard to determine to what extent it has contributed to strengthening the links between European institutions and the citizens of the member states. So far, however, the broader public does not seem to perceive Union citizenship as implying a substantial departure from the national traditions of granting rights. The Constitutional Treaty reaffirms the normative weight of Union citizenship yet does not expand on its previous content.[20] As in 1992, Union citizenship has to be considered essentially as a general category for the limited rights enjoyed by nationals of a member state in the other member states of the Union.[21] It is not obvious that the existence of this category is causing a significant increase in the level of identification of European citizens with the emerging European polity.

2. European identity seems to have attained its most salient dimensions in the domain of political *symbols*. The European flag has become a constant element in the institutional routine activities of all member states of the Union. The circle of 12 yellow stars on an azure-blue background is the official emblem of Europe's unification since 1985. That the number 12 was chosen as a symbol of European identity is related to its special significance in the ancient Greek and Roman world as well as in Christianity (Shore 2000: 47–8). Besides, the EU appears as a visible symbol on European passports, driver's licenses and car registration plates. Citizens of EU member states who travel within the territory of the Treaty of Schengen have learned to appreciate the concrete practical

---

[19] For the complete normative framework currently regulating Union citizenship, see Articles 17–22 in the Consolidated Version of the Treaty Establishing the European Community (*Official Journal of the European Communities*, C 325, 24 December 2002, pp. 44–6).

[20] See Part I, Title II, of the Treaty establishing a Constitution for Europe (*Official Journal of the European Union*, C 310, Volume 47, 16 December 2004, pp. 13–14).

[21] See Meehan (1993) for a systematic analysis of these rights.

advantages connected with Europe's symbolic dimension. It has to be added that the EU is not only an officially visible but also an 'audible' entity. Its hymn is the Ode to Joy, taken from the fourth movement of Beethoven's Ninth Symphony. Finally, we must not forget that the Union has adopted a motto that also appears in the Constitutional Treaty; quite characteristically, it reads: 'United in diversity'.[22]

The history of the EC/EU began with the establishment of an economic community. After several decades, the existence of the Common Market has left deep cognitive traces in the everyday life of average citizens. That there are European standards for product marketing and labelling has an impact on how products are perceived. Thus, the identity of European citizens is closely linked to the identity of consumers. We may expect the common currency to play a central role as a symbol of attachment to the EU. Even before the old national currencies disappeared, preparing for the introduction of the Euro and discussing its effects were already changing the collective patterns of identification all over Europe. In the German-speaking area, for instance, the term 'Euroland' has acquired specific connotations: it refers to the regulatory domain of the Monetary Union. At the same time, it has turned into a widely used category for comparing the economic situation in the EU with the situation in the USA. However, as we will see, the Euro – or, to be more precise, the design of the Euro banknotes – also brings to the fore some of the most characteristic dilemmas and ambiguities of European identity politics.

3. Finally, there are different *programs in the areas of education and culture* which are obviously related to Europe's institutional identity strategies. For instance, since the 1980s, the EC/EU has been making great efforts to promote the mobility of university students via the Erasmus und Socrates programs. The Lingua program was basically conceived as a catalogue of measures designed to lend the cultures of the smaller member states greater visibility within the Union.[23]

Moreover, there have been several initiatives to support European productions in the audiovisual sector, with a special emphasis on television and cinema. Yet, at the same time, in the audiovisual policies implemented by the EC/EU the criteria of market integration, promoting the liberalization of the production and marketing of cultural goods act as a powerful rival to the much-evoked principle of protecting cultural diversity. For more than a decade, critical voices have been raised against a

---

[22] Article I-8 of the Treaty establishing a Constitution for Europe (*Official Journal of the European Union*, C 310, Volume 47, 16 December 2004, p. 13).

[23] For an overview of EC/EU programs in the realms of education and culture, see Vandamme (1994: 256–8) and Shore (2000: 53–60).

creeping tendency to adopt the US cultural model in the policies that regulate the audiovisual sector in Europe (Dumont 1994: 129). Regarding
the official efforts undertaken to develop a cultural identity that becomes
effective at a pan-European level, one should also mention a more recent
series of initiatives in the field of transnational cultural exchange whose
aim is to increase general appreciation of the 'common cultural heritage'
of Europeans. Initiatives of this kind, such as the program Culture 2000,
have been undertaken with increasing regularity by the Directorate General Education and Culture of the Commission. The question now is
what results the EU's 'identity strategies' can show in fostering shared
collective attachments among Europeans.

3.3   Limits of European Identity

In the course of the formation of modern polities, national identity
became the basis of a close relationship between state and citizens which
expressed a complex intermingling of power structures, affective bonds
and patterns of solidarity. The basis itself was not a resource that could
be taken for granted as a quasi-'organic' given but it was the product
of far-reaching institutional efforts. The political challenge was con-
cisely captured by the nineteenth-century Italian nationalist Massimo
d'Azeglio after the *Risorgimento*. Facing the situation of the new nation-
state established on the Apennine Peninsula, he declared that now that
Italy had been made, the order of the day would have to be to make
Italians.

It would certainly be mistaken to analyze the identity dilemmas experienced by the EU exclusively in light of the historical dynamics of nation-
state formation. Nevertheless, it is still tempting to recall the situation
described by d'Azeglio in order to better capture the current quandaries
of political integration in Europe. As an emerging polity, the EU does
indeed face the task of mobilizing collective loyalties 'of its own', that is,
without having to rely on the member states as legitimizing intermedi-
aries. The institutional strategies designed to create and to consolidate
a European identity respond to this challenge. Moreover, the goal of
strengthening a genuinely European layer of political legitimation is an
important feature of the Union's institutional architecture. In contrast
with the Council of Ministers, which is generally regarded as an organ
of the member-state executives, the European Parliament is supposed to
function as the representative body of the citizens of Europe. Yet where
are the Europeans? There are two significant factors which make for a
stark contrast between the current political context in the EU and that in
Italy in the aftermath of the *Risorgimento*.

First, Europeans are not willing to allow themselves to be 'made' without major reservations. In the institutional framework of the European state of the nineteenth century, the political citizenship status was the privilege of a minority. To a large extent, the 'masses' remained excluded from participation in official politics.[24] Things have changed a lot since then. EU citizens do not undergo the Europeanization of their identities as disfranchised political subjects, many of them taking a critical stance towards the process of European polity-building or even questioning it openly. The EU, at the other side, does not possess the institutional means to shape citizens' identities so as to produce effects similar to those the public school system or military service formerly brought about in the nation-states. Second, Europeans of the late twentieth and the early twenty-first century share an attribute which distinguishes them from the bulk of Italy's population around 1860 and complicates all attempts at implementing a collective identity from above: they generally have developed more or less stable national or subnational identities, which so far bear a much greater weight than 'Europeanness'.

Since 1973, Eurobarometer surveys, sponsored by the European Commission, are conducted periodically in the member states of the EC/EU. Their purpose is to offer an empirical assessment of public attitudes towards European integration and European institutions and to examine the support bases of European politics. Questions referring to the formation of a European identity as well as to how identification with Europe relates to identification with the nation-states have become a regular feature of these surveys. Moreover, citizens are asked to give a specific political evaluation of the EU. Finally, there are several questions which focus on the general interest for issues in European policy and on the level of public knowledge concerning European affairs; indirectly, they chart implications regarding the overall topic 'European identity' as well. When it comes to measuring identities, results such as those produced by the Eurobarometer reports should be regarded with a certain amount of scepticism. In a web of shifting identity options, the empirical pictures of identity patterns captured by surveys may vary widely with contextual factors. This holds not only for the EU but also applies to political units with which we tend to associate a lower degree of institutional complexity. At a given moment in time, an individual may feel more Scottish or more British or, to mention another example, as a Québécoise rather than as a Canadian. The identity definition given at that moment will reflect the extent to which the relationship between the different units of

[24] For most countries, the breakthrough to generalizing suffrage came only after the First World War (cf. Therborn 1977).

Table 3.1. *European and National Identity*

European Union	EU12 (1994)	EU15 (1999)	EU25 (2004)
Identity European only	7%	4%	3%
Identity European and nationality	10%	7%	7%
Identity nationality and European	46%	43%	47%
Identity nationality only	33%	43%	41%
Figures for selected countries:			
	France 1994	France 1999	France 2004
Identity European only	11%	7%	4%
Identity European and nationality	12%	7%	9%
Identity nationality and European	52%	49%	55%
Identity nationality only	22%	35%	30%
	Germany 1994	Germany 1999	Germany 2004
Identity European only	9%	4%	5%
Identity European and nationality	15%	9%	9%
Identity nationality and European	43%	37%	48%
Identity nationality only	29%	46%	36%
	UK 1994	UK 1999	UK 2004
Identity European only	7%	5%	1%
Identity European and nationality	7%	4%	5%
Identity nationality and European	34%	27%	35%
Identity nationality only	49%	62%	55%

Percentage 'don't know' not shown.
Sources: Eurobarometer 42 (1995: 66), *Eurobarometer 50* (1999: 59), *Eurobarometer 62* (2005: 94, 96).

reference is marked by political conflict. In the field of EU politics, where cleavage lines remain fluid, the weight of contextual effects is likely to be even more important. In addition, when those interviewed have to make a choice between fixed identity options, the responses measured may have been induced to a considerable degree by the survey itself. However, let us refrain from such objections for a moment and assume that the Eurobarometer surveys offer a rough empirical approximation to Europe's identity mosaic (see Table 3.1). Which place do the citizens of the EU assign to the European identity dimension, according to this approximation?

In 2004, the only country in which the percentage of persons reporting that they see themselves as solely or predominantly European reached a value above 20 percent was Luxembourg (with 26 percent). In contrast, there were six EU member states where a majority of the population identified exclusively with their nationality: Hungary (64 percent) being the leader in this group followed by the Czech Republic (57 percent),

Greece (57 percent), Finland (56 percent), the UK (55 percent) and Lithuania (53 percent); in five more cases (Portugal, Sweden, Latvia, Poland and Estonia), the corresponding values ranged between 49 and 45 percent.[25] Two older Eurobarometer surveys, realized in 1998 and 1999, introduced an interesting additional dimension in EU-sponsored 'identity research'. In these surveys, the respondents were asked to what extent they agreed with the statement that there is a European *cultural* identity that is shared by all Europeans. The findings offer little variation from one year to another, and scepticism regarding a common culture clearly predominates among Europeans (see Table 3.2). In sum, the figures indicate that the levels of primary identification with Europe have remained low along the path stretching from the old EU12, which ratified the Treaty on European Union, to the EU25 produced by the first round of the eastern enlargement. It is true that multiple identities – combining the European and the national dimension – are an important reality in the Union nowadays. Nevertheless, it is striking how stable attitudes reflecting indifference or even hostility towards the EU have remained over a relatively long time span. Thus Reif (1993: 138–9) discusses survey data from 1990 that show that in the EC comprising 12 member states the portion of those not at all identifying with Europe was 46 percent. This figure is fairly consistent with the findings of the long series of subsequent Eurobarometer reports. Against such a background, one can hardly expect a sudden and substantial shift in the 'identity configuration' which the available empirical data roughly delineate.[26]

The weakness of an autonomous European identity component among EU citizens is important because of its political implications. These can be grasped when we turn to the support citizens express to the membership of their countries in the EU. On the one hand, it should be remarked that at the beginning of the twenty-first century support for membership in the EU maintained a consistent level of approximately 50 percent, whereas the negative evaluations of membership oscillated around 15 percent.[27] On the other hand, however, it is also true that in 2004 only 39 percent of the respondents declared that they would be very sorry if the EU were to be scrapped; 13 percent said that they would be very relieved, whereas the score for those indifferent is 43 percent.[28] A comparison of the averages measured in the EC and the EU since 1973 shows that the percentage

---

[25] See *Eurobarometer* 62 (2005: 96).

[26] See Nissen (2004) for a more detailed assessment which draws similar conclusions.

[27] The figures are for the percentages of respondents who think that their country's membership of the EU is a 'good thing' or a 'bad thing'; for the evolution of these figures between 1995 (EU15) and 2005 (EU25) see *Eurobarometer* 63 (2005: 10).

[28] *Eurobarometer* 62 (2005: 86).

Table 3.2. *European Cultural Identity*

'There is a European identity shared by all Europeans.'	Eurobarometer 50 (fieldwork: 1998)		Eurobarometer 52 (fieldwork: 1999)	
	% Completely + slightly agree	% Slightly + completely disagree	% Completely + slightly agree	% Slightly + completely disagree
EU15	38	49	38	49
Figures for selected countries:				
France	40	53	36	59
Germany	44	44	43	43
UK	28	58	28	53

Percentage 'don't know' not shown.
Sources: Eurobarometer 50 (1999: 60), *Eurobarometer* 52 (2000: 11).

of those relieved and indifferent has even increased slightly over the past three decades.[29]

The results of the surveys conducted under the aegis of the Commission show that the development of an identity dimension which might be regarded as primarily European has been slow and limited until now, in spite of all official efforts invested in fostering feelings of 'Europeanness' within the citizenry. At any rate, one can hardly speak of a strong transnational commitment towards the EU. The evidence indicates rather that the 'permissive consensus' which sustained the dynamics of integration for a long time has crumbled. Nor would a triumphal interpretation of the EU's success as an 'identity project' be corroborated by the levels of political participation discernible at the European level, which have remained persistently low. A clear indicator is the turnout at the six elections to the European Parliament held over the past 25 years. Since 1979, electoral participation was at first stagnant and then decreased, the elections of 1999 and 2004 being two consecutive low points in terms of voter turnout (see Table 3.3).

It may be regarded as paradoxical that the turnout at the elections to the European Parliament steadily decreased between 1999 and 2004. Previously, the indistinct profile and the restricted legislative powers of the chamber had typically been cited as the reason why a large segment of the political public in the EU showed so little interest in its activities. The assumption was that, to the extent that the role of the Parliament

---

[29] See the overview of the evolution of people's attitudes towards the continued existence of the EU given in *Eurobarometer* 50 (1999: 37).

Table 3.3. *Turnout Rates at Elections to the European Parliament, 1979–2004*

	1979	1984	1987	1989	1994	1995	1996	1999	2004
EU Average	63,0%	61,0%	/	58,5%	56,8%	/	/	49,8%	45,7%
DE	65,7%	56,8%		62,3%	60,0%			45,2%	43,0%
FR	60,7%	56,7%		48,7%	52,7%			46,8%	42,8%
BE	91,4%	92,2%		90,7%	90,7%			91,0%	90,8%
IT	84,9%	83,4%		81,5%	74,8%			70,8%	73,1%
LU	88,9%	88,8%		87,4%	88,5%			87,3%	89,0%
NL	57,8%	50,6%		47,2%	35,6%			30,0%	39,3%
UK	32,2%	32,6%		36,2%	36,4%			24,0%	38,9%
IE	63,6%	47,6%		68,3%	44,0%			50,2%	58,8%
DK	47,8%	52,4%		46,2%	52,9%			50,5%	47,9%
EL		77,2%		79,9%	71,2%			75,3%	63,2%
ES			68,9%	54,6%	59,1%			63,0%	45,1%
PT			72,4%	51,2%	35,5%			40,0%	38,6%
SE						41,6%		38,8%	37,8%
AT							67,7	49,4%	42,4%
FI							60,3	31,4%	39,4%
CZ									28,3%
EE									26,8%
CY									71,2%
LV									41,3%
LT									48,4%
HU									38,5%
MT									82,4%
PL									20,9%
SI									28,3%
SK									17,0%

Source: Post European elections 2004 survey. Flash Eurobarometer 162 (2004: 7).

was devalued by the Council's clear dominance in the decision-making process, the citizens would not have a strong incentive to vote in European elections. If we adopt this perspective, we might have expected the strengthening of the European Parliament's institutional position to bring about an increase of the general concern for the only electoral contest conducted at the European level. The truth is that the legislative competences of the Parliament *were* substantially widened in the period after Maastricht (Teasdale 1999: 437). In the meantime, the co-decision procedure, which puts the Parliament on an equal footing with the Council, has become the norm in many important domains of EU legislation. Moreover, the coverage of parliamentary activities by the media has increased considerably since 1999, when the chamber played a prominent role in building up the pressures that caused the collective resignation of the members of the European Commission. However, the Parliament's fresh institutional momentum did not inspire greater motivation among the electorate. Against this background, the hypothesis that the strengthening of the parliamentary dimension of EU politics will have a direct positive effect at the level of citizen participation may well be questioned.

Rather, the low turnout rates at European elections seem to offer additional evidence that the potential of the integration project to generate strong ties with the citizenry remains limited. These limits also become visible when we focus on the diffuse context of political competition between the party federations represented in the European Parliament, where, in general, a great coalition formed by the European People's Party, the Liberals and the Socialists sustains a political will-formation in which the imperatives of consensus are constantly at work. For the party organizations, the elections to the European Parliament apparently do not have much political weight of their own, but are primarily 'second-order national contests' (Hix 1999: 180). Nor has the European level so far evolved into a privileged site for mobilizing the activities of social movements that, even when European issues are involved, continue to seek their addressees mainly within the nation-states when articulating their political demands (Tarrow 2001: 233–51). Thus, the daily business of transnational interest representation is dominated by the numerous and, in most cases, highly specialized lobbies that try to make their voice heard when it comes to the regulation of functional domains relevant for their concerns.

All evidence suggests that the *top-down* attempts of the Commission to bolster the identification of Europeans with Europe are not matched by comparable *bottom-up* processes. One may well highlight the historical importance of the European Movement of the post-war period, with its concrete utopia of establishing a transnational federation, in view of the challenges at present confronting the Union (Niess 2001); nonetheless, this movement was never able to generate levels of popular resonance similar to those produced by Europe's nationalisms in the nineteenth and twentieth centuries. The building of the EU is still frequently associated with technocracy and elitism. It is hardly a coincidence that the attachment to Europe is particularly high among managers, whereas it is strikingly lower among manual workers and the unemployed.[30] In a quite literal sense, the European project appears to be 'top heavy': the complex institutional arrangements configuring the system of transnational governance do not rest upon a solid intermediary level. Regarding the identification of the bulk of European citizens with 'their' polity, things appear even more precarious. The 'diffuse support' in the form of 'identity' dissipates almost entirely in attitudes towards the EU that are predominantly instrumental and measured by such categories as 'benefits of membership' in the Eurobarometer surveys.

As the writer Hans Magnus Enzensberger observed in 1963, in a speech revolving around the problematic character of German history, to pose the question of identity means to focus on the things that we take for granted in our understanding of ourselves and the world that surrounds us; hence, it means to raise a radical question, which cannot be ignored or left open.[31] If we try to tackle the question in the empirical context of European integration, it becomes clear that there is not too much of what we might consider 'taken for granted' in Europe. The EU does not rely upon historical 'certainties' or well-entrenched identity patterns; to a large extent, it does indeed reflect the making of a community in primarily *political* terms. Accordingly, European identity would rather be a symptom of the tensions observable in the interplay among different options of political identification than something 'natural' or 'to be taken for granted'.

Inasmuch as it is seen in the light of the identity syndrome, the democratization of Europe appears to be an issue that transcends institutional aspects. In recent years, the EU's democratic deficit has become a topic regularly covered by the media. Media coverage, however, has thus far not fuelled the formation of a democratic movement unfolding across Europe. The very lack of greater democratic pressure 'from below' may be regarded as one of the most troubling indicators of the legitimation problems confronting the emerging European polity.

---

[30] As the socio-demographic breakdown of Eurobarometer survey results shows; see, for instance, *Eurobarometer* 60 (2004: 30–1).

[31] The corresponding passage can be found in Enzensberger (1992: 9)

3.4   Socio-Cultural Heterogeneity in Multilevel Politics

The issue of European identity reflects how different options for collective identification, all of them enjoying some degree of institutional support, interrelate in complex ways within the framework of multilevel politics. Apart from supranationalism and the nation-state option, 'subnational' loyalties, especially when directed towards nations without a state, can play a significant role in this context as well. In EU member states such as Belgium, Spain and the UK, the territories of Flanders, the Basque Country, Catalonia or Scotland have become the focal points of an identity formation strongly protected by political institutions. In addition, a significant number of minority identities in Europe are linked to different kinds of regional attachments, languages or ethnicities. Finally, the 'new' minorities produced by migration have also attained a substantial weight. Whether in Brussels, Paris, Berlin or London, Maghrebian, Turkish or South-Asian communities nowadays shape the image of whole districts in European cities. To define Europe as a continent of multiple identities, therefore, comes very close to making an utterly trivial statement. Nonetheless, the identity patchwork that we encounter in some specific situations may prove highly intricate on closer inspection. Let us cast a glance at the case of Moroccan immigrants of Berber origin in Catalonia. Here we are dealing with the citizens of an Arabian monarchy who have taken up residence on what the Spanish state considers to be its sovereign territory; at the same time, the autonomous government of Catalonia, which enjoys political competences in the areas of culture and education, may be endeavouring to take these migrants' specific ethnic background into account when it comes to organizing education for their children in their mother tongue. Thus, we are dealing with a group whose members have to find an equilibrium – if not to establish priorities – between four different identity options defined by particular linguistic, ethnic, cultural or national ties (Berber – Moroccan – Spanish – Catalan). Comparable contexts, with several politically relevant identities which overlap and, to some extent, are also likely to collide, are not as exceptional as it may seem at first sight. A Kurd living in Brussels or a Sikh in Glasgow is also exposed to parallel cultural pressures rooted in their regions of origin (Kurdistan vs. Turkey, Rajasthan vs. India) and in their host countries (Flanders vs. French-speaking Belgium, Scotland vs. Britain). For the individuals concerned, to live 'multiple identities' may well be experienced as a difficult balancing act. In the realm of politics, therefore, the concept of multiple identities should not be taken for a magic formula for generating consensus. There is no automatism that would always make for a harmonious combination of all the colours that compose the European mosaic of identities.

What is the current situation in Europe at the *institutional* level as regards the articulation of collective patterns of identity against the background of a sociologically highly differentiated spectrum of identities? The EU is often described as a heterogeneous, segmented or polycentric political formation.[32] Showing sensitivity to and coping with structural diversity in decision-making processes is generally regarded as an essential feature of multilevel politics. The European multilevel system can be understood as a complex, integrated negotiating system comprising various policy arenas which exhibit territorially and functionally specific features but are nevertheless interconnected; the resulting institutional complexity means that there is a strong tendency among social scientists to define the EU as a political order *sui generis* (Grande 2000b: 12, 14). The assertion that the EU is a highly complex polity is not especially controversial. By contrast, it seems more problematic to categorize the EU as *sui generis*, that is, as a completely unique political entity that deviates radically from all known forms of statehood, and thereby to lend the analysis of the Union the character of a specialized discipline that develops more or less independently of comparative politics or political sociology. The assertion that the EU has 'long since become a state',[33] can be understood under current circumstances primarily as a provocative expression of calculated optimism. Nevertheless, when viewed from a comparative perspective, political Europe may be less exotic than the *sui generis* label would suggest. The EU does exhibit some features of statehood; as a multilevel system or multiform political order, it has been conceptually affiliated with both federations (or confederations) and consociations.[34]

As regards the federal aspect, viewed in light of conventional analyses of interstate and intrastate relations, the EU does not as yet constitute a union of individuals into a political association; at the same time, however, it is more than a mere alliance of states. It is situated so to speak in the grey area between a federation and a confederation. The EU is not a state and hence also not a federal state. Nevertheless, it possesses a number of federal characteristics; among them are, for example (Burgess 2000: 29, 41),

---

[32] See, for example, Hooghe and Marks (2001: 66), Lepsius (1999: 220), and Preuß (1999: 165).

[33] As maintained by the three social-democratic members of the European Parliament Willi Görlach, Jo Leinen and Rolf Linkohr (2000).

[34] On the comparison between the EU and federal models see, among others, Burgess (2000), Koslowski (1999) and Scharpf (1994); interpretations of politics in the EU inspired by the consociational approach are offered by Chryssochoou (1998), Schmidt (2000) and Taylor (1990).

- decision-making via cooperation and co-decision that includes both intergovernmental and supranational institutions;
- the direct election of the European Parliament as a body representing the voters in the Union not just as members of the European states but also as citizens of Europe as a whole;
- the strong institutional position of the European Court of Justice whose jurisdiction overrides national law; and
- the introduction of citizenship of the Union and the associated legal status throughout the EU.

Clearly the EU already explodes the traditional political-institutional framework of a confederation; however, this does not mean that it is evolving into a federation on the model of the 'United States of Europe'. There is no teleology leading from the European alliance of states to the European federal state. However, we must at the same time acknowledge that the categories of federation and confederation are by no means opposed concepts founded on substantial qualitative differences; they could reasonably be construed as different expressions of an overarching 'federal moment'. Moreover, as regards how its institutions function, the EU can conform de facto to federal patterns without for that reason having to be categorized as a federation from a formal point of view (Koslowski 1999: 563). Federal norms can also shape political relations even where a federal state in the strict sense does not exist.

Analyses of the political structure of the EU have also drawn on the concept of consociation.[35] Consociational institutional arrangements arise in societies which exhibit cleavages among different, socio-culturally defined segments. In such societies, they are supposed to facilitate modes of decision-making which fulfil the criterion of reflecting the interest of an overall political community, on the one hand, while preserving the autonomy of the individual segments, on the other. In general, consociations can be identified by the following features (Schmidt 2000: 41):

- power is divided among the segments when regulating political issues of common concern;
- in all other questions, the segments for the most part preserve their decision-making autonomy;
- the principle of proportionality holds for political representation and appointments to public offices; and

[35] In the history of ideas the concept of *consociatio* can be traced back to Johannes Althusius and his *Politica Methodice Digesta* (1603). It finds its way into contemporary comparative political science through the works of Lijphart who distinguishes consociational democracy from majoritarian democratic systems (see, for example, Lijphart 1977). Lehmbruch (1983) uses the phrase 'concordance democracy' in a similar context.

- the segments are accorded veto rights in areas of concern for their existential interests.

Typical examples of democracies operating in accordance with consociational rules are the Netherlands (until the mid-1960s), Belgium and Switzerland. In contrast to these cases, according to Schmidt (2000: 43), 'the European Union still lacks a proper sovereign people', even though it must be granted an element of statehood. The result is a structural democratic deficit. Accordingly, Schmidt (2000: 34) does not categorize the EU as a democratic state but as 'a bureaucratic consociational state'. In fact, bureaucratic-administrative rule is undoubtedly of major importance in the institutional system of the EU. However, we should not underestimate the political legitimation pressure to which institutional action in the EU is in the meantime exposed. Otherwise it would be very difficult to explain the strategies adopted by the Union to foster a European identity as discussed earlier. In Europe, bureaucratic politics cannot rely on the protective mantle of an authoritarian power apparatus. Schmidt's assessment needs to be supplemented in that the bureaucratic-consociational structures of the EU have only very limited leeway in avoiding the pressures of an essentially 'protodemocratic' mode of justification. In contrast to the era of Jean Monnet, a democratic reform of European governance is today also on the agenda within important elements of the political and administrative control centres of the EU.

Thus, it makes perfect sense to regard the EU, notwithstanding its institutional peculiarities, in terms of proven comparative categories. Viewed in this way, the institutional mechanisms of the vertical (territorial) division of powers within the European multilevel system exhibit a federal logic, at least in outline. In addition, the effects of differentiated integration – in particular, the degree of Europeanization of policy areas which may vary from one member state to another – lend the confederal-federal structures of the EU a pronounced asymmetrical character. On the resulting picture, the semi-federal diversification of policy levels is overlaid with the consociational imperative not to violate the autonomy of the member states comprising the segments of the Union.

I acknowledge the heuristic fruitfulness of analyses of the EU in terms of federal or consociational models, and I am also well aware that there is no lack of new proposals for conceptualizing the specific political features of the EU. Hence, I do not at all intend to bring additional categories into play for their own sake. Nevertheless, I regard it as imperative to highlight an aspect of the context sketched here that remains strangely neglected in comparative classificatory studies of the EU, namely, the fact that the political and institutional heterogeneity of the Union is a specific product of its multinational character. The EU is a multinational community. The socio-cultural heterogeneity and the territorial and political differentiation primarily highlighted by comparative approaches influenced by theories of federalism or consociationalism are features of a multinational order.

3.5   The 'Multinational Moment' in Europe's Institutional Order

For many years, the multinational dimension received scant attention in the numerous analyses of EU politics put forward by social scientists. Where the European institutional framework was not primarily regarded as an intergovernmental regime set up to coordinate economic interests, the dominant tendency was to disaggregate the multilevel system into different policy arenas, each of which was characterized by a variable degree of Europeanization according to its specific functional attributes. In the meantime, however, the intensification of the constitutional debates since the 1990s has increasingly brought the 'multinational dimension' into focus as well. From the angle of constitutional politics, the Union's multinational shape comes to the fore as a central feature of the European political order.

How does the multinational factor impact on the institutional context of the EU? To answer this question, it seems useful to start with a general assessment of the attributes that can be considered typical of multinational democracies in the West today. According to an overview offered by James Tully (2001: 2–6), democratic multinational states (such as Canada, Belgium or the United Kingdom) exhibit the following characteristics:

- We are dealing with a constitutional association that comprises two or more nations or 'peoples'. In principle, these nations are granted the same official status.
- The association has both federal and confederal features. The spheres of political participation and representation overlap with the citizens' national and multinational identity patterns.
- The different nations, as well as the multinational community they constitute, share the commitment to respecting the rule of law and democracy.
- Multinational democracies are multicultural as well. This means that the nation cannot claim absolute priority as a template for the political articulation of socio-cultural identities.

- In a multinational political association, the principles of freedom and self-determination imply that the constitutional rules of accommodation and recognition become a matter of periodic negotiations, which may lead to their modification. There is no 'definitive' agreement on how reciprocal recognition is to be institutionalized.

Since the EU cannot be considered a democracy, we must be careful when using such a list of features in analyzing its politics. In many respects, however, the qualifications will only be of a gradual kind. For the EU, the growing need to legitimize integration in a both common and diverse political space has similar effects to the pressures experienced by multinational democracies.

Focusing on the aspect of legitimation in particular, the German sociologist M. Rainer Lepsius maintains that the heterogeneous structural foundations of the EU foreclose the possibility of European integration following the patterns of political development observable in the formation of nation-states; instead, he argues, a potential model for the Union might be the 'nationality state'. For Lepsius (1993: 281), the interests of the different nationalities in a nationality state cannot be defended by the majority principle, since all nationalities must be regarded as structural minorities which lack the option to become a majority at some point. Hence, what is required is a stable system of minority protection. The citizens of a nationality state must be politically represented both as citizens of the overarching political association and as citizens of a component association. In the corresponding system of representation, all nationalities are to be granted an equal status. Lepsius adopts a view which does not make a distinction between nation and state, thus conflating the nationalities in the institutional order of the EC/EU with the nation-states. From his perspective, the EU's raison d'être is not to overcome the nation-states but to coordinate their interests. The multinational model he depicts should rather be seen as a 'multistate' model. In contrast to Tully's approach, the multinational political association turns into a 'state of nation-states'. This entails an amalgamation of sociological and normative considerations, which connects 'multinationalism' and intergovernmentalism and emphasizes the dominant role of nation-states when it comes to the institutional articulation of collective identities in the EU. The approach thereby evidences the implicit statism in the EU's response to heterogeneity; however, its rigid way of linking nationalities to the political form of the nation-state seems questionable. As is often the case in intergovernmental analyses of EU politics, nation-states attain an almost essential quality, and the moment of dynamism and change which is an important part of Tully's perspective on multinational politics is lost.

Nevertheless, a state-centred interpretation of the multinational moment in the EU, as put forward by authors such as Lepsius,[36] offers interesting insights if it is not connected with an a priori normative stance in favour of nation-statehood. When we examine the declarations of political intent made by some of the foremost founding fathers of the EC/EU, the desire to transcend the negative historical record of nationalism in twentieth-century continental Europe was one of the major driving forces of European unification in the period after the Second World War. The ideas of putting an end to a period of nationalistic atrocities, of overcoming ancestral Franco–German rivalries, and of making Germany an integral part of a European peace system were important elements in the discourse of those who advocated a federated Europe (Loth 1996: 13–22). At the same time, however, integration was never supposed to question the continuity of the nation-states involved in the project of integrating Europe. A statement delivered in 1964 by one of the main architects of the nascent EC/EU, the former French foreign minister Robert Schuman, put it quite bluntly: 'Our European states are a historical reality; it is psychologically impossible to eradicate them'.[37] The institutional consequences of this 'psychology' make for an element of tension within the multinational moment: on the one hand, the process of integration constitutes a highly ambitious political attempt at overcoming all extreme forms of nationalism in Europe; on the other hand, one may argue that a 'thin' version of nationalism has been structurally built into Europe's institutional setting from the very beginning of the integration process, and that it remains an important aspect of European politics.

What does 'thin' nationalism mean? By using the term 'thin', I want to highlight that the perspective adopted here does not focus on nationalism as a political ideology based on an elaborate catalogue of 'thick' normative assumptions.[38] It conceives of nationalism rather as a general organizing principle of modern societies. In such a 'thin' sense, nationalism is an omnipresent and indeed 'banal' phenomenon that permeates our everyday lives and structures our cognitive approach to politics.[39] A 'thin' view of nationalism will tend to be normatively agnostic and sceptical of simplistic dichotomies according to which a clear-cut dividing line can be drawn between 'ethnic' and 'civic' national affiliations. In a nutshell, to speak of thin nationalism simply means to acknowledge the strong links that have been established between processes of political

---

[36] See also Lepsius (1990: 264–9) and, for a similar argumentation, Streeck (1996: 72–4).
[37] Quoted in Moravcsik (1998: 86).
[38] For recent attempts at defending nationalism as a normative standard see Tamir (1993) and Miller (1995).
[39] See Billig's *Banal Nationalism* (1995).

integration and cultural standardization in modern times. The links seem particularly important when it comes to the interplay between cultural identity and political representation. Implicitly or explicitly, some type of cultural affinity has typically served as the foundation of political unity in modern, differentiated societies (see Chapter 2, Section 2.4, and Section 3.1 in this chapter). In the name of the nation, culture is politicized, while politics are simultaneously culturalized. Nationalism's rationale is that sharing a culture is the foundation for building a polity and that integrating a polity requires a common culture. As Gellner (1997: 3) wrote succinctly: 'Nationalism is a political principle which maintains that similarity of culture is the basic social bond.' For those who adhere to a 'thick' nationalism, this is a normative claim, whose validity is supposed to be universal and perennial. In the notorious language of the extreme versions of thick nationalism, 'the basic social bond' assumes quite a literal meaning: *'Deutschland über alles'*, *'todo por la patria'*, *'my country, right or wrong'*. From the contrasting angle of thin nationalism, the connection between culture and politics may well have normatively ambiguous or problematic qualities, but it nonetheless reflects a blunt sociological reality, the relevance of which may vary with the historical and the political context. Thus, the weight of the national bond becomes a contingent factor and does not correspond to any prior normative commitments.

We must recall that state-building and war-making were closely interrelated processes in modern European history (Tilly 1990). European integration, to the contrary, received a significant initial impulse from an explicit 'supranational' agreement upon breaking with a centuries-old legacy of interstate rivalries over regional geopolitical hegemony. This did not mean, however, that the states joining the EC/EU were eager to give up their sovereign authority for the sake of Europe. The 'pooling' of sovereignty and the coordination of policies were meant rather to define a new frame for articulating national interests and identities.[40] In this respect, it is no wonder that the institutional evolution of the EC/EU's specific domains of governance offered only few traces of an open and visible exercise of political power. One of the defining characteristics of the *méthode Monnet* was the effort to hide political decision-making behind inconspicuous technocratic routines (Featherstone 1994). Political authority was successively shifted to the European level with great discretion, so that the growing scope of integrated policy-making appeared to be an almost unintended effect of routine bureaucratic operations. This corresponded to the logic of the famous maxim that *petits pas* would be the best strategy to adopt if one wanted to bring about *grands effets*.

[40] Of course, the obligatory reference here is Milward (1992).

At present, European integration has reached a stage that goes well beyond the establishment of a Common Market. The political implications of Union membership are an issue that dominates the political agenda in all states that have joined or plan to join the EU. The EU constitutes a polity in its own right, a political system *sui generis*, as we have become accustomed to hearing. Even the most orthodox intergovernmentalist would be reluctant to classify the EU as 'just another international organization'. The Union has evolved into a multilayered and contradictory institutional field, marked by the uncomfortable cohabitation of the principles of supranationalism and intergovernmentalism. It is hardly surprising that the interplay of the competing political forces underlying the EU's institutional development reverberates in the politics of cultural identity in Europe. In the present constellation, the nation-states tend to take every precaution against any tendency that might provide the EU with state-like powers, as far as the connection of political and cultural identities is concerned. Whenever it is at work, intergovernmentalism places great emphasis on the importance of the member states' national cultures in the European context. In contrast, European transnationalism may encourage the articulation of cultural identities below and beyond the nation-state level and thereby contribute to a new political configuration of identity options. Thus, the tension between 'thin' nationalism and 'transnationalism' plays a significant role in the debates on the institutional reforms which an enlarged (and still enlarging) Europe needs to undergo in order to be able to meet democratic standards.

3.6   An Example: The 'Battle of the Nations' at Nice

The French Revolution was a crucial starting point for the spread of nationalism. The fusion of the state and 'the people' in the name of the nation, which constitutes a political community conceived of as sovereign and indivisible, must be regarded as a decisive turning point in modern European history. During the period of the Napoleonic wars, nationalism for the first time became a powerful instrument of political mobilization on a continental scale. Even traditional dynastic powers began to rely on the national principle in order to underscore their political legitimacy. The national pathos that had paved the way for the victories of the French armies was seen as a model to be imitated. If one wanted to prevail against the French, France had to be fought making use of the very same weapons that had made France's triumphal campaigns possible (Schulze 1999: 190). In the German lands, for instance, the wars against the French armies were considered to be liberation wars. The battle between Napoleon's troops and the joint forces recruited by

Austria, Prussia, Sweden and Russia at Leipzig in 1813 came to be known as 'the battle of the nations'.[41] If we understand this battle as a protracted struggle between nation-states over hegemony in Europe, it did not come to a real end until the 1950s, when a stable peace settlement was reached at least for the western half of the continent, a settlement that the East has begun to join after 1989.

To which extent can this settlement be properly described as the beginning of a new transnational European order? Almost 200 years after Leipzig, a political event that might be called a 'battle of the nations' as well occupied the centre of Europe's political stage: the event was the EU summit at Nice in December 2000. To speak of a 'battle of the nations' in the context of the Nice conference certainly requires some very substantial qualifications. But let us briefly recapitulate the events first.

The central purpose of Nice was to pave the way for a far-reaching institutional reform, a reform that is unavoidable if the EU is to manage the challenges associated with its eastern enlargement. Moreover, the pressures towards realizing major institutional changes were thought to offer a unique opportunity for achieving higher levels of transparency and efficiency in European decision-making. At any rate, this was the declared goal of the numerous voices that were claiming that the widening and the deepening of the EU were by no means incompatible, but even mutually reinforcing, political objectives.[42] Hence, in more general terms, the main tasks of the meeting consisted in discussing Europe's 'finality' and the general interests uniting all Europeans, ultimately perhaps even in defining such a thing as the European 'common good'. In this respect, hardly any commentator would fail to describe the results of the Nice conference as utterly disappointing. The 'all-European' perspective got virtually lost in an arena of tough intergovernmental bargaining. In the course of the prolonged and difficult negotiations, the representatives of the member states seemed to focus almost exclusively on their respective national interests. The strategy of *sauve qui peut* began to erode the effects of the traditional European *on s'arrange et puis on voit*. Even old cleavages considered typical of the European system of nation-states in an earlier period were apparently re-emerging. As a well-informed inside observer put it: 'For the historically minded, a shadow of the continent's

---

[41] The German term *Völkerschlacht* has somewhat bolder connotations.

[42] For instance, this message was one of the central components of the famous speech delivered by Joschka Fischer, then the Minister of Foreign Affairs of the Federal Republic of Germany, at Berlin's Humboldt University in May 2000 (cf. Fischer 2000).

troublesome past which was characterized by endless struggles about dominance became visible for a moment'.[43]

In the press reports covering the Nice summit, the use of language drawing analogies to warlike situations was quite frequent. Commenting upon the re-weighting of power and the modifications affecting the use of qualified majority voting (QMV) in the EU, newspapers spoke of an intense and open confrontation between France and Germany as well as of a clash between the smaller and the larger countries. In the end, there was much speculation about the winners and losers at Nice and about the forces giving proper support to the tiny compromises reached at the conference. In any case, it was plainly evident that the main players in Europe's institutional setting were still the nation-states. This became especially apparent in the discussions concerning the redistribution of voting power in the Council. The new procedure adopted requires that decisions made under QMV meet three conditions: they must be supported by a qualified majority of weighted votes, count on a majority of member states, and, finally, represent a demographic majority of 62 percent of the EU's population. All in all, the weight of intergovernmentalism in Europe's semi-constitutional structure means that statehood receives a high premium in terms of political representation. In an EU with 27 member states, Germany, with a population of approximately 82 million (17 percent of the total), gets 29 votes in the Council (8.4 percent); for Luxembourg, the corresponding figures are 429,000 (0.09 percent) and 4 (1.16 percent). Thus, when it comes to assigning voting powers in Europe's political system, the principle of equality of states clearly predominates against the principle of equality of citizens. This is also true in the context of the European Parliament: here, for example, a British parliamentarian represents roughly 823,000 citizens, whereas in the Irish case, the ratio is 312,000 citizens per member of the European Parliament.

One of the protocols included in Part IV (General and Final Provisions) of the Constitutional Treaty determines that the weighting of the votes in the European Council and in the Council which was defined in Nice shall remain in force only until 31 October 2009.[44] After that date, the plan was to modify the voting procedure in the two organs in the following way: a qualified majority would then require the support of at least 55 percent of the members of the Council, comprising at least 15

---

[43] Neunreither (2001: 191).

[44] See the Protocol on the Transitional Provisions Relating to the Institutions and Bodies of the Union (*Official Journal of the European Union*, C 310, Volume 47, 16 December 2004, p. 382).

of them and representing member states comprising at least 65 percent of the Union's population.[45] In view of the collapse of the constitutional process in 2005, after the rejection of the Constitutional Treaty by a majority of the voters in France and the Netherlands, the Treaty of Nice retains great significance for the overall functioning of the EU's institutional system. Thus, the summit may ultimately have revealed the very limits of Europe's capacity for institutional reform.

It is not my intention to go into further details regarding the problematic compromises that were negotiated in Nice. Although we have to keep in mind that formal procedures do not necessarily reflect factual political weight, the persistently high profile of the intergovernmental dimension clearly indicates that the nation-states are still the central political players in the EU. Hence, in transnational European politics collective interests continue to be framed basically as national interests, that is, as the interests of nation-states. In spite of the institutional discourses and institutional structures created around 'other' Europes, such as the Europe of the citizens, the Europe of the regions or the Europe of organized interests represented in the Economic and Social Committee, the EU has been constructed as a union of nation-states in the first place. Its institutional structure is permeated by 'thin' nationalism. The commitment to protect cultural identities that are institutionally framed as the national identities of the member states is not simply an exercise in rhetoric; it is deeply embedded in the Union's semi-constitutional architecture. Therefore, it seems to be a sound guess that the EU is far removed from superseding nationalism, at least as far as its 'thin' versions are concerned. The building of Europe entails rather the adaptation of nationalism to a new political setting. Thus far, the very institutional logics of the EU imply a more or less continuous reproduction of national structures. In the context of EU politics, this means basically that political interests are legitimized on the grounds of their relating to entrenched cultural identities, as long as these are the identities of nation-states.

To put it bluntly, the spirit of Nice cannot be taken as an evidence of a general relinquishing of national principles for the sake of a European republic standing on postnational foundations. However, the historical analogy drawn at the beginning of this section should not be overstated either, nor should the picture of a 'battle of the nations' be understood in too literal a sense. The differences between the clash of military forces at Leipzig in 1813 and the events observable two centuries later at Nice are enormous. The taming of nationalism in Western Europe by the

---

[45] See Article I-25 of the Treaty establishing a Constitution for Europe (*Official Journal of the European Union*, C 310, Volume 47, 16 December 2004, p. 21).

transnational framework of the EC/EU is a political reality whose effects can scarcely be overrated. We only have to think of the cautious approach adopted when political disagreement between France and Germany is articulated nowadays, compared to the mutual irritations we would have expected only some 50 years ago. We may also consider the efforts most European leaders put into finding inconspicuous ways of pursuing their national interests within the Union. Or, to give one more example, we may take into account the high symbolic value that was immediately attached to the Charter of Rights of the European Union, even if the document lacked legally binding force. When seen from this perspective, Europe apparently does come close to being a civic community which is based upon a set of common values and stands above single member states. It may not develop state-like qualities, but it may embody a real potential for delineating an institutional frame in which all parties involved are prepared to take the perspective of the other, thereby working towards a reflexive understanding of their own identity. Accordingly, the tension between nationalism and transnationalism which characterizes the EU as a multinational order would generate highly productive political effects.[46] Still, the question is how long these effects can last if the EU is not able to move beyond the status quo and create political structures which are more in line with its multinational differentiation and complex diversity.

3.7   Distinctive Features of Cultural Pluralism in the European Multinational Community

The 'multinational moment' also finds expression in areas of Europe's institutional system in which the logic of intergovernmentalism is not generally accorded a central role. A brief examination of the European Court of Justice (ECJ) and the European Commission as institutions shaped by 'supranational' principles should make this clear.

The ECJ played a decisive role in the development of the EC system into a legal order with pronounced supranational components during the decades following the ratification of the Treaty of Rome (Joerges 1996: 78–80). The task of the ECJ is to ensure a uniform interpretation of community law in the EU. In all questions that concern EC law, its judgments are binding on the courts of the member states. With its conception of the direct effect of EC law and its doctrine of the primacy of Community law over the legislation of the member states, the ECJ

---

[46] In this regard, then, the EU might be able to avoid the institutional failure of historical forerunners which were characterized by a similarly complex diversity, such as the Austro-Hungarian empire (cf. Kraus 2004: 40–2).

blurred the boundaries between the EC/EU and federal models in the legal sphere (Weiler 1999: 19). Nevertheless, the rule that the nation-states should enjoy equal representation also holds in the supranationally oriented European legal community. The judges and Advocates-General attached to the Luxembourg-based ECJ are appointed by mutual agreement by the governments of the member states. Each EU member state appoints one judge to the ECJ.

The European Commission is commonly regarded within the Union as the supranational institution par excellence. According to Article 213 of the consolidated version of the Treaty Establishing the European Community, it performs its tasks 'in the general interests of the Community'. As the custodian of the treaties, the Commission formally enjoys strict independence vis-à-vis the governments of the member states. It is answerable to the European Parliament alone. It derives its political weight primarily from the fact that it has the exclusive right to initiate legislation in the domain of competences related to the regulation of the Common Market and thereby plays a key role in the corresponding decision-making processes. In the Europe of the 15, the Commission had 20 members (in addition to the President): Germany, France, the United Kingdom, Italy and Spain as the larger states appointed two commissioners each, whereas the remaining states appointed one member each. Thus, the principle of equal representation of the nation-states was also discernable here, although with a slight tendency towards proportionality. The criterion of equal state representation has not been substantially modified by the efforts undertaken against the background of the eastern enlargement to facilitate the long-term effective functioning of the Commission and to restrict its size. According to the Constitutional Treaty (Part I, Article 25), when the transitional regulations which hold during the accession phase for new members cease to be valid, the principle of parity between states must be honoured in such a way that the equal rotation of commissioners among the member states must be combined with the appointment of commissioners without voting rights. The goal is to secure at least a symbolic presence of all member states in the Commission. Thus, structural characteristics nourished by the logic of 'thin' nationalism remain securely anchored even in a supranational institutional context.

The multinational factor is not only an important component of the institutional mechanics of the EU. The Treaty on European Union, the Charter of Fundamental Rights, as well as other basic documents of European unification also accord it symbolic weight when they refer to the subject or subjects of the process of integration. In the preamble to the Treaty on European Union, the parties express the desire 'to deepen the solidarity between their peoples while respecting their history, their culture and their traditions'. Article 1 of the Treaty then asserts:

This Treaty marks a new stage in the process of creating an ever-closer union among the peoples of Europe, in which decisions are taken as closely as possible to the citizen. (. . .)

Its task shall be to organize, in a manner demonstrating consistency and solidarity, relations between the Member States and between their peoples.[47]

The Constitutional Treaty worked out by the European Convention seems to enhance the status of 'states' in Europe vis-à-vis that of 'peoples'. Article I-1 (Establishment of the Union), for example, speaks of 'the will of the citizens and States of Europe to build a common future'.[48] To be sure, the Charter of Fundamental Rights of the EU which has been incorporated into the Constitutional Treaty continues to identify the 'peoples of Europe' as the subject 'of an ever closer union' in its preamble, which we have already quoted at length (see Section 3.2). It seems reasonable to assume that by the 'peoples of Europe' are implicitly meant the national peoples (i.e., the 'peoples of the nation-states'). However, neither the Charter nor the treaty documents offer a more precise specification of the identity of the European peoples.

It is worth noting in this context that the EU in its official 'self-representation' seems to have a tendency to avoid employing any symbolic points of reference that could potentially arouse historical or cultural associations pointing to particular nation-states. The *multi*national moment is reflected in the design of EU symbols insofar as references to *individual* peoples are excluded. We already discussed the relation between European identity strategies and the symbolism of integration in Section 3.2. In what follows, I would like to address briefly a dilemma of European identity politics that is closely bound up with the multinational structure of the EU. In selecting a range of identifications, the European institutions have to draw on a store of symbols that abstract from concretely localizable political-cultural horizons of experience and hence remain of necessity semantically anaemic and diffuse. A good illustration of this is the design of the Euro banknotes. We were accustomed to seeing typically portraits of historical figures or pictures of well-known monuments on the banknotes of European national currencies such as the Deutschmark, the French franc or the Spanish peseta. In different ways, a country's

---

[47] Treaty on European Union (signed in Maastricht on 7 February 1992), consolidated version incorporating the changes made by the Treaty of Amsterdam amending the Treaty on European Union, the Treaties establishing the European Communities and certain related acts, signed at Amsterdam on 2 October 1997 (European Union 1999: 11–68).

[48] *Official Journal of the European Union*, C 310, Volume 47, 16 December 2004, p. 11.

currency gave visual expression to symbols of cultural identity regarded as important by public institutions. Things are quite different with the design of the Euro banknotes whose most striking feature is that they do not portray any human beings or any concretely identifiable buildings or landscapes.

In the official view of the European Commission and the European Monetary Institute, the Euro was intended to become a salient symbol of European identity and to serve as an instrument for forming a European consciousness (Shore 2000: 112–15). The stipulation that no national preferences should be expressed, which was supposed to be rigidly observed in producing the designs of the Euro, ultimately meant that a strategy of avoidance was followed in the visual representation of moments of identification. The banknotes represent a series of architectonic motifs which remain abstract: bridges, archways, gates and glass façades which apparently embody different European architectural epochs from ancient times to the present, but which make no reference to actually existing monuments. Euroland thus appears as a world cut off from specific traditions, as a collection of geometric forms in a depopulated space. It has to be said that, in the end, even the semiotics of the Euro make a concession to the nation-states, though it remains restricted to the coinage. The front (number) sides of the eight Euro coins have uniform European motifs with variations on the map of Europe and the EU flag. In return, the member states were allowed to choose their own national motifs for the design of the reverse side.

The multinational character of the EU is deeply inscribed in its political-institutional structure and also shapes the discursive-symbolic modes of expression of European politics. At the same time, the articulation of multinationality in the EU exhibits a number of quite essential peculiarities that clearly differentiate the Union from traditional kinds of multinational states. They follow from the absence of a hegemonic integrating force, the Union's pronounced polycentric character and its open constitutional form.

In the overarching European order, all component units are in a minority position. Even the cultures of the large nation-states are minority cultures in the EU (Lepsius 1999: 219). The Union is a multinational construct without a titular nation. Among the institutionally supported cultural identities within this construct, there is no structural majority. A politically authoritative force for integration cannot be identified in the EC/EU. The incorporation of new members into the community occurred in principle on the basis of the equal status of the parties concerned. Until now, accession negotiations have been conducted for the most part under the banner of an often-laborious search for consensus between the accession candidates and the representatives of the European institutions. The absence of direct geopolitical coercion and of a hegemonic integrating force differentiates the uniting of Europe radically from the processes of nation-state building on the continent (Marks 1997). Ultimately, this also means that the EU is free from a burden that typically weighs on multinational states, namely, the experience of historical injustice suffered by minorities who were forcibly incorporated into the territorial domain of the dominant majority.

The fact that in the EU there is no hegemonic integrating force to counteract a highly developed cultural-territorial differentiation brings me to the second peculiarity of the European multinational constellation. The political structure of the Union has a pronounced polycentric character. Notwithstanding the indisputable special role of Brussels, there is no clearly identifiable territorial-political centre in the EU in which the threads of political, economic and cultural power run together. The EU does not have a capital city in the classical sense but many centres; it is, in the terminology of Stein Rokkan (1999), a polycephalic construct. Political-administrative, economic and cultural centres are strewn across its whole territory and no region enjoys a monopoly of control over the social resources relevant for the formation of a single European centre. Thus far attempts have also been made to accord symbolic recognition to the polycentric structure of the EU in the geographical allocation of its institutions. As the seat of the European Commission, Brussels is indeed regarded as the secret capital of Europe. However, as is well known, the public plenary sessions of the European Parliament are held in Strasbourg. The ECJ, in turn, is located in Luxembourg. A key European institution of more recent origin, the European Central Bank which came into existence with the Economic and Monetary Union, has its headquarters in Frankfurt. As for the most important decision-making body of the EU, the European Council, it does not even have a fixed meeting place; the country which holds the rotating EU presidency serves as the host of the regular summits of the heads of state and government. With its conspicuous institutional decentralization, the EU not only deviates markedly from all paths typically pursued by nation-states; it also exceeds by far the degree of spatial dispersal of competences that characterizes some heterogeneous federal states.

Finally, in comparison with state-like polities – and also in comparison with multinational states – the EU exhibits an open and flexible constitutional structure. It is difficult to do justice to this openness within a formalized constitutional design. The constitutional 'shape' of Europe which can be traced in the EU treaties attests to the process character of European unification which neither freezes the political status quo nor is moving towards a fixed end state laid down in advance. Europe's insecurities as regards its 'own' identity are reflected not least in the notorious difficulties in offering a prospective definition of the European project's external boundaries. Already the growing trends towards differentiated integration or 'enhanced cooperation' indicate that the institutional multidimensionality of the EU is not likely to remain a transitional phenomenon. This multidimensionality answers, on the one hand, the demands to assure the political efficacy of the multilevel system. Viewed in the multinational context, it permits, on the other hand, the adjustment of the degrees of integration to the political readiness for integration within the member states. Thus it contributes to defusing the potential virulence of conflicts over whether a part belongs to the overall association, which are not untypical for multinational states. Where integration was not coerced there is no reason to place the bases of political unification in doubt.

My intention in highlighting a number of distinctive features of the European multinational constellation to conclude this chapter was to show that the political logic of the construction of the EU need not necessarily be exhausted by its offering a forum for the intergovernmental balancing of interests, which is an integral part of Europe. Rather, an internal tension that can be observed more or less throughout the course of the development of the EC/EU feeds off the dialectical relation between a 'thin' nationalism and the 'overcoming' of the nation-state model produced by the process of unification. The nation-state was undoubtedly one of the supporting pillars of integration but it has in the meantime been substantially transformed by the outcomes of this very integration process. The peculiarities just described, therefore, also represent an opportunity to found a multinational political community that is also in fact novel by normative criteria. The political ethos of the European project would then consist in determining the common good in a transnational political system on the basis of political game rules that at the same time enable the various component units of the Union to retain their sovereignty in pursuing their 'specific' common good. The component units referred to here are not necessarily nation-states. In the domain of cultural identities, in particular, we should avoid a statist foreshortening of the definition of legitimate collective interests. At the end of this study I will examine some concrete proposals concerning how the multinational moment in Europe could be dealt with in a politically productive way. However, I would first like to deepen the considerations developed here in the following chapters by providing further empirical support for our still rather general findings, with particular reference to the language question in the EU.

4   Language and politics:
A challenge for Europe

Whenever it comes to defining 'hard' criteria of cultural heterogeneity in Europe's multinational constellation, the terrain of language is almost unavoidably brought into focus. At this point, suffice it to say that at present, after the first two rounds of eastern enlargement and the admission of 10 new members in 2004 and 2 new members in 2007, 27 member states within the European Union (EU) make for 23 languages which all enjoy formal equality. In addition, there is a long list of languages which have an official or semi-official character at the subnational level. Language may well be regarded as the principal factor of cultural differentiation in the EU. Accordingly, the imperative to respect cultural diversity, which plays a pivotal normative role in EU treaties and declarations, becomes in the first instance an imperative to respect linguistic diversity.

As a salient differentiating feature within Europe, language is at the same time a differentiating factor of a quite special kind, since the ability to speak, which is a constitutive attribute of the human species, finds concrete expression in manifold forms. Humanity speaks, yet it speaks in different tongues.[1] Since the universality of language (in the singular) and the difference of languages (in the plural) are parallel phenomena, the linguistic medium is a symbol of cultural diversity with peculiar properties. Ultimately, the particularism of the mother tongue, which in the case of individuals with a multilingual socialization may become the particularism of a limited repertoire of 'own' languages, is a particularism common to all people in different ways. Compared with other expressions of cultural identity in modern societies – such as belonging to a religious community or to a subculture sharing a distinctive way of life – language is a source of especially strong individual and collective attachments. For individuals, it tends to act as a factor providing cognitive

---

[1] Linguists calculate that, while the total number is declining, at the beginning of the twenty-first century there are still approximately 5000 languages spoken in the world (Hagège 2000: 9).

continuity through successive periods of socialization. For groups, it implies the possibility to communicate across several generations. To the extent that human nature has a linguistic foundation, language is a central concern for philosophical anthropology (Taylor 1985: 216). Regarding the questions at stake in that field, the following sections deal with a topic which, at first glance, may seem relatively simple. They are devoted to language as a *political* issue.

From a historical perspective, the politicization of language is a fairly recent phenomenon, which is closely intertwined with the rise of national identities.[2] Language was of great importance in a process of modernization that combined the functional integration of societies with the standardization of cultural identities (as described in Section 2.4 of Chapter 2). It structured the overall framework of communication in which the dynamics of social, economic and political change could unfold. However, the significance of language in the context of modernity must not be reduced to functional aspects. As a source of expressive authenticity, language also has to be assigned a key role in the formation of modern forms of self-perception. Both aspects come together when a democratic public sphere is constituted. In the area of language policy, it has therefore always been difficult to distinguish the defence of instrumental interests from the struggle for the recognition of identities. Language is a substantial component of a group's cultural capital in modern societies. Under democratic conditions, language policy is not only a tool for establishing an extensive frame of communication but is also directed towards protecting the status or the 'honour' of the members of a linguistic community and overcoming collective resentment in institutional contexts marked by cultural heterogeneity.

This chapter offers an introduction to the main issues of language policy in present-day Europe. I begin by showing how important linguistic questions are for understanding what the 'politics of recognition' is about and by assessing the normative significance of language diversity. My next step is to analyze the implications linguistic diversity has for the constitution of a democratic political order. An overview of the different approaches to language policy adopted by Western European states leads to the analysis of the conflict potentials typical of multilingual political settings. The chapter concludes with an assessment both of recent tendencies to establish a stable link between the protection of linguistic identities and civil rights provisions and of the consequences this has for the process of European polity-building.

---

[2] Burke (2004) explores the relationship between languages and political communities in early modern Europe before the French Revolution.

4.1   Language as a Social and Political Bond

Modern societies are societies based upon complex communication. Functional differentiation and the social division of labour led to an enormous increase in routinized large-scale interaction. Such interaction usually required people to communicate in a standardized common language. At the same time, by connecting structural social transformations to specific prerequisites of communication, modernization generally ensured that culture, as the resource sustaining comprehensive social communication, became politicized.[3] The revolution in the field of information technologies we are currently experiencing is apparently endowing the role of cultural identity in processes of social and political integration with additional relevance.[4]

Under functional aspects, language has to be considered an absolutely central element of modern cultures. The infrastructure of industrial and postindustrial societies can't work properly if there is no lingua franca. The functional perspective highlights the *instrumental* dimension of language from which language appears primarily as a medium that designates things and facts. By using language, people are able to communicate in order to meet specific purposes. The instrumental component of linguistic communication becomes patent in virtually all domains of modern societies. In extreme cases, to have the possibility to communicate instrumentally can become a matter of life or death. Thus, in March 2001, several people were killed in a train collision in Belgium. The accident happened in an area close to the linguistic border that runs between the country's Flemish and Francophone territories. According to press reports, one of the reasons why last-minute attempts to avoid the tragedy failed was that the two railway employees in charge of controlling the points in the two stations located on either side of the border were only fluent in French and Dutch, respectively, and therefore could not communicate effectively with each other on the telephone.[5] Only a few weeks later, a front-page feature of the *New York Times* was devoted to the problems state security services face in the USA when it comes to hiring personnel fluent in foreign languages. According to the newspaper, the analysis of the *first* World Trade Center bombing in February 1993 had

---

[3] The intertwining of social, economic and cultural mobilization in the process of modernization is a topic dealt with extensively in classic studies of nationalism, such as those of Deutsch (1966) and Gellner (1983). Benedict Anderson (1991) emphasizes the importance of 'print capitalism' in the formation of 'imagined communities' that were to become the typical manifestations of modern collective identity.

[4] This is one of the main theses advanced by Manuel Castells (1996, 1997, 1998) in his thorough interpretation of the coming 'information age'.

[5] The case is taken from an article published in the newspaper *El País* on 31 March 2001.

proved that there were not enough qualified staff members to listen to tapped telephone conversations in Arabic.[6] Such examples may not be fully representative of our everyday communication routines, yet they show to what extent the information systems in our societies depend on securing a quick understanding based on a shared linguistic repertoire.

However, language cannot be reduced to its instrumental side. Language also has an *expressive* dimension that goes far beyond the mere designating of objects and facts.[7] Many things come into existence only when we move within the expressive dimension of language. It is in this sense that language makes a central contribution to how we gain our conception of ourselves and frame our way of life (Taylor 1985: 10). Expressive meaning can never be completely detached from its linguistic medium, as it only becomes graspable in the reflexive use we make of this medium. Finding an appropriate approach to the expressive dimension of language not only has far-reaching implications for our understanding of language use; it also has a substantial bearing on our understanding of the subject of language itself. In this context, Charles Taylor (1985: 232–4) emphasizes the seminal contributions Johann Gottfried Herder and Wilhelm von Humboldt made when they pointed out the links between language and expressivity. These two representatives of an intellectual current blending Enlightenment concerns with Romantic sensitivities shared the view that language is created and transformed by human communication – by speech. To the extent that language is to be conceived as an activity, its primary locus is conversation. In consequence, language develops in a *linguistic community*; it can be considered a paramount example of a good that is irreducibly social (Taylor 1995: 135). In his *Treatise on the Origin of Language*, Herder (2001 [1772]: 80) argues that human autonomy is basically constituted by language and affirms that humans, as free-thinking and active beings, are creatures of language. As language can only flourish within a linguistic community, its proper sustaining force is a people. Wilhelm von Humboldt (1963 [1830]: 414, 434) adopts Herder's view when he considers language as virtually the outward manifestation of the 'spirit of the peoples'. For Humboldt, the expressive dimension of a language refers to specific social relations and ways of life; it follows that learning a new language is equivalent to acquiring a new standpoint from which to view the world.

Both Herder and Humboldt highlight the social component of the expressive dimension of language. From their perspective, language

---

[6] *New York Times*, 16 April 2001.

[7] In distinguishing between instrumental and expressive dimensions of language, I follow Taylor (1985: 9–11, 218–19; 1995: 101–3); see also Réaume (1991: 45).

provides a key to understanding humanity as unity in differentiation. On the one hand, language is seen as a resource that is constitutive of human autonomy and freedom. On the other hand, this autonomy is socially embedded and relates to the collective practices of a language community. Language creates an elemental social bond. Thus, in a certain sense, individual speech acts always refer to a speech community. At the same time, it is ultimately language itself that defines and sustains the speech community. Wilhelm von Humboldt uses the image of a web (*Gewebe*) to describe how language simultaneously shapes and is shaped by human communication.[8]

Humboldt is particularly aware of the genuinely social dimension of language. While conceding that language finds its ultimate form only at the level of the individual, he highlights the impact former generations of speakers have had on shaping a language. In this respect, for Wilhelm von Humboldt (1963 [1830]: 438) the power of the individual against the power of language must be considered very slight. Humboldt's theory of language anticipates the dichotomy of *langue* and *parole* which would become with Ferdinand de Saussure (1972 [1916]) the basis of twentieth-century structuralist linguistics. The 'given' structure of a language as *langue* limits the possibilities we have for articulating ourselves. At the same time, we modify these limits when we speak and actualize language as *parole*. Moreover, the early version of the expressive theory of language, as put forward by Humboldt, hints at the 'duality' of structure which Giddens (1984) would take as the foundation of his theory of structuration. The web constituted by language frames our communicative repertoire: we cannot speak outside language. Yet, by relying on the structure of language, we also find the freedom to articulate ourselves.

The political relevance of the *instrumental dimension* of language is obvious: we have to be able to employ language in conformity with the specific functional requirements of different situations in all kinds of everyday contexts. How we realize our life chances depends to a considerable extent on our linguistic competence. As learning languages involves costs, the right to use our mother tongue in as many social domains as possible has an instrumental character. It is the *expressive dimension*, however, that gives language its particular political salience, a salience which is frequently intermingled with claims for 'recognition' (Taylor 1992). Language is a resource we need for individual communication. By acquiring this resource, we are attached to a specific, culturally defined community. If a language, as a line of reasoning running from Herder and

---

[8] The corresponding views are elaborated in Herder (2001 [1772]: 80–95) and von Humboldt (1963 [1830]: 414–39).

Humboldt to Taylor holds, forms an irreducible social web, securing potentials for individual development and freedom becomes a matter of a collective support that, in modern polities, translates into institutional provisions devoted to reproducing this web. Thus, if the dignity of individuals is to be respected, the linguistic and cultural identity of their communities of origin must be recognized to a satisfactory extent as well. When the cultural bases which underlie our personal development and which we regard as authentic are institutionally ignored, negated or even repressed, our self-esteem, which is an asset of great significance in the process of building up and protecting our individual autonomy, will be severely hampered, too.

The very example of language shows that the protection of individual dignity may well stand in a complementary relationship with the acknowledgement of membership in a cultural group. By recognizing a language we do not recognize language 'in itself'. The point rather is to recognize a linguistic community and, ultimately, the individual speakers who form the community. Its importance as a social bond is one of the main causes that made language a recurrent point of reference in nationalist mobilizations since the nineteenth century. In some cases, language and nation became virtually interchangeable concepts. As the great sociolinguist Joshua Fishman (1973: 82–5) asserts, one does not have to be sympathetic towards nationalist approaches to language to understand that they are deeply rooted in social reality, and that this rootedness lends them a force that must be taken very seriously. Writing three decades before our entry in a new 'global' millennium, Fishman anticipated that, in the realm of culture, the extension and intensification of international and transnational linkages would entail a successive political activation of particular identities all over the world. In his view, the struggle for authenticity has hardly lost the impetus it has had since the dawn of the age of nationalism; therefore, social scientists would make a big mistake if they underplayed the persistence of this strife or limited their analytic efforts to offering a derogatory assessment of its foundations. Fishman (1973: 83) writes:

The need for identity, for community, to make modernity sufferable, is greater than it was and will become greater yet, and woe to the elites – in universities, governments, and industries – who do not recognize this or, even worse, who consider it to be only a vestigial remnant of nineteenth century thinking.

Against this background, it is to be stressed that there is nothing anachronistic or 'primordial' in the quest for authenticity described by Fishman, nor in the claims to have this authenticity recognized in the political realm. The wish to be authentic is a highly significant element in the motivational configuration of our *modern* selves (Taylor 1989). Hence, the quest for *linguistic authenticity* should not be misinterpreted as a longing for perennial and quasi-'organic' identity patterns. In modern societies, linguistic identities must not be considered an outcome of 'natural' processes of evolution. On the contrary, they reflect in the first instance the dynamics of processes of political integration.

Both at the individual and the collective level, cultural authenticity and political self-determination are correlated. The strong bond of language is by no means to be regarded as a straightjacket. Its elasticity may not be unlimited, yet linguistic identities are malleable; this opens the space for language choice, language planning and language policy. The members of a diaspora group, for instance, may deliberately decide to make preferential use of a new language, thereby initiating a process in which, within one or two generations, language change will denote a change of identity. Language policy has generally been an important factor in the making of modern political communities. The example of Israel, where great collective efforts were made after independence to revive Hebrew as the official state language, may be regarded as particularly striking.[9] In many states that emerged in the south after the end of colonialism, language planning has maintained a prominent role on the political agenda. As the term itself suggests, a mother tongue draws its special meaning from its being closely connected to our experience of primary socialization. But in contrast with ascriptive group attributes, languages can be learned (with more or less facility, depending on the educational background of a person). Seen from a global perspective, multilingualism is a common phenomenon, both at the individual and the collective levels. Often, the multilingual option implies that the instrumental and expressive dimensions of communication are by and large assigned to different languages. At any rate, this is frequently the situation of individuals who belong to a linguistic minority. To cite just one example: in all likelihood, a Sorbian-speaking mother will try to raise her children in Sorbian. However, even on her home territory[10] she will not be able to rely exclusively on her Slavic vernacular, unless she is prepared to limit the scope of her possibilities for instrumental communication radically.

There is plenty of evidence that linguistic identities can be transformed, at least within certain limits. The – relative – changeability of linguistic

---

[9] For an analysis of the circumstances leading to the revival of the Hebrew language see Hagège (2000: 271–341).

[10] That is, in two relatively small areas located in the southeastern part of the former German Democratic Republic.

identities, however, does not reduce the political relevance of the expressive dimension of language. That a person is *understood* in a context of linguistic communication does not necessarily mean that her particular linguistic identity (e.g. bilingual in Sorbian and German) is *recognized*. In a certain sense, what makes for a good part of the political salience of linguistic identities is their very malleability. The weight of expressivity is typically highlighted in multilingual settings, where claims for the recognition of collective identities that are felt as authentic and related to specific linguistic communities generally go hand-in-hand with claims for the recognition of an autonomous institutional frame of political and cultural relations. Language is a field of social practice that shows us how futile attempts at establishing a rigid and dichotomous opposition between the 'ethnic' and the 'civic' bases of political integration can ultimately be. Peoples speak – irrespective of their having constituted themselves as cultural nations or as state nations – and the expressive dimension of language is always part of this speaking. Accordingly, linguistic and political culture cannot be separated from each other; in effect, linguistic culture *is* political culture. This leads me to formulate a first thesis concerning the language issue in the EU: regardless of the institutional level at which it is implemented, European language policy must not ignore the quest for authenticity but must rather pay attention to its diverse manifestations. Neither the instrumental character of market integration nor the functional requisites of political integration can offer a justification for tearing apart Europe's communicative 'web'.

4.2   Mill's Verdict

Within a language group, the expressive and the instrumental dimensions of language tend to reinforce each other. On the one hand, linguistic nationalisms all over the world, while invoking expressive motives, have provided formerly subordinate languages with an official status, thereby increasing their instrumental value. On the other hand, enhancing a language's instrumental utility contributes to meeting the 'authenticity needs' of the members of the linguistic community. In multilingual contexts, however, the relationship between the instrumental and the expressive sides of linguistic communication may be characterized by a tension. Let us evidence this potential tension by getting briefly back to the example of the train crash in Belgium. In the Belgian case, the recognition of the distinct identities of language groups led successively to a political rearrangement of the country's administrative structures along linguistic lines. In addition to the bilingual Brussels area, two main regions were constituted, each of them considered to be monolingual in French or

Dutch, respectively.[11] Thus, both communities have a stable territorial frame for preserving their linguistic identity. In the end, however, to the extent that the press reports on the train accident are trustworthy, this form of recognition may entail a limitation of the repertoire of resources required for instrumental communication across the linguistic border.

By bringing up this example once again, I do not intend to offer any dramatizing critique of the Belgian compromises on the language issue. The efforts that have been put into securing the political coexistence of different linguistic groups in Belgium have a sound normative basis. Moreover, the losses of communicative effectiveness at the functional level would have to be weighed against the potential costs caused by an intensification of linguistic conflicts. Nevertheless, the Belgian example begs a question which is of great relevance, not only in Belgium but also in the overall context of European language policies: how can the recognition of diverse linguistic identities in a multilingual setting be made compatible with the creation of an encompassing structure of communication? The problem stretches beyond the domain of functional communication and affects the whole complex of political integration in democratic systems exposed to claims for recognition which are raised by different language groups.

The classical liberal way of 'escaping' the political challenges posed by cultural diversity has been to consider statehood as culturally neutral and as transcending the identities of particular groups.[12] Generally, the postulate that the equality of citizens had to be linked to the institutional neutrality of the state regarding the cultural attachments of its population played a central role in the process of formation of liberal-democratic rule. The separation of church and state, of religious and secular layers of identity, had a pioneering function in this respect. When it comes to linguistic heterogeneity, however, the liberal strategy of separation is unviable from the very beginning. As Zolberg (1977: 140) remarks succinctly, a modern state may pretend to be 'blind' (regarding religion, for instance), yet it cannot possibly behave like a 'deaf-mute' (when it comes to language). The specific features of languages as markers of cultural identity set them apart from other expressions of cultural differentiation. Language shares the expressive aspect with other patterns of collective identification, such as religion or ethnicity. As was pointed out in the preceding sections, however, language has a substantial instrumental aspect as well. Its instrumental use always entails the possibility of activating

---

[11] For the sake of clarity, I am leaving out the small German-speaking territory. For a general overview of the language issue in Belgian politics see von Busekist (1998).

[12] Barry (2001) offers a recent restatement of this position.

the force of its symbolic expressivity. Thus, the classical modern relationship between politics and religion has no equivalent on the terrain of language. We may assume, rather, that the political significance of linguistic issues increases progressively in the course of modernization due to the requirements of large-scale societal communication.

It is symptomatic that liberal-democratic theory has traditionally remained rather unresponsive to the political dilemmas posed by linguistic diversity. It seems that in the realm of normative theory the prevailing view was to take the historically dominant model of the nation-state for granted, thereby linking democratic sovereignty to the existence of political units conceived of as culturally homogeneous. To the extent that the problems of linguistic diversity can be discounted, language obviously ceases to be a phenomenon of greater political concern. To put it in the jargon of our times: the premise for developing democratic programs was that the linguistic software needed wherever these programs were to be implemented had already been standardized.

Generally speaking, normative theories of liberal democracy rarely dealt extensively with the implications of linguistic and cultural diversity. When they did tackle the language issue, they tended to do so in a sceptical vein. Let us consider one of the seminal texts of modern liberalism. In the *Considerations on Representative Government*, John Stuart Mill (1972 [1861]: 392) wrote:

> Free institutions are next to impossible in a country made up of different nationalities. Among a people without fellow-feeling, especially if they read and speak different languages, the united public opinion, necessary to the working of representative government, cannot exist. The influences which form opinions and decide political acts are different in the different sections of the country. An altogether different set of leaders have the confidence of one part of the country and of another. The same books, newspapers, pamphlets, speeches, do not reach them. One section does not know what opinions, or what instigations, are circulating in another.

If one adopts such a viewpoint, the prospects of sustaining representative forms of rule depend on the degree of national and linguistic unification previously attained within a given political unit. For Mill, a collectively rooted 'fellow-feeling' is a crucial requisite for the successful institutionalization of democratic politics. His view is grounded on the assumption that a liberal democracy will be able to cope with situations of intense political conflict only as long as its citizens share some basic identity patterns, as manifested by language and culture. In Mill's model, language works as the cement of a shared political culture. Such a shared culture is needed if the institutions of a liberal democracy are to function in a proper way. Thus, to a substantial extent, cultural homogeneity, or at least a minimum degree of cultural affinity, becomes a requisite for the exercise of civic solidarity.

An interesting aspect of Mill's often-quoted assertion is that it points to the instrumental and expressive dimensions of language, although without using these categories explicitly, and situates them in the context of democratic theory. Language is seen as an expressive symbol, as one of the most characteristic manifestations of national identity. Accordingly, Mill interprets linguistic differentiation as a symptom of a lack of political cohesiveness. Yet language pluralism is also a negative feature in instrumental terms, as it is an obstacle for the flow of political communication beyond nationality borders and it inhibits the formation of a common public sphere. What is described in the *Considerations* can thus be called a vicious circle of non-integration: the lack of foundations supporting a common identity leads to rigid communicative barriers; such barriers, in turn, obstruct the process of forming a shared political identity.

Mill's approach entails a clear normative preference for creating democracies that are homogeneous along linguistic and cultural lines, as cultural diversity is taken to be a major impediment to civic solidarity. During a long period of time, lasting far into the twentieth century, this preference remained a standard ideological orientation for liberal nationalists, who tended to adopt the approach *one people, one state*. This approach attained a quasi-official character as a guideline for the political restructuring of Central and Eastern Europe after the First World War. The former territorial domains of imperial rule were subdivided in accordance with Woodrow Wilson's interpretation of the nationality principle. The restructuring of Europe in accordance with the Wilsonian formula had questionable consequences, to say the least, as the principle of nationalities was often implemented opportunistically. All over the eastern half of the continent, significant minorities emerged who saw themselves as victims of the political concessions made to new titular nations provided with their 'own' states. The whole interwar period was marked by intense conflicts resulting from this situation (Galántai 1992). As far as Mill is concerned, we should keep in mind that according to his line of reasoning the preference for cultural homogeneity has rather the status of an a priori judgment than the quality of an empirically derived conclusion. In other passages of the *Considerations* in which nationality issues are discussed, it becomes clear that one major focus of preoccupation for Mill is the Austro-Hungarian domain of rule, which the English liberal views with little sympathy. Thus, his argumentation does not scrutinize more closely the extent to which there actually exists empirical evidence which could lend the homogeneity preference a robust foundation.

What can be said today, some 150 years after the original publication of the *Considerations*, about the prospects for democracy in the context of linguistic differentiation when we look at the findings made available by research in the field of comparative politics? Robert A. Dahl (1971: 105–7, 120–1), one of the leading contemporary theorists of liberal democracy, took up the language issue in a wide-ranging empirical study that tries to determine the conditions of stability of democratic regimes. In the study, multilingualism is regarded as a typical feature of subcultural pluralism, a category that also includes the effects of religious, ethnic and regional differentiation. According to Dahl's findings, such a structural pluralism, which is characteristic of multinational states, often imposes major restrictions on the capacity of democratic systems to integrate different groups politically. Dahl (1971: 108) refers explicitly to the Mill hypothesis and observes:

That subcultural pluralism often places a dangerous strain on the tolerance and mutual security required for a system of public contestation seems hardly open to doubt. Polyarchy in particular is more frequently found in relatively homogeneous countries than in countries with a great amount of subcultural pluralism.

Similarly, Dankwart Rustow (1975: 56–8), one of the pioneering figures of contemporary 'transitology' (i.e. the research on transitions from authoritarian rule to democracy), argues that the combination of modernization, democratization and linguistic heterogeneity gives rise to severe political challenges. Rustow does not say that these challenges cannot be mastered. Yet, in his view, political actors in multilingual democracies must show an extraordinary flexibility and ability to learn in order to overcome group antagonisms that are often based on different linguistic identities. Finally, David Laitin (2000), to mention the author of a more recent study, analyzes a data set covering 148 countries and arrives at a conclusion that can hardly be taken as a confirmation of Mill's thesis. According to Laitin, language conflicts tend to be more conducive to institutional mediation than other politically salient forms of cultural heterogeneity. Moreover, their potential for instigating a dynamics of ethnic violence seems to be remarkably low compared to expressions of cultural differentiation that are not language-based. However, as the study focuses primarily on the phenomenon of violence, the effects that linguistic cleavages have on the quality of democratic rule are of secondary importance in the analysis it puts forward.

All in all, the overtly sceptical attitude characteristic of Mill has certainly not disappeared from present-day discussions devoted to political cohesion in linguistically segmented democracies. Mill's thesis continues to be very influential. Yet, at the same time, our knowledge about the mechanisms of integration available in democratic polities that have only 'weak' communicative foundations, since they lack a common language, is still highly fragmentary. There is remarkably little research at our disposal that shows how, in linguistically segmented contexts, processes of political communication work at the micro-levels of society. Against this background, the picture we get when we look at the political implications of multilingualism is, at any rate, a complex one. To put forward a categorical and rigid assessment when describing the interplay of linguistic diversity and democratic politics, as Mill did in 1861, does not look like a very promising strategy today. Hence, I would like to mention two points which seem to be especially important in the present context.

First, it has to be emphasized that an adequate approach to language politics must take into account the overarching cultural framework in which the identities of linguistic groups are embedded. This concerns the relationship of linguistic identity patterns and other features of differentiation such as religion, ethnicity or nationality, as well as, to an even greater extent, the intention and direction of language policy programs, which may aim at preserving the status quo, as in the case of the *francophonie* approach adopted by the French state, or be part of a set of comprehensive measures aimed at social transformation, as may be the case with the language planning initiatives pursued in countries of the south under the banner of decolonization.[13] Second, all attempts to shed light on the interplay of democracy and the structural factors relevant for language policy must pay great attention to institutional mechanisms. Where languages call for a high level of political institutionalization as icons of cultural identity, linguistic diversity may imply increased potentials for conflict.

The following sections give a general assessment of how linguistic issues have been politically regulated by Western European states. The regional focus reflects the circumstance that Western Europe is the original historical and cultural setting in which the EU was formed. At the same time, as we will see, this region, composed of consolidated democracies with a comparable socio-economic profile, is characterized by a wide variation in institutional strategies in the field of language policy.

4.3   The Language Policies of European States

That language can be regarded as a salient feature of cultural differentiation in Europe is not so much due to the quantitative dimensions of the

---

[13] A classification of different types of political language planning can be found in Weinstein (1990).

linguistic diversity which we find across the Old Continent. According to the figures presented by linguists, approximately 225 vernacular languages are spoken in Europe. This is not much in view of the numbers given for Africa or Asia, which are estimated to be above 2,000 in each case.[14] It is also still far below the linguistic diversity level of the Americas, where about 1,000 languages are registered. However, to a great extent, political factors compensate for the modest force of numbers in Europe, as a quick comparison of the 'Old' with the 'New' World reveals.

On a trip from Alaska to Patagonia, one will manage to communicate fairly well almost everywhere by relying on just two languages: English and Spanish. Additional fluency in Portuguese and French would almost maximize the opportunities for making oneself understood. Whoever plans to travel across Europe from north to south or from east to west and to address the local population, in contrast, will have to master a broader linguistic repertoire. In the larger cities, as well as when talking to younger people, the traveller can probably rely on the world language English in many situations. Moreover, in the continent's central regions, the knowledge of a regional lingua franca, such as German or French, will be a good starting point for communicating with the natives. However, things might get complicated in more remote areas, such as Lapland, the delta of the Danube or Andalusia, where neither English nor German nor French are likely to serve as tools of an unhindered communication, and our traveller will need additional linguistic skills or the help of an interpreter if he or she wants to engage in conversation with a local farmer or a fisherman.

Evidently, the decisive point when we compare Europe to the Americas is not linguistic diversity as a brute fact. The point rather is that the political geography of European modernity is reflected in a high degree of overlapping of linguistic and administrative boundaries. In Europe, language was an eminently important factor in the processes of nation-state formation. It hardly seems a coincidence that very few European states have a linguistically 'neutral' official denomination: Belgium, Britain and Austria are the examples that come to mind in the context of the EU, and one may well speculate concerning the extent to which this neutrality points to a deviation from the 'normal' patterns of nation-building in Europe. At any rate, the cases of Austria (after the First World War) and Belgium stand for specific problems on the path to political integration.

When we focus on the relation between language and statehood, European history, at a first glance, seems to corroborate the claims of

---

[14] Compare the information on the site *L'aménagement linguistique dans le monde*, which is regularly updated (Leclerc 2005a).

those theorists of liberal democracy who, following Mill, argue that the making of a political community is concomitant with the development of a shared cultural identity. When the age of modern mass democracies began towards the end of the nineteenth century, the processes of linguistic-cultural standardization were already entering an advanced stage in many cases. Typically, the first phase in the formation of European nation-states consisted in the military and administrative penetration of a delimited territory by a political centre. In the subsequent phase of standardization, the centre strove to establish a uniform communicative space across this territory, thereby securing the effective administration and control of its domain of rule (Rokkan 1999: 163–76). The imperative of standardization acquired particular significance in the course of the formation of the larger Western European territorial states, such as France, Spain and Britain. However, the goal was not pursued with the same intensity everywhere.

A paradigmatic case of a persistent and rigid policy of linguistic standardization is France. In 1539, the edict of Villers-Cotterêts prescribed that French should be the language of all written legal acts within the domain of royal rule. Nonetheless, we may assume that the measure was not implemented uniformly, as a significant portion of the administrative personnel in the provinces lacked sufficient knowledge of the language of the court. The ambition to create a linguistically homogeneous territory, which had already been a guideline in the absolutist state, became even more important with the revolution of 1789. From the revolutionaries' point of view, the minority languages spoken in the rural peripheries represented a threat for the unity of the newly created nation. A report prepared for the Welfare Committee, dated *8 pluviôse an 2* (27 January 1794), stated that federalism and superstition spoke Breton, emigration and hatred of the Revolution, German, the counter-revolution, Italian and fanaticism, Basque. Accordingly, Jacobin zealots travelled across the country in the years after 1789, denouncing the *patois* which they associated with the *Ancien Régime* and praising French as the language of the revolutionary New Order.[15] However, even the Revolution did not bring about an immediate large-scale change of the situation in the Republic's peripheries. Historical evidence suggests that in the initial years of the Third Republic, promulgated in 1873, French was a foreign language for about half of the country's adult population, who spoke it only poorly, if at all (Jacob and Gordon 1985: 115).

The scenery began to change with Jules Ferry and his reforms, which led to the creation of a public system of elementary schools covering the

---

[15] Compare the accounts in Jacob and Gordon (1985: 109–14) and in Maas (1989: 33–41).

whole country. The school system introduced between 1879 and 1889 was built upon a curriculum conceived by Ferry himself. Its aim was to link the production of national mass loyalty to the spread of a unitary French language standard. The use of local idioms in educational institutions was subject to sanction. For those affected, Ferry's strategy entailed significant psychological and social costs, as schooling alienated them from the communicative practice they experienced at home (Maas 1989: 41). Yet, little by little, the strategy did bring about the intended effects. The republican school system implied an enormous push towards linguistic homogenization. The second major institution deployed to achieve linguistic unity within the French citizenry was the military service, which exposed recruits from different parts of the country to a uniform communication routine. In sum, compulsory schooling and conscription were the main supports of an official identity regime designed to foster unity. Under the banner of the republic, there was no place for linguistic and cultural diversity. The situation is succinctly described by the philosopher Jean-Marc Ferry, who writes: 'In France, the political category of "integration" always wears a uniform'.[16]

According to the official view, cultural unity is constitutive for the unity of the Republic, and republican unity materializes in the unity of culture. Whereas majority culture and republican culture become all but interchangeable concepts, the members of cultural minorities face high assimilationist pressures. In manifold ways, the 'regionalist revolution' (Lafont 1967) of the 1960s and 1970s as well as the sharp increase of ethnic differentiation caused by successive waves of immigration from the Maghreb contributed to reopening the debate on the political significance of cultural pluralism in France's republican order. However, the main features of the French model of integration did not change substantially. The upshot is that, in the meanwhile, the French polity exhibits a rather peculiar approach to diversity. In its external relations, the French state behaves as an ardent defender of the *exception culturelle*. It takes the stance that the EU must form a bastion against the standardizing tendencies of a global mass culture which, from the French political elites' viewpoint, is nothing but a vehicle for reinforcing Anglo-American hegemony. To speak of a 'republican schizophrenia' (Laborde 2001: 727) in this context does not seem exaggerated. For embracing cultural diversity on the terrain of interstate relations lacks credibility against the background of the fixation on achieving cultural unity within the French nation-state. The contradictions involved here will be brought into focus again

---

[16] Be it in the colour of military or in the colour of school clothing, we may add. For the citation see Ferry (1994: 35–6).

when we discuss the transnational context of European language policy (cf. Section 4.5).

France notoriously exemplifies the implicit tensions between the nation-state and multilingualism. Modern states are characterized by a strong propensity for ruling and administering in one language. This propensity reflects, in the first place, the criteria of bureaucratic rationality, as had already become patent in the French case in 1539 with the Villers-Cotterêts edict. From the perspective of a political centre in the process of nation-state formation, making concessions to multilingualism at the administrative level would imply a loss of efficiency. To be able to stabilize their structures of rule in the long run, however, modern polities not only need to function efficiently; they must be legitimate as well. The second important political dimension of language here comes to the fore. It points to the motivation that drove the Jacobins' push for homogenization after 1789: inasmuch as languages are seen as forces that give cohesion to different groups, claims for linguistic authenticity have to be put under the control of the state. Language-based dividing lines between civil society and political society must be abolished. In a context in which the postulate of promoting bureaucratic and administrative efficiency, on the one hand, and the strategies used to secure political and cultural legitimacy, on the other, are as closely bound up as in France since the sixteenth century, the state turns into a linguistic assimilation machine. It becomes, in effect, a 'glossophagic' state, that is, a state which aims at imposing a system of public monolingualism and at devouring minority languages (Laponce 1987: 201).

However, the historical experiences of France, as well as those of other larger territorial states in Europe, should not be generalized without qualification. To suppose that there has been *one* standard European model for the organization of rule by the nation-state would be misleading (Ebbinghaus and Kraus 1997: 339–44). If we examine the degrees of congruence among political and cultural integration patterns in European countries, it becomes apparent that there are fairly sharp differences between the paths of state formation. It is true that especially those European national polities which succeeded the larger absolutist states made significant attempts to combine the goals of territorial integration and cultural homogeneity when applying the principle of sovereignty within their territories. Yet in view of the long-term results of these processes, the success story of the European nation-state appears to a large extent to be a myth (Tilly 1992), even if in some cases the attempts at homogenization were really far-reaching. A monopoly of centralized state control in the realms of language and culture was especially hard to establish in countries that experienced only a limited 'nationalization' of collective identities before entering the period of modern mass politics. In these cases, the institutional negation of pluralism by the state would arouse the protest of already mobilized ethnolinguistic groups.[17]

European paths of state building have produced different levels of cultural standardization and language rationalization. The political guideline *cuius regio, eius religio* and its natural companion *cuius regio, eius lingua* did not remain uncontested principles in the making of the European state system. There is a high degree of variation in the interplay of language (or languages) and political integration in Western European nation-states. This is not to deny that Europe's contemporary linguistic landscape has been shaped by political institutions in substantial ways. In modern societies, linguistic communities can hardly survive without a minimum of institutional support. Obviously, such a support necessarily goes far beyond the realm of a life-world which would be immediately accessible to ethnographic observation; it means that a language is used in the educational system and its presence is guaranteed in the media. Thus, linguistic bonds should not be seen so much as the reflection of a primordial identity firmly rooted in the past, but rather as the expression of a political culture that is subject to continuous transformations.

In contemporary Europe, we find a very broad range of constellations in the field of language policy. Some cases are characterized by a high degree of congruence between the monolingualism of the state and the country's socio-linguistic reality. Iceland could be mentioned as an example in this respect; among EU member states, Portugal might come close to such a situation. In other cases, state monolingualism does not reflect the profile of a society, but rather articulates the political goal of ignoring societal multilingualism for the benefit of an officially sanctioned collective identity. Apart from France, Greece is another older EU member endorsing such a position with regard to language policy. In general, however, the member states of the EU tend to pay formal tribute to the existence of different languages on their territory. They do so by implementing measures that begin by making minor symbolic concessions towards linguistic minorities and can extend as far as guaranteeing the full bilingualism of public institutions.

The following overview discusses the institutional strategies adopted by European states that officially acknowledge the existence of different

---

[17] Following Stein Rokkan, one could argue that the persistence and revival of peripheral identities are as characteristic for Western Europe as their dissolution or eradication; compare Rokkan (1975) as well as Rokkan and Urwin (1983).

linguistic groups within the citizenry in dealing with the language issue. The main focus is on the more established democracies in Western Europe. Depending on the specific political context, the principle of territoriality and the principle of personality can be used as the elementary instruments for the institutional regulation of language pluralism. Moreover, regarding the scope of the societal domains subject to multilingual arrangements, language rights can be granted by applying comparatively restrictive or comparatively generous criteria. To the extent that there is any official recognition of linguistic heterogeneity, we obtain a simple typology of the language policies implemented by European states by combining the principle of recognition with the functional scope of official multilingualism (see Figure 4.1).[18]

I. Provisions protecting the members of language communities are an option chosen particularly in settings where the targeted groups have become a minority even in the core areas of their traditional home territory. Typically, the groups falling under this category are numerically very small. The Sorbs in the German *Länder* of Saxony and Brandenburg (approx. 60,000) or the Croats in the Austrian Burgenland (between 20,000 and 40,000) are examples that spring to mind here.[19] The two minorities of Slavic origin enjoy cultural rights guaranteed by the state especially in the spheres of local administration and education; they are meant to alleviate the strong pressure towards assimilating into the German-speaking majority which both groups have to confront. Often, the practical effects of the minority provisions in everyday life are largely symbolic because of the undisputed dominance attained by the majority language. Hence, minority members have to make great concessions in their communicative routines, and the question is whether minority protection can bring a silent assimilation process to a halt or only manage to slow it down.

II. The principle of linguistic autonomy is applied within a limited portion of a state's territory, where it ensures the formal equality of minority and majority languages. Both Catalan in Catalonia and German in South Tyrol, to cite two examples, share an official status alongside the respective state languages (i.e. Spanish and Italian). Formal equality, however, is restricted to the regional context. Regarding its overall symbolic appearance and institutional framework, the state is committed to a more or less exclusive use of the majority language. The challenges of bilingualism

---

[18] Compare Kraus (2000: 147); a detailed description of institutional language policies in Western Europe is provided by Siguan (1995: 59–91).

[19] The figures are taken from Haarmann (1993: 67) and Hilpold (1996: 138–9).

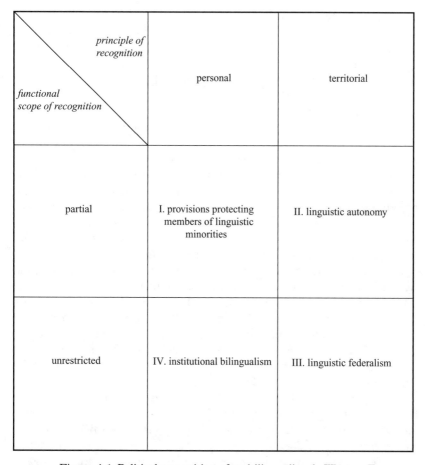

	principle of recognition	
functional scope of recognition	personal	territorial
partial	I. provisions protecting members of linguistic minorities	II. linguistic autonomy
unrestricted	IV. institutional bilingualism	III. linguistic federalism

Figure 4.1 Political recognition of multilingualism in Western European states

thus become primarily a matter of regional concern. Depending on socio-linguistic background and political context, the ranking of levels of linguistic recognition give rise to prolonged conflicts.

If attachments to different language communities are concomitant with different patterns of political loyalty, a linguistic status experienced as unequal on the side of the minority will easily give rise to demands for compensation. Many Catalan nationalists, for instance, think that struggling for the cause of Catalan within their 'own' domains of sovereignty continues to be a paramount task, because they perceive the Spanish state as a Spanish-speaking entity (which indeed it tends to be).[20] They take Catalonia's demographic weight (more than 6 million people, a majority of them speaking Catalan) to be important enough to maintain that the autonomy regime should work de facto on the basis of a 'small state' model in the field of language policy. This would imply a local regulation of linguistic affairs which would no longer have to take into account the prerogatives of the central state.

III. In contrast with the autonomy approach, linguistic federalism does recognize several languages as state languages. This is the status of Dutch, French and German in Belgium, one of the founding members of the European Community/EU.[21] In Switzerland, Article 4 of the constitutional text revised in 1999 defines German, French, Italian and *Romantsch* as national languages. According to Article 70, German, French and Italian are official at the federal level; at the same time, *Romantsch*, which is the variety of Rhaeto-Romanic spoken in the Grisons canton, is granted the constitutional status of a regional official language.[22]

Linguistic federations aim at a consistent application of the principle of territoriality. To this end, the state is subdivided into political and administrative units which are by and large classified as linguistically homogeneous. To the extent that we move from the political macro-level to the micro-level, the institutional approach towards multilingualism tends to become less generous. Thus, in Belgium, official bilingualism in the strong sense is limited to the capital city of Brussels. Of the 23 Swiss cantons, 19 are monolingual.[23] Three cantons are considered to be bilingual in French and German. The Grisons canton is the only administrative subunit which is officially trilingual (German – Italian – *Romantsch*). Both Belgium and Switzerland can be classified as democracies with marked consociational features. Their linguistic federalism is interwoven with other important layers of cultural and ideological segmentation (McRae 1986: 335). In everyday political communication the interaction beyond the borders of linguistic communities rarely plays

---

[20] An analysis of the dynamics of language politics in Catalonia can be found in Kraus (2007: 206–16); see also Kraus (1996: 252–60).

[21] This represents a very rough summary of a complex situation. According to the constitution of 1994, the Belgian federation comprises three communities (the French community, the Flemish community and the German-speaking community), three regions (Wallonia, Flanders and the Brussels region) as well as four linguistic regions (the French-speaking region, the Dutch-speaking region, the bilingual region Brussels-Capital as well as the German-speaking region); the numerous articles of the Belgian constitution which are relevant for language policy are listed in Leclerc (2005b).

[22] See Leclerc (2005c) for an overview of Swiss language policy regulations.

[23] There are 14 monolingual German and 4 monolingual French cantons. The Ticino canton is Italian-speaking.

a central role. To maintain the balance in the realm of language policy requires that none of the state languages should represent a majoritarian threat to the other languages. Unlike linguistic autonomy regulations, linguistic federalism – at any rate in its Belgian and Swiss versions – implies that the state refrains from enforcing the use of a lingua franca.[24]

IV. In principle, institutional multilingualism does not restrict the official use of different languages by subjecting it to territorial critieria. For practical reasons, this kind of approach is generally limited to not more than two languages. The EU members Finland and Ireland guarantee the equal use of the two respective state languages (that is Finnish and Swedish in the first, English and Irish in the second case) as communicative tools of public administration. It has to be added, however, that in Finland the application of the personality principle is qualified by its complex conjunction with rights defined on a territorial basis.[25]

The examples of Ireland and Finland are of great interest, not only for those devoted to studying linguistic legislation, as they show that belonging to different linguistic groups is not necessarily an indicator for contrasting patterns of national identification. At present, Irish is the mother tongue of not more than approximately 10 percent of Ireland's population. In spite of the intensive efforts the Irish state has put into reviving the autochthonous language since the Republic's independence, socio-linguists argue that Irish is at best leading a rearguard battle against English (Hagège 1996: 204–6). Nonetheless, many Irish, although not fluent in the vernacular, continue to regard the Irish language as a symbol of Irish identity and therefore are highly supportive of the policy of official bilingualism.

In Finland, the Swedish-speaking minority comprises slightly less than 6 percent of the population.[26] Traditionally, the language issue has been very relevant in Finnish politics; up to now, the linguistic minority has maintained its 'own' parliamentary representation by means of the Swedish People's Party (SFP). If we look at the evolution of the vote

---

[24] Even if, according to a report published by *The Economist* ('Fifth tongue, fifth column', 18 November 2000), English is increasingly employed de facto in such a function in Switzerland.

[25] Municipalities may be defined as monolingual Swedish or monolingual Finnish. If the rate of the (Finnish- or Swedish-speaking) minority population in a municipality reaches the level of 8 percent, a municipality is considered to be bilingual. The corresponding classification can only be reversed when the rate of minority population falls below 6 percent. The figures are obtained by asking for the citizens' self-classification. Depending on the linguistic definition of a municipality, the local administration has to make for a more or less extensive bilingual profile of its services. The linguistic status of a municipality is especially significant in the realms of education and culture (cf. Leclerc 2004).

[26] The exact figure for the year 2004 was 5.58 percent (cf. Leclerc 2004).

since the first general elections in 1910, it is striking to observe that the percentages obtained by the SFP generally differ only very little – the range is between 0.5 and 1 percent – from the proportion of the Swedish-speaking Finns among the whole population.[27] Yet, the minority identity and the loyalty towards the Finnish nation-state stand in an unquestionable complementary relationship. This view is widely shared by the Finnish-speaking majority. Quite symptomatically, in the presidential elections of 1994, the SFP candidate Elisabeth Rehn came very close to the results of her Social Democratic competitor Martti Ahtisaari, who won the contest; accordingly, she received the support of almost half of the Finnish-speaking segment of the electorate.

The paths taken by Finland and Ireland in the field of language policy also make apparent that the institutional position of a language is not the most decisive factor determining the language's fate in the long run. The Finnish state adopted a policy towards the Swedish-speaking minority which is very generous by all comparative standards. Nevertheless, in the period stretching from 1910 to 1990, the Swedish language, to some extent identified with the country's former elites, kept receding against Finnish, the relative number of Swedish speakers going down from 12 to 6 percent (McRae 1997: 86). In Ireland, on the other hand, the massive political revaluation of Irish after independence did not instigate the language's renaissance; English, the language of the former colonial power, continued to expand its hegemonic position.

The previous discussion of Mill's verdict showed that a multilingual social structure is a challenge for modern democratic polities. In a nutshell, the challenge consists in finding a way to weaken the foreseeable tensions between promoting administrative efficiency, on the one hand, and the requirements of democratic legitimation, on the other. The two aspects can be related to the instrumental and the expressive dimensions of language, respectively. Mill's hypothesis captures the challenge well: functional barriers to communication obstruct the formation of a shared political identity; at the same time, such barriers are likely to remain high as long as the common political will to transcend them is lacking. However, the model of the 'glossophagic' state is certainly not the only viable response to the challenge. Often enough, multilingualism served as a starting point for distinctive paths of institutional pluralism. Institutional pluralism must not be considered a priori as an obstacle to the process of consolidating a democracy. Countries such as Switzerland, Belgium and Finland have a democratic record that is definitely not below

---

[27] Here, I am relying on the overview of electoral results and linguistic census data prepared by McRae (1997: 193).

'average' by Western European standards. Viewed in the light of their political experience, the 'problem' does not reside in the institutional specificities of multilingual democracies. The problem, rather, is that the more or less canonical contributions to the theory of liberal democracy were formulated in a context that made, albeit implicitly, cultural and linguistic homogeneity a background condition of political integration.[28] From the corresponding angle, diversity was typically perceived as an anomaly to be erased by relying on the appropriate forms of institutional engineering. Thus, the 'dogmatic monolingualism' characteristic of mainstream modern theories of liberal democracy has little to offer when it comes to conceiving innovative ways to manage diversity within institutional settings which are supposed to meet democratic standards.

4.4   From Linguistic Pluralism to Linguistic Recognition

The models of language policy discussed in the previous chapter dealt exclusively with vernacular languages (i.e. with languages that have an autochthonous origin). Accordingly, they do not apply to the languages of immigrant groups. This may seem problematic, since it implies the omission of a phenomenon of remarkable scope, as is proven by the examples of Turkish in Germany or dialectal Arabic in France.[29] In cities such as Berlin, Brussels or Paris, entire districts are shaped by immigrant communities whose members predominantly use the language of their region of origin to address each other. In general, the receiving states are disposed to make some minimal concessions to these groups in matters of language policy, be it by subsidizing mother tongue courses for immigrant children or by sponsoring some broadcasts in the languages of the immigrants in the public media.

Nonetheless, language policy initiatives targeting migrants are generally subordinated to the broader goals of immigration policy and subject to the deficiencies observable in this field. In the German case, for instance, it is frequently criticized that because of political negligence school children with a non-native background become 'semi-lingual' and end up lacking a sufficient functional knowledge both of German and of

---

[28] See Tully (1995: 58–98), who describes the ideological universe of early liberal constitutionalism as an 'empire of uniformity'.

[29] Approximately 2.5 million people of Turkish origin were resident in Germany in 2000. The figure includes 400,000 naturalized former Turkish citizens and may offer a rough estimate of the size of the German Turkish-speaking community (however, it does not list the speakers of Kurdish separately). In France, the number of people speaking one of the Maghrebinian (Moroccan, Algerian or Tunisian) varieties of Arabic was about 1.4 million at the end of the 1990s. For the German figures, see Beauftragte der Bundesregierung für Ausländerfragen (2002); for France, see Leclerc (2005d).

their family's language.[30] Moreover, language policy programs developed especially for immigrants usually do not have the protection of cultural diversity as their main objective. They are not designed primarily to provide institutional protection to the identity of a minority group, but rather aim at mitigating the social and economic discrimination of minority members by facilitating their integration in the majority society.[31] At the level of de facto language policies, Western democracies make a clear distinction between immigrants and autochthonous groups when it comes to assessing the legitimacy of claims to cultural protection; accordingly, the languages of immigrant communities are still far removed from being assigned any kind of official status in European states. To differentiate between minorities can be considered the standard approach in the normative theory of citizenship rights as well. Thus, Kymlicka (1995: 96) argues that demands for collective rights raised by 'national minorities' bear greater weight than similar claims articulated by 'ethnic groups' produced by migratory movements; in his view, deciding to emigrate can be considered a conscious act, which includes being prepared to make a substantial effort to adapt oneself to a new cultural environment. Nevertheless, there is increasing empirical evidence that the changes of the socio-linguistic constellation brought about by the 'new' minorities will have a substantial impact on the democratic fabric of Western polities. In the long run, they might well lead to modifying the normative premises upon which minority policies were based until now.

To draw attention to the specific features of different types of minority is a good starting point for clarifying the political rationale that underlies the dynamics of institutionalizing linguistic pluralism in the context of European democracies. In a pioneering comparative study dealing with the causes and political implications of the 'ethnic revival' in modern, industrialized Western European societies, which is still a highly recommendable reading, the Finnish social scientist Erik Allardt (1979: 43–7), after analyzing a broad sample of empirical cases, maintains that the mobilization of territorial linguistic minorities in the developed West cannot generally – or, at any rate, cannot anymore – be interpreted as a reaction against types of discrimination which are linked to social exclusion and bear negative material consequences. In contrast to the ethnic groups constituted by immigrants, Europe's 'autochthonous' linguistic minorities were in most cases not struggling to overcome a situation of direct social and economic subordination. They were rather struggling

---

[30] For the concept of 'semi-lingualism' see Crystal (2000: 79).
[31] Bilingual education programs for children with a Hispanic background in the USA, for example, follow this normative orientation (cf. Ricento 1998).

for recognition, as Allardt (1979: 44) literally put it in the late 1970s, thereby anticipating the debate led in political theory after 1990. From Allardt's viewpoint, by making such claims for recognition, their primary goal is to have their self-categorization accepted by the majorities.

For the bulk of the minority groups in question, this self-categorization is not so much related to socio-economic background conditions; ultimately, its core consists in a distinctive cultural identity whose principal symbol is language. In particular, groups with a high capacity for political mobilization – such as the Tyroleans in Italy, the Basques and the Catalans in Spain, the Walloons and the Flemings in Belgium or the Swedish-speaking Finns – cannot be adequately characterized by attributing them an inferior position in the system of cultural division of labour. What they strive for are political and institutional provisions that allow them to reproduce a collective identity which they consider as specific.[32] We are dealing with groups exposed to a peculiar dialectic of socio-economic equality and cultural differentiation. Simplifying, we can conclude that the major issues on Europe's current language policy agenda are less related to questions of material status than to questions of self-respect and 'honour'.

For the approach adopted here, recapitulating Allardt's account of the mobilization of linguistic minorities in Western Europe is an illuminating exercise that allows us to tackle some substantial political issues currently raised by cultural and linguistic diversity in the EU. If we want to achieve a comprehensive understanding of the conflict structures characteristic of multilingual contexts we must be prepared to take an important additional step: it consists in establishing a connection between the role of recognition in language policy and a prominent research tradition in socio-linguistics that has focused on the study of *diglossia*. The concept of diglossia refers to linguistic settings in which two or more languages occupy clearly separate functional domains within the same society. What is more, this functional separation generally overlaps with a social hierarchy. Typically, in this hierarchy a 'high' language used in the realms of education, administration, finances and the media can be distinguished from a 'low' language.[33] As Fishman (1971: 286–8) points out,

---

[32] For general overviews of Western Europe's new regionalisms and peripheral nationalisms focussing on their political goals see also Puhle (1995) as well as Tiryakian and Rogowski (1985).

[33] When Ferguson (1959) introduced the concept of diglossia, his aim was to designate a 'high variety' and a 'low variety' of the *same* language; accordingly, he mentions examples such as classic vs. popular Arabic and High German vs. Swiss German. The concept was given a broader meaning by Fishman (1967), who uses it to analyze situations in which the functions of the higher and of the lower code in intrasocietal communication

societal bilingualism and diglossia can combine in different ways. Shifts in the relationship between different languages and between speech communities therefore reflect the dynamics of political and cultural change at work in a country. In the case of France, for example, French had already attained an exclusive role as the functionally 'high' language well before the final decades of the nineteenth century, when Jules Ferry's educational reforms reinforced its hegemony across the whole country. Nonetheless, according to the historical account on how 'peasants' were turned into 'Frenchmen' presented by Eugen Weber (1976), around 1850 it was still the rule that the rural population in the peripheries only spoke the regional *patois*. Thus, a peasant in Brittany would only be fluent in Breton and hardly speak any French. Hence, to the extent that there was no encompassing language community based on the use of French, the situation was characterized by diglossia without bilingualism. Today, in contrast, we will observe a co-occurrence of diglossia with (a limited) bilingualism in those areas of France with surviving regional languages. The Breton peasant may still speak Breton, but he has certainly acquired a solid knowledge of French as well. The regional languages have retained their subordinate status. Yet, in the meantime, everybody is able to communicate fluently in the 'high' language.

In connection with theories of recognition, the concept of diglossia makes an important contribution to our understanding of linguistic conflict in Western democracies. Claims for recognition raised on the terrain of language policy are to a significant extent claims made in order to attenuate, or sometimes even to overcome, the effects of diglossia. By mobilizing for linguistic equality, the members of the groups exposed to diglossic institutional settings want to expand the range of the social and functional domains in which they have the possibility of using their vernacular language. Linguistic recognition then implies that individuals who belong to a minority group are given the option to live an everyday life that is not too far away from the communicative 'normality' that the members of the dominant culture are used to. In this context, it is revealing that bilingualism is experienced as particularly problematic within groups whose members experience diglossic situations as situations of status inconsistency. In the recent past, examples like those of the Québécois in Canada, the Catalans in Spain or the Flemings in Belgium exhibited this very pattern. In the cases mentioned, the discontent caused by the functional subordination of the 'own' language regarding the dominant language (English, Spanish and French, respectively) fuelled demands

correspond to *different languages* (Spanish and Guaraní in Paraguay or French and Breton in Brittany, for instance).

for full political and cultural equality. It may be considered symptomatic that the linguistic mobilization of the three groups gained significantly in strength after they had gone through periods of intense modernization, which were accompanied by the formation of a new middle class greatly exercised by questions of cultural status.[34]

In the meantime, the Breton peasant who is not proficient in the dominant language belongs to a distant past. Nowadays the members of Western Europe's linguistic minorities are generally bilingual. Frequently, their knowledge of the majority language may even be better than their competence in the mother tongue. At the same time, however, they are frequently quite determined to defend their vernacular and to resist their complete linguistic assimilation. In the case of Ireland, the massive public support for a policy upholding an official bilingualism (Irish and English) indicates that the allegiance to the 'own' language even reaches well into the large segments of the population who were assimilated linguistically generations ago. Many people perceive language as a key to the realm of authenticity, as a symbol of collective identity that must not be renounced by any means. Consequently, in a socio-cultural context characterized by diglossia, struggles over recognition often involve conflict over the status of languages. The history of European nationalisms offers many examples for the political tensions involved in situations of diglossia. In a book devoted to the case of Finland, the philo-nationalist historian John Wuorinen (1931: 53) wrote several decades ago:

[T]he Finns could never become a fully united nation while the upper classes were separated from the lower by a linguistic gulf. The gulf could be bridged and the people united only by reversing the process which had made the upper classes increasingly Swedish. In a word, they would have to adopt Finnish as their mother tongue.

With hindsight, one can argue that in Finland the attempts to turn the popular language into a vehicle of higher communication – in other words, at ending a state of diglossia in which Finnish was predominantly used as the lower idiom – were successful without implying a violation of the linguistic identity of the members of the Swedish-speaking community. This is not to say, however, that the bridging of the gulf between two spheres of communication which had been separated for a long time, as Wuorinen puts it, was a process free of conflict.[35] In many other cases, the policies directed at equalizing the status of languages

---

[34] For a discussion of the dynamics underlying linguistic mobilization in Québec, Catalonia and Belgium, see Gagnon (1984), Balcells (1991) and Leton and Miroir (1999).

[35] McRae (1997: 9–103) has a useful historical overview of language politics and policies in Finland.

within a country contributed to getting rid of old resentments held by speakers of the formerly lower language variety but also created new resentments felt by members of the linguistic community which had been previously associated with a high status.[36] According to the thesis put forward in the introduction to this chapter, a democratically grounded language policy must aim at overcoming collective resentments, thereby furthering the integration of different cultural groups within a common institutional framework. To take such an objective seriously means to be aware of the multiple challenges it involves.

Where linguistic communities can be recognized by application of the principle of territoriality, the establishment of officially unilingual spaces may make it possible to circumvent a good part of the problems posed by diversity. Generally speaking, the will to institutionalize the equal coexistence of two (or more) languages within a shared territorial unit is likely to require greater efforts; from the perspective of socio-linguistics, societal bilingualism without diglossia appears to be relatively unstable (Laponce 1987: 33–42). On the one hand, to make sure that different languages have a more or less equal standing in all relevant functional domains of a society is a demanding political task. On the other hand, the 'costs' of bilingualism are often unevenly distributed among different language groups. In the case of the officially bilingual Brussels region, for instance, there seems to be an imbalance that mainly affects the members of the Dutch-speaking community, who complain about their having to switch to French in many communicative contexts (Arel 2001: 187).

By relating the issue of recognition to the phenomenon of diglossia, we acquire a better understanding of the identity conflicts that revolve around language. This does not mean, however, that establishing the link between recognition and diglossia takes us directly to an institutional standard formula for addressing the political challenges of multilingualism. If we want to find a normatively sound equilibrium between the imperatives of instrumental communication and the commitment to protect diverse linguistic identities in multilingual settings, we must be prepared to work out a political analysis which includes thick socio-linguistic evidence. When we enter the field of recognition, designing an adequate institutional response to the challenges of diversity requires a careful appraisal of contextual factors, which necessarily vary from case to case. In this respect, language policies are no exception. Still, bringing diglossia into

---

[36] The developments observable in some of the successor states of the Austro-Hungarian monarchy, which entailed bitter tensions between the new titular nations and German- or Hungarian-speaking minorities of imperial origins, are a case in point; compare Jászi (1961 [1929]: 453–5).

focus may be of considerable help if we are to grasp the context which gives conflicts over linguistic recognition their specific shape. Hence, the interplay of recognition and the (latent) problems of diglossia should be regarded as an important aspect of the politics of language in the EU. Before getting there, however, there is one more question to be addressed. It concerns the significance of linguistic rights as elements of an internationally approved catalogue of basic cultural rights in contemporary Europe.

4.5 Language and the Protection of Minorities in the Context of a European Human Rights Regime

Thus far, we have analyzed the language policies of European states as the outcome of endogenous developments. The evidence presented shows that a broad range of institutional strategies exists for dealing with linguistic and cultural pluralism. Against this background, one important aspect still to be discussed is the impact of international law on the regulation of linguistic diversity in Europe. To what extent has a minimal normative consensus emerged regarding the rights that must be granted to linguistic minorities, irrespective of the great differences between the specific regulations we may find across European states?

Human rights are universal rights. They are rights individuals possess as members of the human race, regardless of where they may find themselves on the planet. However, the bearer of these rights is not a human identity defined in abstract terms. Universality means that concrete men and women are protected in their dignity, in ways that take into account the specific historical, linguistic and cultural embeddedness of their existence. Hence, the human rights postulate of universal equality has to be complemented by the obligation to respect cultural difference, as long as the latter does not place the unity of the human species in question (Ignatieff 2000: 2, 43). The category of cultural rights makes this complementarity manifest, as it relates rights – that is, something all of us share – to patterns of cultural identity, which may well be attributes of specific groups. Language is an obvious case in point.

The cultural aspect is relevant, albeit implicitly, for virtually all human rights legislation (Toivanen 2000: 213). The right to free speech, for instance, has an undeniable linguistic dimension. Accordingly, to prohibit the use of a language in public is to restrict free speech. On the other hand, to cite another example, freedom of assembly is a necessary precondition of the ability of groups to protect their cultural identity. International organizations such as the United Nations or the United Nations Educational, Scientific and Cultural Organization have recently exhibited an increasing tendency to emphasize the independent character of cultural rights vis-à-vis civil, political, economic and social categories of human rights.[37] In the Western world, in particular, a new political discourse on rights and recognition, which establishes a close connection between issues concerning the material dimensions of citizenship and questions related to the field of symbolic representation and cultural identity (Fraser and Honneth 2003, Pakulski 1997), has had a great impact on redefining the legal status of minorities.

In Europe, after the end of the Cold War, the protection of linguistic and national minorities has gradually become a matter regulated by an emerging transnational human rights regime. Since the constitution of the Council of Europe in 1949, one of its main goals has been the promotion of human rights. The Council's activities in the area of human rights acquired additional relevance when the Eastern European states began joining the body after 1989. It should be noted that the corresponding initiatives always had the unconditional, active support of EU institutions. In the 1990s, the Council devoted a good part of its activities to defining a set of minimal standards for protecting minorities (Aarnio 1995). Its starting point in this regard was to establish a close connection between the field of cultural recognition and questions of human rights, as can be seen in the Convention for the Protection of National Minorities introduced in 1995. The Council had already made an initial path-breaking move in terms of setting cultural rights standards several years before with the European Charter of Regional or Minority Languages, whose elaboration was completed in 1992. In the present-day European human rights context, the Charter should actually be considered a key document establishing a catalogue of general norms for dealing with linguistic diversity.

The Preamble to the Charter stresses the great weight assigned to the principles of democracy and cultural diversity within the framework of the national sovereignty and territorial integrity of the Council of Europe's member states. Moreover, it states that the protection of minority languages must not be detrimental to the official languages of these states. In Part I of the Charter (Articles 1 through 6), regional or minority languages are defined as those languages that are 'traditionally used within a given territory of a State by nationals of that State who form a group numerically smaller than the rest of the State's population'.[38]

---

[37] Symonides (1998: 561–5) and Toivanen (2000: 214–25) list the principal international declarations and conventions containing such a view.

[38] European Charter for Regional or Minority Languages. The document is available in English and French on the website of the Council of Europe. The quotations are taken from the English version (http://conventions.coe.int/Treaty/en/Treaties/Html/148.htm).

Thus, dialects of an official language or the languages of migrants are not taken into account. Nor are the languages falling under the definition listed explicitly. Although the Charter comprises a catalogue of concrete obligations which are to be met by the signatory states, it does not provide the subjects of language rights with the possibility of lodging a formal complaint when a state fails to guarantee a sufficient level of minority protection. Instead, an expert committee acts as a controlling organ. In spite of having a binding character, the Charter is a highly flexible legal instrument. Part II (Article 7) lists the common objectives and principles which all the parties to the treaty have to accept. The states are expected to recognize regional or minority languages 'as an expression of cultural wealth' and to make sure that these languages are not exposed to any discriminatory measures. The Charter has an 'à la carte' structure. Accordingly, the signatories have to choose a minimum of obligations out of the inventory given in Part III (Articles 8 through 14). To put it in more concrete terms, the states that ratify the Charter must accept and implement at least 35 out of the 68 options indicated there. Of these 35 options, at least three have to relate respectively to the areas delineated in Articles 8 ('education') and 12 ('cultural activities and facilities'). Moreover, at least one measure must be chosen from Articles 9 ('judicial authorities'), 10 ('administrative authorities and public services'), 11 ('media') and 13 ('economic and social life'). The options selected refer exclusively to the language or languages which have been determined by a signatory state.

The Charter's main guidelines had already been worked out prior to 1989. Accordingly, the document's priorities mainly reflected the situation of Western European states. Nonetheless, the Charter acquired additional salience following the collapse of communist rule, when minority problems intensified all over the eastern half of the continent. Frequently, experts assessing the contribution that the legal text makes to the protection of minorities tend to be sceptical. Blumenwitz (1996: 185), for instance, argues that the document is bound to have little practical impact because of the conditionality of many of its clauses; in his view, the Charter can serve as a proper framework for minority protection only in those states that had in any case already adopted a generous approach in their dealing with minority issues. A somewhat more optimistic view is offered by Tomuschat (1996: 102), who argues that if all the members of the Council of Europe were committed to implementing the Charter's program extensively, virtually no demand made by a linguistic minority would be left unsatisfied. At any rate, we may interpret the Charter thus far as a European treaty that explicitly works against all kinds of state activities aimed at the repression or assimilation of minorities.

Towards the end of 2006, the Charter had been ratified and entered into force in 21 member states of the Council of Europe, 13 of whom were at that time EU members (Austria, Cyprus, Denmark, Finland, Germany, Hungary, Luxembourg, the Netherlands, Slovakia, Slovenia, Spain, Sweden and the UK).[39] Regardless of its deliberately moderate tone and the flexibility of its provisions, which leave quite a lot of space for nation-states to maintain their prerogatives, the treaty aroused serious reservations in several European states, both outside and within the EU. In this context, again, a closer look at the French example, marked by protracted and severe political controversies over the Charter, is especially instructive. France signed the Charter in May of 1999. The Socialist Prime Minister Lionel Jospin had acted as one of the main advocates of this symbolically important declaration of political intent. Before signing, there had been a long period of preparations and consultations, devoted to making sure that the articles adopted from the Charter were compatible with the Constitution of the French Republic. Symptomatically, when putting together its specific catalogue of measures for the area of language policy, the French executive remained very cautious, signing only 39 of the 68 articles, thereby scarcely going beyond the minimum level of 35 which is juridically required. In domains that seemed to be particularly 'sensitive', such as justice and administration, the self-imposed concessions had a rather restricted character. Thus, regionalist spokesmen complained that the foreseeable reforms were disappointingly modest. At the same time, however, from the perspective of some Gaullists and other guardians of republican orthodoxy, assembled around the figure of Jean Pierre Chevènement, the changes were considered an unacceptable expression of 'a communitarian view of society'.[40]

Although France did finally sign the Charter, the signing was not followed by the necessary ratification of the document. Immediately after the signing, the Gaullist Jacques Chirac, in his function as the President of the Republic, appealed to the *Conseil constitutionnel* for an assessment of the treaty's conformity with the French constitution. In June 1999, the *Conseil* ruled that the contents of the Charter were not compatible with the republican constitution. According to the view adopted by the judicial body, the Charter's preamble violates the constitutional principles which affirm the indivisibility of the Republic, equality before the law and the unity of the French people. Thus, the treaty's entry into

---

[39] Status as of 20 September 2006; source: Council of Europe, Treaty Office (http://conventions.coe.int/Treaty/Commun/ChercheSig.asp?NT=148&CM=7&DF=9/20/2006&CL=ENG).

[40] See the article 'La France signe la Charte européenne des langues régionales', published in *Le Monde*, 8 May 1999.

force would require a modification of the constitution. Between 1999 and the present, the process of ratifying the Charter in France, otherwise a staunch defender of cultural diversity in international forums, has remained stalled.

Even when handled with great political care, as was the case with the Charter, the issue of language pluralism apparently impinges on core areas of the French republican creed. In 1992, Article 2 of the constitution had been changed. Since that year, the article reads: 'The language of the Republic is French'. With the introduction of such a statement, France became the only EU member state to affirm explicitly a single official language without also mentioning other languages that are present on its territory (Birnbaum 1998: 355). For those voices who call for a firm upholding of the republican tradition, the Charter – as well as most of the body of documents which the Council of Europe has elaborated to deal with minority problems and to address questions of local and regional autonomy – represents a frontal attack on the spirit of the French constitution. They suspect that the Council backs the activities of 'national-regionalist lobbies'. From their perspective, the Charter for Regional or Minority Languages, opened for signature in 1992, plainly manifests an 'ethnicist and communitarianist inspiration',[41] thereby challenging the most sacrosanct postulates of French constitutionalism.

Notwithstanding the political vicissitudes of the Charter in France up to the present, we have to keep in mind that important obstacles to adopting the treaty had initially been removed even in the French case. In the overall context of the European Union, France may be located at one end of a fairly broad political spectrum, which covers a significant amount of variation of institutional approaches to managing cultural diversity. Thus, for countries like Finland, Spain or Hungary, ratifying and implementing the Charter did not entail any substantial difficulties, as they had previously already made far-reaching concessions in the area of cultural and linguistic rights for domestic political reasons. Seen in this light, the Charter is the expression of a minimal consensus on redefining former nation-state prerogatives in the field of institutional identity politics in Europe. It should be noted that EU institutions have been very much involved in formulating this consensus. The EU's Committee of the Regions, for instance, called on the member states to ratify the document in an opinion adopted at its own initiative on 13 June 2001.[42] The Charter also consistently received the support of the European

---

[41] This is a paraphrase of the position adopted by Anne-Marie Le Pourhiet (2001: 213–14), a public lawyer at the University of Rennes.

[42] Bulletin EU 6–2001, 1.4.19 (europa.eu.int/abc/doc/off/bull/en/200106/p104019.htm).

Parliament from the very opening of the signature process. In February 1994, the European chamber passed the Killilea Resolution, which urged all member states to work towards a quick ratification of the treaty, by a majority of 321 votes to 1 with 6 abstentions (Grin 2000: 17). Viewed against this background, the Charter should be considered to be more than a mere additional instrument of international law, designed to avoid minority conflicts in the traditional sense of the term, namely, as conflicts involving minorities in the first instance. The efforts undertaken to define common European standards for managing linguistic diversity in a manner that corresponds to a deeper understanding of human rights also seem to have great relevance for members of larger (non-minority) language communities. These standards consider men and women not as abstract speakers of language *tout court*, but as speakers of *languages* which relate them to specific socio-cultural life-worlds. The Charter recognizes that these life-worlds have a normative weight of their own and possess a legitimacy that must not be overruled by the imperatives of *realpolitik*. Accordingly, it defines the elementary bases for a European language regime that may be considered just from the perspective of both minority and majority members.

5 The language question in the institutional complex of the European Union

Since its inception in the 1950s, European integration has been a multilingual undertaking. This is true, in the first instance, in a quite trivial sense: relations between states are communicative relations. Interactions among political and administrative elites who belong to different language communities generally necessitate translation. The domain of international politics is, after all, also a domain of interpreters, and Europe is no exception to this rule. But beyond this, the European Union (EU) differs markedly from other more or less well-established arenas of interstate cooperation in that it officially accords multilingualism a very prominent place in its institutional architecture. In this chapter I will focus on the political background of the institutionalization of the EU's language regime and the practical implications of multilingualism for the European institutions.

For many years, the language issue occupied a rather inconspicuous place on the European political agenda. If newspapers had highlighted the 'Brussels language problem' in their headlines 20 or 30 years ago, politically informed readers would have assumed that they would find a report on the conflict between the Francophone and Dutch-speaking communities in the Belgian capital. Today, by contrast, many readers would be more likely to associate such headlines with the language situation in the EU. In fact, since the signing of the Treaty establishing the European Union, public interest in the European language regime seems to be increasing steadily, at least if one goes by press reports. German newspapers, at any rate, have recently devoted much attention to the subject. The reason for this development is obvious: since Maastricht, 'Brussels' – the 'European' Brussels, that is, not the 'Belgian'– is no longer seen exclusively as the site of a highly specialized and technocratic administration; it appears, rather, as the institutional germ of a transnational political order that must be judged by democratic standards. With the increase in intensity of the conflicts over the political form of the EU and with the constitutional debate in particular, the importance of the language question has increased dramatically as well. Against this background, the question can no longer be reduced to the purely instrumental aspects of communication. When what is at stake is the justification of a common political identity, the expressive aspect of linguistic communication comes to the forefront of discussions concerning the European language regime.

The language question in the EU can be divided, roughly speaking, into two components. On the one hand, there is the regulation of the *internal* modes of communication, which essentially means how multilingualism is 'processed' in the context of the regular political and administrative routines within the European institutions. On the other hand, the language question concerns the sphere of *external* communication: how do the EU institutions communicate with European citizens? In the same connection, we must also ask what foundations existing language policy provides for constructing a European civil society. Even though the internal and external areas in reality overlap, in my view it makes sense to separate them for the purposes of analysis. The role of language policy in constituting the European public sphere will be addressed in greater detail in the following chapter. This chapter will concentrate on the field of internal communication (i.e. communication within the European institutions). I will first trace the development of the official language regime of the EU. Then I will examine the practical side of the official multilingualism and highlight some of the problems and contradictions that mark the current situation. Finally, in an interim conclusion, I will discuss possible approaches to alleviating the problems of institutional multilingualism.

5.1   The Institutional Path to Multilingualism

Several dozen autochthonous languages are spoken on the territory of the EU. There is considerable variation in the size of the language communities linked to these languages: at one end of the spectrum, we find the examples of German, with some 90 million native speakers in the EU today (the figure does not include the German-speaking Swiss)[1]; on the other hand, we come upon tiny linguistic islands as those constituted by Sorbian in Germany (60,000 speakers) or by Sami in Sweden and Finland (about 20,000 speakers in Finland and Sweden). In the 27 states which are EU members at present there are 24 state languages: German,

---

[1] German is followed by French, English and Italian, which are the respective mother tongues of 55 to 60 million EU citizens each.

French, English, Italian, Spanish, Polish, Romanian, Dutch, Hungarian, Portuguese, Greek, Czech, Bulgarian, Swedish, Danish, Finnish, Slovak, Lithuanian, Slovene, Latvian, Estonian, Irish, Luxembourgian and Maltese. In addition, 6 languages enjoy an official status at the regional level: Catalan, Galician, Basque, Welsh, Frisian and Sami.[2] Finally, there are legal provisions protecting the speakers of several other minority languages (such as Sorbian in Germany or Croatian in Austria). One of the most characteristic features of European linguistic diversity is that it represents not just a socio-linguistic problematic but, above all, a political one. How is this political issue dealt with in the European institutions?

The 'linguistic constitution' of the European Community (EC)/EU is based on a studiously brief article of the Rome Treaty of 1957 and a directive issued by the Council the following year. The European Economic Community (EEC) Treaty limited itself to specifying procedural rules for clarifying the language problematic; Article 217 of the Treaty read as follows:

The rules governing the languages of the institutions of the Community shall, without prejudice to the provisions contained in the Rules of Procedure of the Court of Justice, be determined by the Council, acting unanimously.[3]

In fact, in April 1958 the Council issued a directive regulating the language question for the EEC. It included the following eight articles[4]:

Article 1. The official languages and the working languages of the institutions of the Community shall be Dutch, French, German and Italian.

Article 2. Documents which a Member State or a person subject to the jurisdiction of a Member State sends to institutions of the Community may be drafted in any one of the official languages selected by the sender. The reply shall be drafted in the same language.

Article 3. Documents which an institution of the Community sends to a Member State or to a person subject to the jurisdiction of a Member State shall be drafted in the language of such state.

---

[2] State languages which also have an official or semi-official status outside their 'own' national territory, as for instance German in South Tyrol or Italian in some municipalities of Slovenia, are not taken into account here.

[3] In the Treaty establishing a Constitution for Europe, the article duly appears in the following version (as Article III-433): 'The Council of Ministers shall adopt unanimously a European regulation laying down the rules governing the languages of the Union's Institutions, without prejudice to the Statute of the Court of Justice of the European Union'.

[4] Cited from Coulmas (1991a: 38–9).

Article 4. Regulations and other documents of general application shall be drafted in the four official languages.

Article 5. The Official Journal of the Community shall be published in the four official languages.

Article 6. The institutions of the Community may stipulate in their rules of procedure which of the languages are to be used in specific cases.

Article 7. The languages to be used in the proceedings of the Court of Justice shall be laid down in its rules of procedure.

Article 8. If a Member State has more than one official language, the language to be used shall, at the request of such State, be governed by the general rules of its law.

Article 217 of the EEC Treaty made the formation of the European language regime into a matter for intergovernmental consensus. Nothing has changed since then. Since 1958, the consensus requirement and the clear commitment to a plurality of working languages serve as the guidelines for regulating issues relating to language within the European institutions. Along the path leading from the founding of the EEC to the successive enlargements of the EC/EU, the criterion that the official languages of the member states should be accorded equal status has retained its validity as new members have joined. Luxembourgian is the only official language which has a special status, as it is not used as routine working language of the organs of the Community; before 2007, this was the case with Irish, too. Otherwise, the text of the regulation of April 1958 has been repeatedly adapted to the language profile of the member states. With the first rounds of the eastern enlargement in 2004 and 2007, the number of European languages enjoying unrestricted official status increased from the initial 4 to a total of 23. Thus, the number of language combinations that have to be catered to by the translation and interpretation service of the Community has increased from 12 (4 official languages in 1958) to 506 (23 official languages in 2007). It is striking that Article 1 of the 1958 regulation governing the language question speaks of 'official languages' and 'working languages' but that none of the subsequent seven articles offers an explanation of the distinction. Hence, the introduction of this conceptual pair ultimately lacks concrete legal relevance. Theoretically, all official languages also enjoy equal status as working languages. Thus the language regime of the EU formally accords remarkable linguistic tribute to the principle of the equality of states. The 'language constitution' of the EU entails an integral multilingualism at the institutional level.

The distinctive multilingualism of the EU is clearly intended to set it apart from the traditional communicative parameters of international organizations. The United Nations uses English, French, Spanish, Russian, Arabic and Chinese as its official languages and English and French as its working languages. It employs approximately 120 permanent interpreters. The member states of the Association of Southeast Asian Nations and the European Free Trade Association do not employ interpreters and use English as the sole working language at their meetings. In the Council of Europe, French and English serve as official languages and German and Italian as additional working languages. The Organization of African Unity, which comprises 50 members, employs English, French and Arabic as its working languages.[5] Thus, the pronounced multilingualism of the EU fulfils a highly important symbolic political function and, especially as regards the language regime, attests to the Union's aspiration to be more than 'merely' an international organization. Upholding the principles of integral multilingualism ultimately reflects the 'protodemocratic' claim to make will-formation processes at the European level linguistically comprehensible for all citizens of the Union.

In principle, integral multilingualism is reflected in all of the EU institutions. Thus, for example, Article 14 of the Council's Rules of Procedure (CRP) states the following with regard to the regulation of languages[6]:

1. Except as otherwise decided unanimously by the Council on grounds of urgency, the Council shall deliberate and take decisions only on the basis of documents and drafts drawn up in the languages specified in the rules in force governing languages.
2. Any member of the Council may oppose discussion if the texts of any proposed amendments are not drawn up in such of the languages referred to in paragraph 1 as he or she may specify.

In the Comments on the CRP, the provisions of the article are explicated as follows:

Pursuant to paragraph 1 of Article 14 of the CRP, except as otherwise decided unanimously, 'the Council shall deliberate and take decisions only on the basis of documents and drafts drawn up in the languages specified in the rules in force governing languages' (. . .). The term 'drafts' refers, in particular, to Commission proposals that must be submitted to the Council in the 11 official languages. This provision allows a delegation to oppose discussion of an item if, when the

---

[5] See the overview in Coulmas (1992: 155).
[6] Quoted from: *Official Journal of the European Communities*, L 149, 23 June 2000, 149/26.

Council brings up the item, the relevant documentation is not available in the official language it prefers.

Paragraph 2 of Article 14 of the CRP also enables each member of the Council to oppose discussion if the texts of any proposed amendments are not drawn up in such of the languages referred to in paragraph 1 as he or she may specify (...).

If a document is not yet available in all 11 official languages, it can nevertheless be the subject of a 'political agreement' on the substance. However, subject to the possible derogations set out below, that text may be adopted only if it is available in good and due form (i.e. finalized by the legal/linguistic experts) in the 11 official languages.

It is to be noted that:

- a regulation or directive addressed to all Member States or a decision addressed to all Member-States cannot enter into force (nor, therefore, be published nor the Member States be notified of it) unless the text exists in the 11 official languages (Article 4 of Regulation No 1);
- a common position of the Council adopted pursuant to the procedures referred to in articles 251 and 252 of the TEC is not forwarded to the European Parliament unless it is available in all 11 official languages.[7]

The extensive quotations from the CRP and from the internal Comments on the CRP demonstrate the great importance attached to the factor of linguistic diversity in the European decision-making process. Aside from the Council, the European Parliament, as the second, though still comparatively subordinate, arm of the EU legislature, is the institution in which integral multilingualism has the greatest impact. No other community body has dealt more intensively with questions of linguistic diversity or has made a stronger commitment to respecting linguistic pluralism than the Parliament. In its rules of procedure of February 1999, it requires that all parliamentary documents must be drafted in the official languages. Moreover, it specifies that a speech delivered in one of the official languages must be translated simultaneously into all of the other official languages and into other languages as well, if the administration of the Parliament regards this as necessary.[8] By 'other' languages are meant primarily minority languages like Gaelic, Catalan or Basque (Labrie 1993: 118).

---

[7] Quoted from: Council Guide. Internal Document II. Comments on the Council's Rules of Procedure, September 2000. DG F – Information Policy, Transparency and Public Relations, Luxembourg: Office for Official Publications of the European Communities, 2001, 17–18.

[8] See Article 79 of the Rules of Procedure of the Parliament reproduced in Labrie (1993: 374).

In contrast with the Council and the Parliament, the Commission apparently does not take a position in its rules of procedure on the use of official languages in the conduct of its business (Labrie 1993: 94). This is amazing since the European Commission can be justly regarded as the nerve centre of the multilingual circuits of communication within the Union. In the year 2000, the institution employed a good one-third of the translators (1,250 of 3,000) and almost 70 percent of the interpreters (653 of 951) in the service of the EU; together they accounted for almost half of the total 'language personnel'.[9] The quantitative dimensions of the language services of the European supranational control centre are viewed as unique worldwide. One need only compare the 120 interpreters who work for the UN with the almost 1,000 interpreters in the service of the EU.[10] Nevertheless, multilingualism in the internal communication of the Commission is subject to concrete limits, as we shall see presently. Finally, according to Article 217 of the Treaty of the European Community, the European Court of Justice (ECJ) is the only Community body authorized to decide independently on its language regime. Although experts and witnesses are always permitted to use their own language before the court, for each case a language of procedure is specified in which, for example, the court records are kept. Moreover, the effective working language of the ECJ for the internal deliberations of the judges is French (Labrie 1993: 129–32).

The 'linguistic constitution' of the EC/EU seems to be characterized at first sight by the fact that the 'major' agreements of Rome and Maastricht factor out issues regarding the regulation of language. Ultimately, the entire language regime of the Union rests exclusively on the 1958 decree. Of course, this does not mean that the language issue is not in urgent need of additional regulation. As a glance at the commentary to the rules of procedure of the Council reveals, the linguistic aspect is a central factor in the daily workings of the European institutions. Even though the EC/EU has thus far declined to adopt a clearly delineated language policy, its *official* discourse is dominated by an insistent plea for multilingualism. The multilingual credo is defended emphatically, indeed almost passionately, in a webpage entitled 'Multilingualism: The Key to

---

[9] Source: European Commission. Joint Interpreting and Conference Service, 2001: Info/Web/Media – 6 March 2001 (internal fact sheet).

[10] In the context of the 2004 enlargement, the official estimate was that 80 interpreters would be required for each new language. See *Frankfurter Allgemeine Zeitung*, 18 January 2005 ('Fieberhafte Fahndung nach Dolmetschern und Übersetzern' ['Feverish search for interpreters and translators']).

Success' devoted to the self-presentation of the interpreting service of the Commission.[11] It is worth quoting at length:

Language is one of the most obvious (audible rather than visual) signs of diversity, which characterize mankind. The global society in which we live is moving more and more towards the three major economic poles, Europe, the United States and Japan, Europe being the continent of greatest diversity and, by the same token, the one with the greatest need for a language policy in its common endeavour.

The European Union wants to preserve, defend and foster language diversity and has realized that a desire for political unity is not enough to bind together heterogeneous peoples. The best way to bring peoples together is to respect their differences rather than to coerce them into unity.

[. . .]

The European Union's sense of cultural diversity is one of its strong points and one which will help it to move towards a greater interdependence of globalization whilst safeguarding its differences. Anyone who feels that his or her cultural identity, and that means primarily language, is protected, will not feel that identity threatened. Such a threat would have been anathema to the founding fathers of the European Union.

The pronounced normative content of this text draws a close connection between the multilingual orientation of the European project and the political primacy of protecting cultural diversity. As we have seen in Chapter 3, the treaties of the Union and the Charter of Fundamental Rights do in fact accord this primacy a very prominent role. The appeal to the spirit of the 'founding fathers' in defending institutional language pluralism is by no means drawn out of thin air either. For the first president of the Commission, the German Walter Hallstein, the integration process represented a departure from monolithic notions of national membership likely to foster the emergence of new political loyalties on a European scale. However, he did not think that this would imply a tendency towards the homogenization of linguistic and cultural identities – far from it. Thus, Hallstein wrote (1973: 112):

Europe is diversity. We want to preserve its wealth and diversity of characters, of talents, of beliefs, of habits, of customs, of taste. (. . .)
    Even the fact that the Europeans do not speak the same language should not bother us. Switzerland provides the classic example that linguistic variety is not a constraining, but rather an enriching, factor and our wish for our Belgian friends is that they can soon be cited as another example. The multiplicity of languages

[11] European Commission. Joint Interpreting and Conference Service, 1995–2002: Multilingualism (europa.eu.int/comm/scic/multi/multi_en.htm). Here cited in the version of 18 February 2002.

is not an obstacle but an incentive. The experiences with our European officials in Brussels . . . prove this.

The commitment to preserving multilingualism was inscribed in the evolutionary path of the EC/EU institutions from the beginning. The protection of linguistic pluralism can be understood in the first place, as the quotations demonstrate, as obeisance before the cultural diversity of Europe. In this sense, language policy in the EU is a genuine expression of the multinational constellation. To be sure, the multinational constellation proves to be primarily a 'multistate constellation' in the area of language. The striking generosity of the EU's institutional recognition of language diversity is ultimately a tribute to the very important European tradition of national languages. Note that by national languages are meant exclusively the languages of nation-*states*. The formal recognition of the equal status of all official state languages results from the desire to erect an effective symbolic barrier to the resurgence of nationalistic animosities. Since the ratification of the Treaty of Rome, the dominant view among the ranks of the elites who have set the pace and direction of the integration process is that hard-won gains should not be jeopardized by allowing the language issue to become politically overcharged (Coulmas 1991a).

However, it would be mistaken to see the EU's defence of cultural and linguistic diversity as merely the result of typical intergovernmental tactics. The principles governing language policy in the European institutions have in the meantime developed an independent normative dynamic that transcends the boundaries of cultural identities tied to the nation-state. Regional and minority languages have benefited of this development, for the European Parliament has enjoined the member states to protect them in several resolutions. The Commission, for its part, provides financial support to the European Bureau for Lesser Used Languages (EBLUL) founded in Dublin in 1982 (De Witte 1993: 169). The EBLUL functions primarily as the advocate of the interests of native minority language groups in Europe and seeks to promote better access to domains such as education and the mass media for these groups. In addition, there have been repeated initiatives by the European institutions to accord due consideration to members of migrant groups when shaping programmes and recommendations in the area of language policy (Labrie 1993: 225–74). The original priority was to ensure instruction in the mother tongue for the children of migrants whose parents came from another member state of the EC/EU. This fostered the tendency within the Commission to promote the goal of instruction in the mother tongue in general, that is, independent of the country of origin of the migrants in question. As a consequence, the logic of recognition tends to be extended to linguistic identities that do not have the backing of a nation-state.

5.2   Official and Real Multilingualism

The impression created by the *de jure* regulation of the language issue in the EU corresponds in only a very qualified way to the *de facto* situation in the Brussels institutions. For everyday communication within the institutions conforms not to the standards of integral multilingualism but to an often highly selective multilingualism. The distinction between official and working languages, which is not further explicated in the official EU 'language constitution', acquires great importance in practice. The EU bodies do not by any means strictly uphold the principle of the equality of all official languages in their internal communication. Following the foundation of the Community of the Six in 1957, French for many years enjoyed undisputed pre-eminence as the actual working language of the European bodies (Gehnen 1991: 53). Where empirical data concerning language use in the European institutions are available, they show that French has been able to defend to the present day its position as a dominant medium of communication, in the Commission in particular. According to a survey conducted by Schloßmacher (1994: 106–12), which covers the Council of Ministers, the Commission and the Parliament, in the 1990s French was used as the working language for both spoken and written communication around 60 percent of the time by the officials and employees in EU bodies. The concept 'working language' does not have an official meaning in this context but merely signifies the language which is actually used at work. English accounted for one-third of the instances cited. German followed a long way behind with around 5 percent. All remaining languages were so little used that they can in practice be ignored.

The data presented by Schloßmacher describe a situation that could already be more or less read off from the results of earlier investigations (Gehnen 1991, Haselhuber 1991). The traditional dominance enjoyed by French in the Community bodies resulted in the first place from the fact that French organizational models served as templates for the construction of the political and administrative apparatus in Brussels. In addition, the fact that the European institutions operate in a Francophone environment exerts an obvious influence. But French has apparently forfeited much of its historical strength as the preferred lingua franca of the EU bodies in favour of English in recent times. English was already the dominant working language among the deputies of the European Parliament by the mid-1990s. Its 'communicative share' here was 46 percent; for French, the figure was 38 percent; for German, 8 percent.[12] As regards the Commission, English also seems to have overtaken French particularly among the younger officials and employees (Gehnen 1991: 60). The importance of English in the European institutions has increased steadily since the accession of the United Kingdom, Ireland and Denmark in 1973. With the northern enlargement in 1995, this tendency received a further boost. The eastern enlargement is again leading to a sharp increase in the de facto importance of English as a working language in the European bodies. Thus, the negotiations with the membership candidates were conducted exclusively in English, though this does not signal an official change in the language regime.[13] If at all, there were only weak links between the group of Commissioners nominated by the new accession countries in 2004 and the world of the *francophonie*.

German is accorded a largely symbolic function in the internal administrative activity of the EU as a third working language. Since the end of the 1980s, the German government has been more explicitly committed to strengthening this position vis-à-vis French and English (Ammon 2004: 3–6). But notwithstanding the recent increase in disputes over language policy to which we will return presently, German remains weakly anchored as a working language in EU bodies. Finally, all the remaining 'smaller' European official languages are already relegated to a position 'not far removed from that of folkloristic remnants' (Haselhuber 1991: 49) in the domain of internal communication.

Thus, the equal status of the official languages often proves to be a fiction in the practical activity of the EU institutions. In situations in which communication processes can be conducted without the direct aid of the interpreting or translation services, the multilingualism at work remains very selective. Officially, there is no basis for this practice in the regulations. However, the departure from a system of integral multilingualism in the semi-official shaping of the institutional language regime is a norm supported by the Commission. As early as in November 1984, in an internal document that addresses the language problematic in the wake of the accession of Greece and prior to the imminent entry of Portugal and Spain, one finds that the Commission advocates 'pragmatic

---

[12] See Schloßmacher (1994: 109–11) for a detailed breakdown.

[13] Personal communication of a leading official in the General Directorate for Enlargement, Brussels, March 2001. While the original language in which Commission documents were drafted was still French in 40 percent of the cases in 1997, the figure had fallen below 30 percent in 2004; see *El País*, 17 April 2004 ('La lengua de Europa es la traducción' ['Europe's language is translation']).

formulas' based on 'actual needs' [*besoins réels*].[14] This pragmatism tailored to actual needs is primarily designed to make it possible to differentiate between meetings of holders of political or social mandates, on the one hand, and interactions between officials and employees of the Community and experts in specific fields, on the other. For the latter cases, the recommendation is to operate with a simplified language regime that orients itself to the customary standards of international organizations. For the remainder, 'asymmetrical' solutions should be adopted whenever possible – in other words, arrangements which make it possible for all participants to express themselves in their own language while the interpreting service restricts itself to a small number of languages. It is clear that by the languages generally used in international organizations are meant the de facto working languages of the European institutions: English and French.

Even when the conference service covers the full palette of official languages at a meeting, which under the language regime currently in force means simultaneously interpreting from 23 languages into 23 languages, one should not conclude that all of the resulting language combinations can always be individually catered for. That would far exceed the capacity of the EU language services. For comparatively 'exotic' language pairs such as Greek–Finnish or Slovene–Maltese, qualified personnel may generally be in short supply. After the incorporation of nine additional official languages to its language regime in 2004, the EU was apparently facing a 'translation crisis', with a backlog of approximately 60,000 pages of untranslated documents.[15] When it comes to interpretation, the problem can be circumvented to some extent by 'relay' interpretation. Taking the combination Greek–Finnish as an example, this means that the Greek is translated into English; English then serves as a 'relay' from which what was said is then interpreted into Finnish. As a general rule, the more widely used languages serve as relay languages.[16] The relay system makes possible a maximal representation of all official languages in conference situations but inevitably leads to a multiplication of inaccuracies and information loss. The lag it causes in direct communication tends to be commented upon within the European institutions with jokes

---

[14] Commission européenne: Extrait du PV 760, 2ème partie, du 28.11.1984. The precise text reads: 'En ce qui concerne l'interprétation, la Commission . . . se prononce à faveur de formules pragmatiques qui ne se fondent que sur les besoins réels, qui assurent le maintien du haut niveau qualitatif et de l'efficacité du système d'interprétation et qui permettent de n'écarter aucune langue'. See also van Hoof-Haferkamp (1991: 67).

[15] *BBC News*, 26 May 2004 ('EU tackles translation "crisis"'); (http://news.bbc.co.uk/go/pr/fr/-/2/hi/europe/3751079.stm).

[16] Personal communication of a representative of the Joint Interpreting and Conference Service, Brussels, March 2001.

like 'The Danes laugh last'. Before the eastern enlargement, moreover, in order to simplify the language regime a variety of modalities short of the 'full' 11:11 variant were employed, such as 9:6 or 9:11, for example. But notwithstanding the 'pragmatism tailored to actual needs', the demands imposed by the institutional language regime for the Joint Interpreting and Conference Service of the Commission are very considerable. According to information provided by the long-time director of the service (van Hoof-Haferkamp 1991: 67), she assigned on average approximately 11 interpreters per community meeting in 1989 when there were still only 9 official languages. Under these circumstances, even finding suitable conference space is often a massive organizational challenge.

The primary problem most often associated with institutional multilingualism by those outside the European committees, however, concerns the financial costs of interpretation and translation. What role does language play as a political-administrative cost factor in the EU? Those expecting an exorbitant expenditure will be surprised by the figures actually presented by the Joint Interpreting and Conference Service. According to its calculations, the total costs incurred by the Commission for translation and interpretation in 1999 amounted to 0.3 percent of the total budget of the EU. If one includes all of the EU institutions, the figure rises to 0.8 percent (€686 million out of a total of €85,557,748,703). The press office of the language service of the Commission concludes from this that multilingualism costs each citizen of the EU just 2 Euro per year.[17] These figures are within the range of other available calculations. Coulmas estimated that the portion of the administrative budget devoted to financing the language regime in the Europe of the Twelve amounted to around 40 percent. One should keep in mind in this connection that the sum allocated by the EC in its budget for its own administrative activities was relatively low. At the beginning of the 1990s, for example, the Community as a whole employed no more administrative personnel than the city of Cologne. Accordingly, Coulmas proceeded on the assumption that the expenses generated by the 'language constitution' around 1990 did not exceed 2 percent of the total EC budget.[18] Thus, although the costs of multilingualism in the EU should not be ignored, there does not seem to be any reason to get overexcited about them either. The Commission expected an increase of the translation budget by 46 percent in the aftermath of the accession of 10 new members in 2004.[19]

[17] Source: European Commission. Joint Interpreting and Conference Service, 2001: Info/Web/Media – 6 March 2001 (internal fact sheet).
[18] Coulmas (1991a: 23); compare also Gerhards (1993: 103, n. 19).
[19] *Avui*, 18 February 2004 ('Una Babel sense el català' ['A Babel without Catalan']).

Against this background, it may seem understandable that the European Parliament has consistently voted against revoking the directive that all official languages should be treated equally for financial reasons (Kraus 2000: 152).

Nevertheless, one should keep in mind that the expenditures on interpretation and translation are not the only costs generated by language pluralism in the EU institutions. Thus, staff members of the Commission in Brussels point to the 'hidden costs' of multilingualism which cannot be represented in purely monetary terms. Under this heading fall the many delays resulting from the need to conform to the official language regime. For example, meetings have to be postponed because insufficient interpreters are available, or decisions are deferred because a document is not available in all of the official languages by the appointed time. In general, it must be assumed that the necessity of using several languages entails a considerable additional burden of work for the majority of European officials.[20] Even in a communicative environment dominated by 'technical' problems, which the Brussels bureaucracy has become used to address in its own professional jargon called *Eurospeak*, tensions can ultimately arise between the instrumental and expressive dimensions of linguistic interaction. The more language diversity demands official recognition in the daily workings of the institutions, the less room is left for 'straightforward' communication.

Notwithstanding all of the problems sketched, one must emphasize that the multilingualism of the EU institutions has positive functional aspects to which all too crude criteria of administrative efficiency can scarcely do justice. The 'political culture of compromise' (Abelès and Bellier 1996), which is a characteristic feature of the work of the Commission, finds expression literally in a 'culture of translation' in which the very willingness to display linguistic flexibility is sufficient to ensure a rudimentary degree of respect for the criteria of the 'inclusion of the other' (Habermas 1998) or of *'audi alteram partem'* (Tully 1995). In fact, the multilingual working environment demands a high degree of pragmatism and good will. The shared experience of an elite socialization is undoubtedly a factor in this regard in that it makes it easier for the officials and employees of the Commission to take a flexible approach to the language question. A further important factor that should be mentioned is no doubt the traditional isolation of the EU headquarters from the customary conflicts of everyday politics.

---

[20] Information provided by staff of the Directorates General for Information Society and Media and for Education and Culture, Brussels, March 2001.

But this perspective in particular also points to the following conclusion: the more the EU institutions (including the Commission) are regarded in the member states as relevant political decision-making arenas, the higher is the symbolic value acquired by the internal language regulations in the perception of outsiders. In the existing multilingual context, the potential for tension between the instrumental and expressive aspects of linguistic communication increases in accordance with the degree to which the EU is supposed to evolve from an international regime into a 'genuine' transnational political community.

5.3 The Politicization of the Language Issue

The institutional language regime of the EU has increasingly become a focus of public discussions in recent years. The topic now commands growing attention far beyond specialists in linguistics. Although a new regulation of the language question apparently remains a taboo subject in official discourse in Brussels, it incites lively speculation in the German, Spanish or British press. It is striking how strongly contributions reflect national standpoints as a general rule.

The widespread view seems to be that the institutional façade of integral multilingualism has begun to crumble, both internally and externally. Even EU employees and officials tend to acknowledge the inadequacies of the language policy status quo, if only in private. The problems generated by the established language regime have functional and normative aspects. The *functional aspect* is most apparent in those domains in which multilingualism deeply shapes the activity of an EU body and in which policy depends heavily on the ancillary support of interpreters and translators. As already indicated earlier, this inevitably leads to a more or less serious loss in organizational efficiency. Decisions have to be deferred because the relevant documents are not available on time in all official languages. Meetings cannot take place because the interpreting service is overtaxed. Language barriers hinder the flow of information both within and between the institutions[21] and hamper a swift and flexible response to sudden changes in the political environment.

The institution in which these kinds of problems are most apparent is the European Parliament. To the extent that the Parliament functions as a forum of public political debate in the EU, its activities should be assigned to the domain of external rather than internal communication. Thus, I will return to the European Parliament in the following chapter.

---

[21] The diverse barriers to comprehension which, for example, the Court of First Instance has to overcome in written procedures are succinctly set forth in Nemitz (2000: 446–7).

The points I am concerned with here have a general connection with multilingual internal communication *within* the European institutions. They are particularly apparent in the context of parliamentary activity, which by definition involves a lot of communication; for the principles of unrestricted multilingualism apply in the plenary sessions which are open to the public. The complaints expressed in a newspaper article by the Trotskyite deputy Alain Krivine (2000), who was elected to the Parliament by French voters in 1999, are clearly related to the language question. Krivine criticizes that the texts and proposed amendments which he needs to perform his tasks are often available only right at the beginning of a session and are not always translated on time. He experiences the parliamentary debates as a 'ceremonial perfectly oiled and regulated by the strict and legitimate working hours of the translators'. The chronometrically monitored speeches of the deputies are restricted to one to three minutes.

The extensive use of simultaneous interpretation inevitably leads to translation errors which have provoked more than a few phantom debates. Mishaps of this kind are unintentional. But the fact that the language question can be readily exploited for tactical purposes also leads to functional blockages. Deputies who are known to be multilingual repeatedly insist on their right to use interpreting services that also cover the official language of their member state, thereby ensuring that sessions are adjourned and votes postponed (Bueno 1999: 330).

The functional wear and tear caused by the EU language regime is impossible to ignore. Even more important, however, is the *normative aspect* of the problems resulting from how the language issue is regulated at the institutional level. It becomes particularly salient where comprehensive multilingualism acquires a predominantly theoretical character because the repertoire of working languages in use is strictly limited. The essential conclusion to be drawn in this regard is that the divergence between de jure regulations and de facto practices ultimately founds a realm of political hypocrisy. According to the political logic governing its construction, the institutional language regime should guarantee the equal status of the official languages. But in reality equality in status proves to be a fiction. In internal communication within the EU, two languages, namely, English and French – or if one adds German, at most three languages – literally 'have the say'. The encomium to multilingualism in how the European institutions represent themselves to the outside world begins to look suspiciously like routine lip service. For, clearly, the way the language regulations are actually applied by rank-and-file EU officials and employees confers undeniable advantages on native speakers of French and, particularly, English. The recent tendency within the EU institutions to target specifically personnel capable of producing error-free English documents has already sparked a legal dispute over language discrimination in Brussels.[22] Even holders of political mandates, such as the members of the European Parliament, must expect to suffer disadvantages within the institutional communication network of the Union if they do not have sufficient proficiency in one of the dominant working languages. It is not always possible to make a sharp distinction between the functional and the normative dimension of the language regime in this context. Hence, it is primarily the members of the smaller language groups who suffer disadvantages on account of the deficiencies of the language services. The difficulties of the European Parliament to present decently translated documents in Finnish, for example, seem to be notorious (Bueno 1999: 323). For those deputies affected who want to acquire as broad a grasp of the issues as possible in advance of political decisions, this can hinder their parliamentary activity in concrete ways.

In the case of the European Parliament, integral multilingualism also mutates into a highly selective multilingualism based on the twin pillars of English and French outside the context of the plenary sessions. Communication in informal working groups or in sessions of special committees is primarily conducted in the de facto linguae francae of the European institutions (Wright 2000: 169). European deputies who are not sufficiently proficient in French or English must rely on the aid of colleagues with the requisite language skills, which inevitably restricts their ability to participate directly in the discussions. Symptomatic of the situation in the Parliament in general is the fact that the vast majority of the official complaints concerning language discrimination are made by members of the smaller language groups, such as the Danes, the Dutch, the Greeks and the Portuguese (Labrie 1993: 127). Clearly, the Community principle 'to show due respect to the languages of all members',[23] which was still emphatically upheld by Jacques Delors while he was President of the Commission, gives rise to considerable difficulties in its practical realization. A central aspect of the normative complications entailed by the official regulation of the language question in the European institutions is the *tacitly* accepted dominance of one to two official languages as working languages. The 'levels of respect' shown towards the remaining 21 official languages thereby take on a rather symbolic character.

---

[22] See the report 'Englisch bevorzugt. Die feierlichen Erklärungen zum "Jahr der Sprachen" und die Wirklichkeit in europäischen Institutionen' ('English Preferred: The Solemn Declarations of the "Year of Languages" and the Reality in the European Institutions'), *Frankfurter Rundschau*, 6 July 2001.

[23] Cited from Volz (1994: 99).

Specifically with regard to the scope of symbolic recognition, a further normatively dubious aspect of the institutional language regulations must not be overlooked. There can be no doubt that the language regime of the EU has exposed itself to criticism on account of its narrowly statist interpretation of the meaning of the recognition of linguistic and cultural diversity. The contrast in status between 'small' official (state) languages and 'big' regional (non-state) languages reveals the political implausibility of this narrow interpretation. Estonian and Latvian (with around one to one and a half million speakers apiece) are official languages of the EU; by contrast, Catalan (with around 6 million speakers) has a subordinate status in the Union's institutional framework.[24] Following the accession of Malta, Maltese (with approximately 0.3 million speakers) is an official language, whereas Welsh, which is spoken by 0.5 million people in Wales, must continue to make do without EU recognition. The languages of larger communities of 'new' Europeans, such as Arabic and Turkish, should not be overlooked in this context either. Ultimately, what is at stake is whether language rights in the Union are understood as rights to be regulated in accordance with nation-state prerogatives or as European civil rights. In light of the argumentation line presented in the previous chapter, the linguistic rights of citizens cannot be appropriately conceived of as a mere appendix to the rights of states.

The functional deficits and normative inconsistencies which characterize the institutional language regime of the EU lead to periodic political disgruntlement. The indignation caused by language policy even reaches into the ranks of the Commission, whose members are in other respects no strangers to compromise. Discontent with the large grey area produced by the juxtaposition of official and unofficial language regulations has been expressed above all by the Germans. German EU officials tend to insist that their language has equal status with English and French as a working language. But at the same time they observe that in the everyday affairs of the European institutions those who do not have a perfect command of French or English are at a disadvantage. They are upset by the

---

[24] In June 2005, the Council of the European Union decided to give Irish, which had previously only had the status of a 'language of the Treaty', the status of an 'official and working language'. The decision was made at the request of the Irish government. At the same occasion, the Council responded to an initiative put forward by the Spanish Zapatero executive by paving the way for a restricted use of Catalan, Basque and Galician in European institutions. The modalities were to be negotiated with each institution individually. The European Parliament, for instance, has limited the use of Catalan to the sphere of written communication. See *Frankfurter Allgemeine Zeitung*, 14 June 2005 ('Irisch wird EU-Amtssprache' ['Irish becomes official language of the EU']), *Avui*, 7 July 2006 ('El Parlament Europeu aprova l'ús del català només per escrit' ['The European Parliament approves only the written use of Catalan']).

fact that German is given short shrift in the internal communication of the EU bodies in spite of its demographic weight in the Union.[25] A resolution passed by the local chapter of Germany's Social Democratic Party (SPD) in Brussels in April 2000 offers an interesting insight into attitudes on this issue. We may assume that the membership of the Brussels SPD chapter is drawn primarily from EU officials and employees. Significantly, the resolution was also concerned with a European political issue, namely, the reform of the Commission. The document addressed to the decision-makers in the Commission and to social-democratic deputies in the European Parliament provides symbolic evidence of the close interconnection between party-political, language-political and European-political positions in discussion in Brussels. The resolution contains, among other things, the following demand[26]:

Urgent measures must be taken to ensure the implementation of the working languages
The reform of the Commission must concentrate on promoting the use of the working languages in the administrative offices especially during the enlargement process. Practical steps in this direction are:

- **Upper-level management positions in the salary groups A1 and A2** should in future be filled exclusively on the basis of demonstration of the relevant qualifications. This includes relevant linguistic skills. Since, at present, an agreement on a single working language is not possible, a successful candidate should have at least passive competence in the three working languages of the Commission (English, French and German).
- **Those who aspire to a career in the civil service** should be expected to acquire basic knowledge of all three working languages within two years.

The resolution adopts the widespread view that German is the third official working language in the Commission alongside French and English. But, as we have seen, EU regulations provide no clear support for this interpretation of the distinction between official and working languages. The very ambiguity of the Union's institutional language regime makes it susceptible to conflict.

This susceptibility became especially apparent when Germany insisted on formally reinforcing the status of German as a third working language. Since the unification of Germany in 1989, the Federal Government has

---

[25] Here I am condensing information drawn from conversations conducted in March 2001 with high-level officials of the Directorates General for Enterprise and Industry and for Research.
[26] Resolution of the SPD Local Association Brussels: 'Die Reform der Kommission: Für eine effiziente und bürgernahe EU-Verwaltung' (Reform of the Commission: For an Efficient and Responsive EU Administration), Brussels, 26 April 2000 (emphasis in the German original).

been eager to promote equal treatment of German in the European institutions (Volz 1994: 95–8). The Finnish–German 'language dispute' presented one particularly striking consequence of this tendency. In July 1999, Finland assumed the rotating presidency of the Council of the EU from Germany. The Finnish government planned to use English and French, in addition to Finnish as the language of the incumbent presidency, as the sole conference languages in a series of informal ministerial gatherings.[27] The German government, by contrast, stubbornly insisted on the right to use German as a conference language as well. When the Finnish government refused to budge, the Germans together with the Austrians cancelled their participation in the meetings.[28]

The language dispute dragged on over the whole summer. Finally, Berlin and Helsinki agreed on a compromise solution: whereas the German participants in the ministerial meetings could speak German, the other working languages would not be translated into German.[29] This attempted resolution of the dispute initiated a new round of language strife within the Europe of the Fifteen. For the Spanish Foreign Minister, Abel Matutes, and his Italian counterpart, Lamberto Dini, now demanded that Spanish and Italian must also be interpreted if there were going to be translations from German. At an informal meeting of the Foreign Ministers in Lapland, Matutes explained in Spanish before switching to English: 'If a further language is used in addition to English and French, then the Spanish ministers will use Spanish'. In a memorandum to the presidency of the Council he added that preventing discrimination against Spanish was 'a matter of principle'.[30] Spain seemed determined not to give up on that matter in the period after the eastern enlargement. In 2005, its government battled successfully (together with the Italian executive) against the Commission's attempts at limiting interpreting at press conferences to English, French and German. Apparently, however, Spain was not able to prevent the Commission from taking on

---

[27] At official meetings at the ministerial level, the interpreting services cover all official languages. At informal meetings, by contrast, a selective regime of working languages is the norm.

[28] On the events in question, see *Berliner Zeitung*, 3 July 1999 ('Bonn bleibt im Sprachenstreit mit Finnland hart' ['Bonn Remains Firm in Language Dispute with Finland']), *Frankfurter Allgemeine Zeitung*, 5 July 1999 ('Zunge zeigen' [lit. 'Sticking Out Tongues']) and *Spiegel Online* (www.spiegel.de/politik/ausland/0,1518,29647,00.html), 2 July 1999 ('Nix will sprecken deutsh' ['No want speak German']).

[29] See *Der Tagesspiegel*, 10 September 1999 ('Neuer Sprachenstreit überschattet Treffen der EU-Außenminister' ['New Language Dispute Overshadows Meeting of EU Foreign Ministers']).

[30] Quoted from *El País*, 10 September 1999 ('España boicoteará los consejos informales de la UE si el alemán se impone sobre el español' ['Spain Will Boycott Informal EU Meetings if German Prevails over Spanish']).

plans to reduce the number of translators within the Spanish service by about one-third.[31]

Evidently, the search for pragmatic formulas regarding the language issue is not confined to the Commission. Thus, it has become customary to offer interpreting services only for a highly restricted repertoire of languages during informal ministerial meetings (as opposed to formal sessions of the Council); however, there is no clear normative basis for determining precisely how many languages should be accommodated in such contexts. Hence, the language dispute can be understood in the first place as a conflict over the proper interpretation of claims founded on 'customary practice'. The unofficial regulation of the language question in the EU institutions was for a long time governed by pragmatism. But as an official of the Directorate General for Education and Culture remarked in connection with the dispute between the Finns and the Germans, nationalism can sometimes trump pragmatism.[32] In fact, the politics of the 'empty chair' briefly taken on by the Germans in the Council was viewed even by sectors of the German public as a mock battle that served as a pretext for adopting a more aggressive stance on Berlin's national interests in the EU.[33] This may be an accurate assessment. But how can one draw a sharp dividing line between legitimate positions on language policy and particularistic national interests? The problem of the EU language regime seems to be just that it fosters the blending of communicative and 'national' criteria of rationality.

In a radio programme dealing with the background to the language dispute of 1999,[34] Wilhelm Schönfelder, the German delegate to COREPER, the Permanent Representatives Committee of the member states in Brussels, presented a particularly vivid account of the political virulence of the language issue. According to Schönfelder, the language regime is a highly charged emotional issue. He went on to specify that, at the level of meetings of the Council of Ministers, there is a range of

---

[31] See   *EurActiv.com*   (http://www.euractiv.com/en/governance/italians-spanish-object-second-division-language-status/article-136115?_print), 3 March 2005 ('Italians and Spanish object to 'second division' language status'); *El País*, 26 November 2005 ('Un nuevo intento de relegar el castellano' ['A new attempt to relegate Castilian'], 19 January 2006 ('Bruselas ratifica la equiparación del idioma español al maltés y al eslovaco' ['Brussels ratifies the equlization of the Spanish language to Maltese and Slovak']).

[32] Personal communication, Brussels, March 2001.

[33] This was the tenor of a commentary in *Die Zeit*, 28, 1999 ('Feindbild Europa. Wer in Brüssel Deutsch sprechen will, muss zuerst europäisch denken' ['Bogeyman Europe. Those Who Want to Speak German in Brussels Must First Think European']).

[34] Broadcast by WDR 3 on 11 February 2001. The account of the contents presented here is based on an English translation of an excerpt, which was kindly made available to me by staff of the Interpreting and Conference Service of the Commission in Brussels.

pragmatic solutions that function as long as nobody explicitly discusses them. Finally, he intimated that the decision not to participate in meetings in which German would not be interpreted was taken at the highest level in the German government. The concern was to defend the status of the German language within the EU.

The statements of the German COREPER delegate provide further confirmation of the peculiarity of the institutional language regime with its convoluted rules of procedure. The official regulations seem at first sight to suggest that the European official languages have equal status. In reality, however, this equality of status can be assured in at most rudimentary ways. Recourse to the repeatedly invoked 'pragmatic solutions', which essentially boil down to using English and French as working languages, is thus common practice. From the official normative perspective, however, the demonstrative commitment to integral multilingualism remains valid. Pragmatism accordingly remains a taboo that must not be explicitly discussed if it is to function effectively in the everyday running of the European institutions. The language issue thereby becomes the object of ongoing and more or less covert struggles for hegemony within the Union. In recent times, however, the issue has forced its way into the political spotlight. It is becoming increasingly evident that the unwillingness or inability of the EU to conduct an open debate on its internal language regime in the end contributes little to reducing conflict.

5.4   The Reform of the Institutional Regulation of Language: A Pending Debate

The institutional efforts to avoid politicizing the language issue had only modest success in the Europe of the Fifteen. As the diplomatic row between Berlin and the Finnish presidency during the summer of 1999 made clear, the issue of language has kept its political explosiveness, in spite of attempts over decades to circumvent it. This makes the reticence of the European Constitutional Convention concerning the language issue all the more striking.

Integral multilingualism seems to have gradually reached the limits of what is technically feasible. For better or worse, the eastern enlargement should prove to be a catalyst for a formalized transition to a more selective multilingualism at the institutional level. Let us examine the situation of language policy in an EU with 27 member states. The accession of Malta, Cyprus, Poland, Hungary, the Czech Republic, Slovakia, Slovenia, Estonia, Latvia, Lithuania, Romania and Bulgaria has implied the extension of the language regime that prevailed in the EU15 from 11 to 23 official languages.[35] For the interpreting and translation service, this represents an increase in the number of language combinations that must be catered for from 110 to 506. At the same time, all of the Eastern European accession countries represent small- to medium-size language groups. The spectrum extends from the around 40 million speakers of Polish to the just over 1 million people who make up the Estonian-speaking language group.[36] This yields a long list of new language couples, which do not belong to the standard repertoire of a normal interpreter's training, such as Swedish–Bulgarian, Slovenian–Portuguese or Hungarian–Lithuanian. Such a constellation makes recourse to relay languages inevitable. However, this also means a dramatic increase in information loss and in awkwardness of communication, which are concomitants of the relay system. The oft-invoked Babylonian confusion of tongues in the EU threatens to assume surreal proportions.

In addition to the genuine translation problems, there are serious bottlenecks in the provision of the necessary infrastructure of meeting rooms. An expert report commissioned by the Council of Ministers came to the conclusion that retaining the regime of integral multilingualism with 23 official languages would raise the required number of interpreters and booths for each meeting from 33 and 11, respectively, in the EU15 to 115 and 23 in the EU27. In the opinion of the experts, it is scarcely possible to make available sufficient meeting rooms with so many booths. They grant that constructing a large off-site interpretation complex is a viable alternative, if adequate audiovisual broadcast facilities are provided.[37] But aside from the ongoing difficulty in finding interpreters who are competent in three to seven languages in addition to their own, this proposal would inevitably lead to a sharp increase in the susceptibility of the conference services to technical mishaps.

The EU administration in Brussels can rationalize part of the work of written translation though the implementation of computer technology. The software developed for this purpose simplifies the translation of technical documents in particular.[38] However, there is little prospect of such aids being employed in the sphere of oral communication for the foreseeable future. The scope for ambiguity that is typical of conversational situations has thus far posed insuperable obstacles for translation

---

[35] See the Articles III-128 and IV-448 of the Treaty establishing a Constitution for Europe.
[36] Details from Haarmann (1993).
[37] On the contents of the expert report, see El País, 9 July 2000 ('El idioma de Europa' ['The language of Europe']).
[38] On the mode of operation of the automatic translation system designed for the transmission of specialized EU texts, see Laurens (1994); for a brief survey of the possibilities of computer translation in general, see Raeithel (2000).

machines.[39] The computer inevitably filters out the multifarious nuances of meaning of communication bound to specific contexts. Hence, those who hope for a technological fix to the problems posed by the EU's institutional language regime will have to be content with at best partial fulfilment of their wish for the present. There is no alternative to a political approach to the problem.

What factors would such a political approach have to take into account? In the first place, it must be made clear that the question of the language regime in the European institutions is by no means a side issue of the integration process which can be safely left in the hands of pragmatically minded translators and interpreters. At the same time, criteria of administrative efficiency should not be accorded absolute priority in deciding this issue. On the contrary, the institutional regulation of language in the EU is a thoroughly political matter. Ultimately, the language regime will always also be at least an elementary reflection of the political identity of the Union. The importance of the language issue will increase in direct proportion to the extent to which the EU evolves beyond an intergovernmental regime into a transnational political community.

Furthermore, we must take into account how the dynamics of the eastern enlargement affects the relative importance of the de facto working languages in the EU bodies. None of the new languages introduced by the accession states approaches the lingua franca potential of English, French and, with qualifications, even German, in the European context. Hence, the current palette of two to two-and-a-half semi-official working languages remains unchanged. Shifts in the 'communication quotas' within this palette are nevertheless to be expected. English will certainly be able to consolidate its position further, primarily at the expense of French, which does not play a prominent role as a foreign language within the bulk of accession states (de Swaan 2001: 162). From the German side, the eastern enlargement is sometimes associated with the expectation that the historical status of German as a regional lingua franca will be restored to some extent (Ammon 2001a). But even if this were to transpire, the hegemony in the meantime enjoyed by English also among the Eastern European political and administrative elites will certainly not be challenged. As already mentioned, English functioned as the sole informal working language in negotiations with the accession candidates.

A third point should also be kept in mind. It certainly makes sense in the context of the EU to distinguish between the domains of internal

---

[39] Personal communication of an employee of the Joint Interpreting and Conference Service of the European Commission, Brussels, March 2001.

and external communication, both from an empirical and a normative point of view. However, this does not mean that there is no connection between the two spheres. Even though the strict separation between communication at the level of institutions and communication at the level of a 'union of citizens' is generally emphasized within the Commission,[40] revoking the formally equal status of official and working languages in the EU bodies would certainly send a signal for the communicative networking of segments of European civil society far beyond the institutional framework.

Hence, proposals for reforming the institutional 'language constitution' cannot be completely separated from the problem of an overarching 'language constitution' or of a European constitution in the usual sense of the term. Here I will limit myself to a couple of general suggestions for modifying the institutional language regulations. I will take up the theme of an overarching 'language constitution' again later.

The issue, therefore, is what standards should inform an *official* regulation of the selective multilingualism in the EU bodies. Ultimately, it is a matter of defining the scope of the internal language regime for the coming decades. Unfortunately, when it comes to the institutional regulation of its internal language regime (or rather regimes, as the regulations vary with the institutional level they address), the Union seems to be highly afraid of entering the realm of politics. Yet for both substantial normative reasons and for practical considerations, a serious debate on the EU's internal language policy is more than overdue. In my view, we should start from two premises. First, the number of languages chosen should indeed be kept small for reasons of pragmatism and efficiency; communicative interaction within the EU institutions that gets by without calling on the interpreting services should be regarded as the ideal case. Second, the number of institutional working languages should nevertheless be greater than one. A minimum degree of multilingualism is necessary as a symbolic expression of the actual diversity of Europe at the institutional level. The Union's internal regulation of the language issue must pay normative tribute to the significance of cultural difference in processes of intercultural communication. To do so does not require what in political theory has been called a mirror representation of diversity: not all particularities of linguistic diversity, but the sheer fact of linguistic diversity has to be represented, to apply an argument developed by Goodin (2004)

---

[40] The following quote from a top official in the Directorate General for Education and Culture can serve as a typical example of this view: 'Even if the Commission applies English only – and this will not happen – this will not mean anything for the situation outside the Commission'. Personal communication, Brussels, March 2001.

to the context of language. But finding appropriate ways to deal with diversity does require *politics*. Finally, after the eastern enlargement, English would undoubtedly be the only realistic option for single-language communication in the EU bodies. However, *global English* is not suited to representing the specific political identity of the Union.

If the institutional standard repertoire is to be of the order of two to three working languages, then there is much to be said for the trio of English, French and German. The fact that the selection clearly coincides with the actual status quo is not the decisive point. Rather, it is a major problem that the current status quo lacks a clear-cut normative basis that could contribute to its political legitimation. What could make for such a normative basis? It is important that there are good reasons for each of the languages taken individually and, above all, that all three share an important commonality when viewed within the European context. Let us first examine the languages individually. The EU bodies have long since had to accept that English has in effect become the principal lingua franca in Europe as well. French has indelibly shaped the development of the European institutions and has secured itself a permanent place within them. As for German, the demographic weight of the language in the EU speaks in its favour. But perhaps of greater relevance than the specific advantages of English, French and German taken individually[41] is a further feature that they share, namely, that they function as *transeuropean hinges*. Each of the three languages is an official language in more than one EU member state: English in Ireland, Malta and the United Kingdom, French in Belgium, Luxembourg and France, German in Belgium, Luxembourg, Austria and Germany. Therein resides their potential to point beyond particularistic national identities.[42]

Moreover, only by preserving a multilingual regime, however restricted, is it possible to combine communicative efficiency with requirements of justice. For linguistic discrimination within the EU institutions could in principle be avoided if, in communication within groups, not just members of language communities which are not catered for,

---

[41] Attempts by linguists to think up a suitable European language regime tend to adopt ecological or historical perspectives on language (see, for example, Haarmann 1991, Hagège 1996). Their proposals do not always distinguish between institutional and extra-institutional communication. I am primarily concerned with the *political* dimensions of the problems posed by the language regime.

[42] Let me hasten to add that the same argument could also be made for Dutch (Belgium and the Netherlands), Swedish (Finland and Sweden) and Greek (Cyprus and Greece). But from a common-sense point of view, the limited number of speakers in these three cases diminishes their importance for transnational communication.

but all participants, refrained from using their mother tongue; this would entail native French speakers using English (or German), native English speakers French (or German), and so forth. Initial steps towards such an arrangement have already been put into practice in COREPER,[43] though here too English and French clearly dominate. Last but not least, the multilingual tradition also contributes to preserving and enhancing an intercultural sensibility in the everyday institutional affairs of the EU, which represents an indispensable resource in the context of transnational communication. This is the very contribution of multilingualism to representing diversity in EU institutions. By comparison, the cognitive strains of working in a multilingual environment must be regarded as secondary, especially since they mainly affect a group to whom the standards of an elite professional socialization apply.

The recommendation in favour of a selective multilingualism based on English, French and German is by no means above criticism. The EU is not a streamlined construct but a heterogeneous and polycentric collection of institutions. Thus, the peculiarities of the EU institutional structure should be given high priority in any regulation of the language issue. To look for a *single* royal road to shaping the European language regime would certainly not be a particularly productive strategy. The English–French–German option is in essence a regulative starting point for developing further institutional language regimes. In general, the following maxim should guide this process: the more instrumental the context of political-administrative consultations, the more selective one may be in defining the corresponding language regime. An expert hearing on controlling air pollutants in the EU member states may not require the same standards as a forum on European constitutional politics. However, one should be under no illusions concerning the possibility of always consistently and consensually distinguishing between the instrumental and the symbolic, identity-related components of language. Hence, every pragmatically motivated effort to reform the institutional language regime must be mindful of the danger of becoming entangled in political controversies over the recognition and protection of different cultural identities. In the transition to a selective multilingualism, we must therefore also reflect on what forms of compensation the EU can offer language groups who are not included in such an arrangement. The symbolic costs unavoidably generated by a restricted language regime in the form of the limited recognition granted to politically significant and legitimate patterns of identity should be counterbalanced as far as possible by a

---

[43] Personal communication of a high-level official in the Secretariat General of the Council of the European Union, Brussels, March 2001.

concerted decentralization and diversification of decision-making processes in the Union in accordance with the subsidiarity principle. In any case, the decisive step to be taken to give diversity a more concrete meaning is to leave the ground of official declarations and informal regulations and to enter the realm of politics.

6   Political communication in the transnational civil society

The contentiousness of language policy within European institutions is closely bound up with the political character of the European Union (EU). Processes of communication within the Union have such a high practical and symbolic profile because they contribute essentially to the progressive constitution of a political community. The EU possesses extensive decision-making authority; European law has direct effects on all citizens of member states; and European politics is conducted within a highly differentiated complex of institutions with an independent executive, legislative and judiciary. Hence, the EU explodes the framework of a traditional international organization. Not only since the introduction of the Euro has its influence on the everyday lives of Europeans become virtually ubiquitous. It extends to a whole range of regulatory domains. In fact, there is scarcely a single policy field in the member states today in which the Community dimension is completely insignificant (Schmitter 1996b: 125). In areas such as agriculture and trade, it has long since become the dominant factor.

The considerable (and growing) importance of political processes in the institutions of the EU for the lives of its citizens cannot be doubted. But how do things stand with the communicative mediation of EU politics? Here there are evidently massive deficits. A constant chorus of complaints connects the political indifference of the subjects of European governance towards the outcomes of this very governance with the lack of information on EU affairs and the lack of transparency of decision-making processes in Brussels. The results of a special Eurobarometer survey conducted in early 2001 can be seen as symptomatic of a general malaise: 4 out of 10 people polled in the EU of the Fifteen declared that they knew nothing about the Nice Summit and Treaty. Only 26 percent expressed an interest in participating in the debate concerning the future of Europe. Almost concurrently with the publication of the results of the public opinion poll, the Belgian Prime Minister Guy Verhofstadt, who was in the process of assuming the Presidency of the European Council on behalf of his country, admitted that a veritable chasm exists between the citizens and the institutions of the EU.[1] The chasm referred to by the resolutely pro-European Verhofstadt is in large part a communicative one. The EU is constantly confronted with the problem that a low level of public awareness of its political tasks and activities is reflected in mistrust and refusal of loyalty. To a significant extent, the constitutional crisis in which Europe found itself in 2005 must be interpreted as a dramatic symptom of this situation.

Evidently, the external communication of the EU as a whole suffers from the fact that the flow of information from the Europe of institutions to the Europe of citizens has until now had little success in stimulating popular political participation. We must now examine to what extent this problem also has roots in the politics of language. Here the connection between institutional will-formation and the communicative substructure of a developing 'European civil society' plays a crucial role. How does the language question impact on the factors which influence the emergence of a political public sphere in Europe? In this context, the category of the public sphere must be understood in a substantive normative sense as the ensemble of intermediary structures of opinion- and will-formation which confer legitimacy on a political order by exposing decision-making processes to the critical examination and judgment of the citizens (Habermas 1990). As such, the public sphere is a key structural element of politics in democratic constitutional states. Accordingly, the language issue points back directly to the debate over the European constitution.

In this chapter, I will first discuss two prominent views of the European problematic of language and the public sphere. In contrast with these positions, I will set forth what I regard as the essential interconnections between questions of language and public political communication in the EU. I will then turn to the main parameters of an EU language policy directed to the external sphere of communication and briefly discuss attempts to circumvent the communication dilemma through the Internet. At the end of the chapter, I will sketch a possible strategy for shaping the relation between multilingualism and a transnational public sphere in Europe.

6.1   Constitution, Publicity, Language

With the constitutional debate which followed the Maastricht Treaty, the problem of how a political communication community could be founded

---

[1] On the Eurobarometer results, see Commission européenne (2001): L'Opinion Publique Européenne Face à l'Élargissement de l'U. E., à la Monnaie Unique et au Future d'Europe. On Verhofstadt's statements, see El País, 3 July 2001.

on the basis of a multiplicity of languages also became the focus of increased attention in European discussions. The prominent constitutional theorist Dieter Grimm, whose analysis of the European democracy deficit I already discussed in Chapter 2, unquestionably played a pioneering role. Significantly, Grimm drew a direct connection between his thesis that the EU lacks a genuine basis of democratic legitimation and the issue of language. In Grimm's own words:

The importance of the language factor for the possibility of European democracy is often underestimated, partly because a democracy concept confined to the area of organized opinion-formation predominates . . . partly because of a failure to perceive the dependency of democracy on communication opportunity. Pointing to multilingual states like Switzerland, Belgium or Finland . . . does not refute this. [A] country like Switzerland had formed a national identity well before constitutionalization and relates its multilingual political discourse to it . . .

By contrast, the absence of a European communication system, due chiefly to language diversity, has the consequence that for the foreseeable future there will neither be a European public nor a European political discourse . . . The European level of politics lacks a matching public (Grimm 1995: 295–6).

From the perspective adopted by Grimm, the fact that the citizens of the EU are not in a position to arrive at discursive agreements regarding their political concerns lends the European democratic deficit a structural character. Grimm (1995: 299) concludes that for the present the possibility of democracy clearly remains tied to the political framework of the nation-state.

The communication-theoretical aspect of Grimm's plea for democracy in the nation-state provoked Jürgen Habermas into a response. Habermas (1998: 160) is not at all inclined to abandon a normatively demanding concept of the public sphere in light of the process of transnational integration and argues that there cannot be a democratic European federal state

unless a European-wide, integrated public sphere develops in the ambit of a common political culture: a civil society encompassing interest associations, non-governmental organizations, civic movements, etc., and naturally a party system appropriate to a European arena. In short, this entails public communication that transcends the boundaries of public spheres that have until now been restricted to nation-states.

In opposition to Grimm, Habermas understands the creation of a public sphere in the EU as an integrative aim to be promoted by means of the appropriate political institutions. He addresses the language question only in passing by casually describing English as the 'second first language' (Habermas 1998: 161) of Europeans.

Habermas takes up the issue of language again in a subsequent intervention in the European constitutional debate, where he treats it in a more differentiated fashion, but without modifying the general position he developed in response to Grimm. He reaffirms the outstanding political function of the infrastructure of the public sphere in a democracy: it transforms social problems 'into the focal topics of discourses so that citizens have an opportunity to relate simultaneously to the same issues in similar terms, and hence to take affirmative or negative stances on the associated controversies' (Habermas 2006: 102). Habermas recognizes that no such arenas of public will-formation exist in Europe at the transnational level. Hence, he proposes that national public spheres should be networked while preserving intact their internal circuits of communication. But this willingness to respect the autonomy of linguistically distinct forums of political communication is once again coupled more or less abruptly with the hope that 'English as a second language' (ibid.: 104) will prevail as the normal medium of communication in the EU.

Leaning towards a Westphalian perspective, Grimm correlates language primarily with the identity of nation-states, conflating the political communication community and the national linguistic community. By contrast, Habermas for cosmopolitan reasons loosens the ties that bind language to a democratic community integrated via processes of public communication. His idea is that communicative bonds which transcend particular cultural and linguistic memberships must develop in the European transnational domain. Grimm tends to align language, as the mode of expression of political culture, primarily with the communicative space of a national collectivity; thus, the nation-state framework creates the preconditions for an apparently harmonious coexistence of the political-instrumental and the political-expressive dimensions of language. For his part, Habermas can scarcely avoid downplaying the expressive binding power of particular linguistic identities in favour of the instrumental requirements of cosmopolitan communication in the transnational domain.

What is striking is that both thinkers base relatively strong political theses on not altogether unproblematic empirical premises. We can detect an interesting inconsistency in the argument in the passage from Grimm cited earlier. For the constitutional theorist, the experience of multilingual democracies such as Switzerland, Belgium and Finland cannot be sensibly projected onto the EU, if only because of the quantitatively different dimensions of language pluralism at the level of the Union. Grimm further specifies that, in Switzerland, the formation of an overarching collective identity historically preceded the political process of constitutionalization. But one might ask how such an identity could have arisen and been reproduced when one of its necessary presuppositions, on which Grimm insists in the case of the EU – namely, a shared language – was lacking. Grimm uses an analytical prism which forces him to make a political equivalence among linguistic community, nation-state and the public sphere.[2] The wide spectrum of variations of linguistic policy constellations in European democracies (cf. Chapter 4, Section 4.3) thereby inevitably receives short shrift.

Habermas, by contrast, tends to underestimate the sociological and normative implications of language pluralism for the creation of a transnational space of communication. 'English as a second language' is a postulate far removed from the everyday lives of large segments of the European population, as we shall see. In addition, it is a *political* postulate and should be made explicit as such. Habermas takes his orientation from the normative desideratum of a European public sphere. But this fails to take account of the fact that the integration of language communities is shaped by processes of political domination (Bourdieu 1991). Accordingly, the introduction of a second first language to serve European citizens as a shared standard of communication must respect constitutionally legitimated regulatory criteria. Moreover, the fact that putting the issue of language on the political agenda creates the potential for conflict should not be overlooked in analyzing possible forms of organization of a transnational public sphere.

In assessing the implications of linguistic and cultural diversity, each author emphasizes a specific dimension of the problem of communication and publicity in the EU. Grimm gives the impression that language, as a politically relevant pattern of cultural identity, is almost hermetically sealed into the nation-state. But he thereby underestimates the capacity of communication communities to diversify internally and open themselves up externally. Habermas, in contrast, for normative reasons tends to dissolve cultural differences in the transnational public domain, so that he has to downplay the potentials for communicative closure in multilingual contexts of political interaction.

---

[2] In fact, the extent to which Switzerland, as a democratically constituted federation of states, possesses the stable national foundations Grimm ascribes to it is a matter of controversy. The Swiss author Adolf Muschg (1998), for example, sees the political development of his country in a different light: 'Switzerland is not a nation and it does not have to become one; it is at once much less and much more: a civic alliance of different peoples, formed to safeguard their differences within a framework defined by human rights and human dignity'. ('Die Schweiz ist keine Nation, und sie braucht keine zu werden: sie ist viel weniger, und viel mehr: ein ziviles Bündnis Verschiedener, geschaffen zum Schutz ihrer Verschiedenheit im Rahmen der Menschenrechte und der Menschenwürde.')

Grimm has the merit that, with his scepticism concerning the relation between language diversity and publicity in the EU, he drew attention to something which had been largely neglected in discussions of European democracy. Assessments of the prospects for a democratization of the Union in political science, in particular, often focus on the system of institutions in the narrow sense, so that insufficient attention is paid to the socio-cultural infrastructure of democracy. Habermas takes up the questions posed by Grimm from a somewhat different, normative point of view, thereby bringing important new perspectives to bear on the controversy concerning the prospects of democracy in the EU. Generally speaking, the positions taken by other authors who at least broach the language question in analyzing political communication structures in the EU overlap to a greater or lesser extent with the conclusions drawn by Grimm and Habermas.[3] Consequently, the discussion only does partial justice to the complexity of the issue of linguistic diversity for European politics. The normative challenges of language pluralism for the constitution of an overarching space of political communication can scarcely be met by a defensive posture inspired by the model of the homogeneous nation-state. However, the offensive strategy – typically involving embracing the English language – of attempting to create a political public sphere without acknowledging the politically controversial character of developing a corresponding communicative infrastructure can provide at best weak impulses for the formation of a transnational political culture which both bridges and respects the diversity of linguistic identities.

6.2   Political Communication in Multilingual Contexts

Although the problems of the political public sphere and of language should not be viewed as congruent in principle, they certainly do overlap. The communicability of political discourses remains inextricably bound up with the medium of language. Thus, before political communication can even take place, the linguistic channels along which it is supposed to flow must first be clarified. This may seem a trivial matter, but in a context of linguistic differentiation its implications are by no means trivial. For the decision over how to communicate is itself already a political decision. Accordingly, the politics of language is an important dimension of Rousseau's paradox (cf. Chapter 2, Section 2.5) in multilingual settings.

---

[3] As regards the requirement to ground a common political space in a shared linguistic identity, Greven (2000), Kielmansegg (1996), Siedentop (2000) and Van Parijs (2004), for example, defend a similar conception to Grimm. By contrast, Eder (2004), Eriksen and Fossum (2000), Kaelble (2001) and Rifkin (2004) tend towards the position of Habermas, though with different emphases.

Chapter 4 provided an overview of how nation-state democracies in Western Europe have dealt with the paradox. At one end of the spectrum is the French version of the republican model. It provides the paradigmatic example of the deliberate creation of a uniform space of political communication 'from above', through the state and its institutions. From the end of the eighteenth century in France, the creation of a public sphere facilitating smooth interactions between political and civil society was almost synonymous with linguistic homogenization. The francophone political pathos which still resonates today is fuelled by the conviction that the enlightened revolutionary heritage of 1789 embodied by the French language transcends all socio-cultural particularism. However, the multilingual democracies of Belgium, Finland and Switzerland represent alternatives to the Jacobin model of integration. In these cases, it is often overlooked that the possibilities of broad-based linguistic communication within the population remained severely restricted even long after democratization. In a survey conducted in Switzerland in 1972, around 40 percent of German Swiss and 50 percent of the Romands (i.e. Francophones) stated that they were fluent only in their own language. There exist census data for Belgium up to 1947.[4] According to the last calculation, the proportion of individuals who were bilingual (i.e. who were capable of communicating both in Dutch and in French) was just 16 percent nationally. Even in Finland, where the territorial language boundaries are much more blurred than in Switzerland or in Belgium, data for the year 1950 show that official bilingualism was not equivalent to societal bilingualism. The number of those who regarded themselves as bilingual amounted to 8 percent among Finnish speakers and 46 percent among Swedish speakers.[5]

To be sure: such data do not provide an adequate basis for constructing a general model of multilingual political publics. Nevertheless, they can be interpreted as indicators that in multilingual societies democratic integration has been achieved under the banner of mutual recognition of linguistically defined group identities. The policies pursued have indeed been marked by regular conflicts; but in the cases examined, they have also led to a sustainable basis for coexistence among political equals who respect each other's differences.[6] In addition, the spaces of political

---

[4] In later censuses a deliberate decision was taken not to make statistical determinations of membership in language groups in order to avoid political controversies (McRae 1986: 35).

[5] The details have been drawn from the meticulous studies of multilingual democracies by McRae (see McRae 1983: 67–8; 1986: 39–40; 1997: 99–100).

[6] For an evaluation of the political significance of multilingualism in Switzerland from the perspective of political philosophy, see Holenstein (1988); on Belgium, see Van Parijs

communication in the countries mentioned reflect in varying degrees patterns of linguistic diversity. For example, the existence of different language communities finds expression in the publicly controlled media as well as at the level of political institutions, where different languages may be used indistinctly. In this respect, polyglot individuals play an important role in mediating discursively between the communities in the formation of opinions and in the processes of reaching political decisions. As it happens, rudimentary attempts to foster a multilingual repertoire in public contexts of communication were also discernable in the later period of the Habsburg Empire, whose language situation easily outstripped the problems of Belgium or Switzerland in degree of complexity, thus coming close to the realities of the present-day EU.[7]

Let us turn once again to the institutional context of the EU in an attempt to throw some empirical light on the problems of language diversity and the public sphere. The European Parliament must be regarded as the main forum for the public presentation of relevant positions on current issues in EU politics. But the level of awareness of the activities and deliberations of the Strasbourg Parliament is clearly well below the level of attention accorded to the activities of parliaments in the member states. The weariness with politics which seems to have infected so many European democracies becomes even more acute when it comes to the formation of opinions at the supranational level. It would certainly be mistaken to make the Parliament the scapegoat for the general lack of interest in European issues. Nor do I want to suggest that parliamentary culture in the political systems of the member states is in rude good health by comparison with Strasbourg.[8] However, even from the point of view of an unreconstructed political realism, the prospect presented by plenary sessions of the European Parliament is generally a rather sobering one. This is especially true for the functions of articulating and disseminating political options which parliaments are supposed to perform in liberal democracies (von Beyme 1999).

The contribution of the European Parliament to making the basic contents of European decision-making public remains modest. The activities of parliamentarians lack transparency and broader political impact. The

---

(2000a). For a comparison with the normatively interesting case of Canada, see Kymlicka (1998) and Taylor (1994).

[7] This claim seems justified at least concerning the Cisleithanian (Austrian) part of the Empire, which undertook initiatives towards a flexible politics of nationalities following the Compromise ('Ausgleich') of 1867; on official policy concerning multilingualism in the regions represented in the Austrian *Reichsrat*, see Goebl (1997).

[8] For a disillusioned analysis of the operation of contemporary parliamentary democracy, see, for example, Bobbio (1988) and Zolo (1992).

Strasbourg parliament is certainly not a site of intense and heated political debates. When important votes are taken, the European People's Party and the Social Democrats typically unite in an informal coalition in the chamber (Hix 1999: 79–82). Preliminary deliberations leading to decisions take place within the Union's institutional complex of the comitology,[9] which includes representatives from the assembly but nevertheless does not accord the Parliament any special status compared with other involved European bodies.

It is obvious that the weak profile of the European Parliament as a public forum for developing a transnational political discourse is also connected with the problem of language barriers. It is not easy to imagine how a lively political debate could be conducted in 23 (or more) languages. Consequently, the contributions of parliamentarians in the plenary sessions are restricted to brief statements on issues delivered as monologues. Podium times are strictly limited due to the need to coordinate sittings with the interpretation services. The effect is like that of a rigidly conducted ritual in which the unavoidable reliance on the machinery of translation leaves little room for the art of political rhetoric.

In fact, the real work of the delegates does not take place in the plenary sessions but in the meetings of the numerous committees and working groups which shape the parliamentary decision-making process. Here, a multilingualism based on the twin pillars of English and French becomes the de facto communication regime. Delegates who do not have sufficient knowledge of at least one of these two languages depend on the aid of colleagues who possess the requisite competence (Wright 2000: 169). Their scope for communication in informal contexts is always severely restricted. Parliamentarians' levels of competence in foreign languages have not yet been investigated in a comprehensive and reliable manner. The Directorate-General for Research of the Parliament planned to conduct an internal study on this issue for statistical purposes after the 1994 elections. But the project was abandoned because it roused the ire of many delegates (Bueno 1999: 312–13). This occurrence is further proof of the explosiveness of the language question. It is extremely doubtful whether parliamentarians who have not mastered the relevant repertoire in the de facto working languages to some extent are in a position to perform their functions satisfactorily. A delegate who speaks only her native language – assuming her native language is neither English nor French – is in effect condemned to silence in many areas of activity, a silence which is

---

[9] 'Comitology' designates a complex system of committees in which national experts defend positions on measures planned by the commission; on the modalities of will-formation in the comitology, see Joerges and Neyer (1998) and Joerges and Everson (2000).

ultimately synonymous with political insignificance. Knowledge of foreign languages is an important criterion in hiring officials and employees of the Commission. However, to make it a selection criterion for the election of political representatives would create major problems from a normative point of view. It is not a coincidence that the European Parliament has consistently presented itself as a bastion of integral multilingualism.

Nevertheless, it is clear that the language problem is of great importance, not just for the *representation* of publicity in the European Parliament but also for its *production*. For a majority of delegates, influencing the will-formation process presupposes competence in foreign languages. But the implications of factual differences in the status of official languages and the corresponding inequality of opportunities for political communication remain a taboo issue even for the Parliament itself. The circle connecting language with the political public sphere here closes once again. The communicative anomalies of the parliamentary public sphere at the European level are reflected not least in the fact that the Strasbourg institution does not play the classical role of a representative body as a locus of conflicts between government and opposition. The modus operandi of the Parliament is essentially tailored to its complementary (and still, to a large extent, subordinate) status vis-à-vis the other European legislative authority, the Council. Political discussion takes place within a network of issue-specific working committees which bring together members of different parliamentary groups (Neunreither 1998: 432–4). This system may indeed foster important political interactions and initiatives on specific issues; but it does not create the impression that the European Parliament is an agora of transnational politics.

The problem of political communication at the level of the European Parliament is just the tip of the iceberg. It shows that the formation of a discursively integrated public sphere among political elites is a slow process. The creation of a common public space in which institutional decision-making processes are embedded seems to be even more difficult in the domain of transnational mass communication. In the EU, the divisions within the sphere of political communication founded on the infrastructure of the mass media continue to reflect the borders which separate nation-states and language communities. On the one hand, there have been initiatives by the European Community/EU to develop a 'European audiovisual space' by promoting cross-border film and television productions. However, they were aimed basically at intercultural dialogue and the preservation of cultural heritage. By contrast, the topic of 'information society', which has recently been accorded a prominent position on the agenda of the Commission, is particularly concerned with laying down uniform European standards for implementing telecommunication systems and new information technologies. Questions of political communication in a narrower sense were expressly excluded in both instances (Schlesinger and Kevin 2000: 221). Moreover, independently of the activities of the EU, private media concerns have until now generated at best weak impulses towards the formation of a European media system.

Let us first consider the print media. There is no question that the readership of European newspapers remains overwhelmingly regional and national. The high-circulation, so-called 'great European dailies', such as *Le Monde*, the *Frankfurter Allgemeine Zeitung* or *El País*, are in the first instance press organs whose editorial policy reflects the political and cultural priorities of the countries in which they appear. The only daily newspaper that can claim to reach a genuinely European public is the *Financial Times Europe*. The readership of this English-language paper is mainly comprised of members of political and, in particular, economic elites. Its reporting is also followed with great interest in Brussels. The European edition of the *Financial Times* (not to be confused with national editions such as the *Financial Times Deutschland*) is reputed to be particularly close to the Commission. In the opinion of a contributor to the *Financial Times*, its addressees belong to a class with both a European and a global outlook, which he describes as 'people with money who don't want to lose it or want to have even more of it'. The editor in chief of the European edition describes the paper as 'neoliberal, but with a social conscience'.[10] The economic incentives favouring the introduction of a European daily newspaper which deviates from a business newspaper format are not generally rated as very strong. Here too, the multiplicity of languages remains one of the chief factors hindering the emergence of a pan-European public (Gerhards 2000: 291).

As regards the audiovisual media, until now the development has been, if anything, even more painfully slow than in the case of the print media. Initiatives to establish a European television channel have failed. Pilot projects such as Eurikon or Europa TV, which were started in the 1980s, were of short duration (Meckel 1994). In the audiovisual media sector, the problem of the plurality of languages is also regarded as a basic structural hurdle to the emergence of European channels (Gerhards 1993: 101–2). Significantly, news channels such as CNN or BBC World which broadcast in the lingua franca English have a 'global' rather than a European orientation (with an emphasis on the USA in the case of CNN and on the Commonwealth countries in the case of BBC World). Other

---

[10] Quotes from an article on the *Financial Times Europe* in *Die Zeit* 29/2001 ('Mächtig, trocken, rosa' ['Powerful, Dry, Pink']).

lingua franca programmes which can be received in Europe, such as the music channel MTV, use the linguistic medium relatively sparingly. By contrast, the news channel Euronews has a policy of broadcasting a single core repertory in several languages (English, French, German, Spanish, Italian and Arabic). The multilingual channel has for the present found very limited acceptance with the public, though it is regarded by media experts as having good growth potential (Schlesinger and Kevin 2000: 227).

The main problem we encounter when considering the structure of media-generated publics in the EU is, in essence, that the communicative exchange between the European political stage and the European public is fragmentary on account of the structure of the media landscape. Thus far, there have been only weak initiatives towards developing the requisite media infrastructure for a transnational communication community. The EU does not yet satisfy the standards of an interculturally networked space of political communication which fulfils the minimum requirements of a critical public sphere (Glotz 1995). If, in contrast with someone like Grimm, the problem of publicity and communication in Europe is not regarded from the very beginning as a major hindrance to further political integration, then two general argumentative strategies can be deployed. The first appeals to alternative forms of publicity in the transnational domain, the second to a possible Europeanization of national public spheres.

On the first approach, issue-specific public spheres formed by experts and interest groups take the place of an overarching public sphere integrated communicatively through the connection between politics and media (Eder 2000). Such partial public spheres develop in the context of decision-making processes in which the EU-typical procedural rules of comitology play a decisive role. In areas such as BSE (Bovine Spongiform Encephalopathy, i.e., in a more popular jargon, the 'mad cows disease') or migration, for example, they create the preconditions for the emergence of transnational resonance structures for political debate. Of course, this tells us nothing about how communication unfolds within these resonance structures. Moreover, as a general rule it will prove very difficult to specify systematic and normatively robust criteria for where to draw the line between deliberative expert public spheres and closed arenas of elite decision-making. Let us examine again the segment of the public represented by the readership of the *Financial Times Europe*. The portrait painted of it refers, among other things, to how 'a small group of influential and educated people' are playing a pioneering role in the construction of a common European public sphere. However, from a normative point of view, one might have doubts about a perspective for which an elite of the happy few, who 'today spend their evening in Barcelona, tomorrow in Berlin and next week in Stockholm', provides the standards of a transnational political discourse which apparently can get along fine without any link to a democratic general public.[11]

The second approach presents the Europeanization of national public spheres as a viable option for dealing with the problem of public communication on a European scale (Ernst 1998, Gerhards 1993). What is envisaged is more intensive attention to European issues within national media systems informed by a perspective which draws connections between national and European political dimensions. A certain scepticism is also appropriate in assessing this approach, because, in the final analysis, the problem of a European public is not really addressed by falling back on communication within the nation-states. The overarching context which relates these different public spheres to each other still has to be discursively produced if there is to be something more than a mere juxtaposition of Europeanized public spheres. One of the main concerns of free public communication in pluralist democracies is to foster at least a provisional specification of the common good.[12] Comparable processes of working out a conception of a European common good are scarcely conceivable in the absence of a shared framework of political communication.

Ultimately, we know far too little about the basis and the rules of political communication in multilingual democracies. In view of the situation in the EU, it would be helpful if we could draw on empirically well-documented models which illuminate the *micro*-structures of publicity under conditions of cultural and linguistic differentiation. In considering discussions of publicity in the social sciences, we typically encounter a problem that is characteristic for treatments of the relation between communication and politics in democratic theory in general: language is treated as an exogenous factor in the political process. However, the very clarification of the preconditions of communicative understanding is often itself already a political issue. Even under conditions of cultural heterogeneity, a democratic public sphere must be able to produce a framework for political cohesion by determining a conception of the common good, however precarious and provisional such a conception may prove to be. For the time being, we may assume that in multilingual democracies this takes place through a horizontal nesting of publics in which both political and civil society actors relate their respective concerns to each other. Intercultural mediation processes – 'translations' in quite a literal sense – are clearly highly relevant in this connection.

[11] Quotes from *Die Zeit*, 29/2001 ('Mächtig, trocken, rosa' ['Powerful, dry, pink']).
[12] On this, see the position set forth by Häberle (2000: 10–12).

In view of the tendencies observable in the domain of transnational communication, there is a danger that in the EU a vertical shift (from bottom to top) of publicity will take the place of horizontal exchange. This danger implies that experts and elites become isolated and seal off whole areas of decision-making into specialized forums from which the majority of citizens are excluded. The persistence of such a situation would seriously undermine the normative force of the project of integration in the medium term and set the project itself on shaky foundations. For, in the final analysis, politics, like language, has an expressive as well as an instrumental dimension. The integrating power of a political order ultimately depends on the fact that political events unfolding on the 'public stage' are made comprehensible for a broad public by being presented in a symbolic-dramatic form (Geertz 1980). But without a comprehensible communicative context, this integrative force remains ineffectual.

6.3   Europe's Linguistic Landscape and the External Language Policy of the European Union

How should we assess the linguistic foundations of transnational communication in Europe? In the first place, the question concerns how knowledge of languages – in particular, of foreign languages – is distributed in the EU. As regards the relation of individuals in member states to their respective official languages, it is generally assumed that all individuals who have completed the obligatory period of schooling have acquired the minimum linguistic competence required to make an autonomous exercise of their civil rights. If we consider the linguistic prerequisites for the unhindered exercise of the right to freedom of information and communication, this is by no means a trivial assumption. Thus, in officially multilingual contexts, the basic principle holds that membership in one of the recognized language groups should not entail any political disadvantages – in other words, civil rights speak the mother tongue. In many cases, this linking of civil rights with language follows the principle of territoriality. Immigrants who want to become citizens of the host country are typically expected to be willing to acquire a new 'political native language'.[13] We thereby assume that citizens are able to communicate in the national official language or in one of the national official languages.

---

[13] The emphasis new legislation on the integration of immigrants in countries such as Germany or the Netherlands places on language acquisition makes this point evident; see Maas et al. (2004) for the German case. In 2006, the President of the German Parliament, the Christian Democrat Norbert Lammert, started an initiative to anchor the official status of German in the constitution; compare *Spiegel Online*, 30 September 2006, 'Lammert will Deutsch als Landessprache im Grundgesetz'

The situation is more complicated in the European communicative space. Granted, the equal status of the official languages also remains an authoritative guideline in the context of EU citizenship. Nevertheless, as we saw in the case of the members of the European Parliament, transnational political communication on the basis of one to two dozen official languages of equal status is a chimera. For the majority of participants, transnational communication consistently means communicating in a foreign language. But knowledge of foreign languages cannot be as straightforwardly assumed as the mastery of an official language by citizens, as is shown by the available data that support conclusions concerning the competence of EU citizens in foreign languages.

In 2001, the Directorate-General for Education and Culture of the European Commission for the first time issued a special Eurobarometer report on 'Europeans and Languages'; a total of 16,000 citizens from the (at that point still) 15 EU member states were interviewed for the report.[14] A second special Eurobarometer on languages followed in 2006.[15] Based on a total of around 26,000 interviews, the 2006 survey gives a picture of the linguistic situation in the EU25; moreover, it includes data for Romania and Bulgaria, which were expected to join the Union in 2007, as well as for Croatia and Turkey. According to the data the 2006 report presents for the EU25, 56 percent of the respondents claimed to be fluent in a language other than their mother tongue, and 28 percent said that they were fluent in two languages in addition to their mother tongue. By far the most widespread foreign language was, as expected, English: 38 percent of EU citizens stated that they had sufficient skills in English to have a conversation. The corresponding figure for French and German was, in both cases, 14 percent.[16] English also was the foreign language used most frequently on a regular basis (i.e. almost every day) with 31 percent, followed by German and Spanish with 22 percent each.[17] The strongholds of English knowledge were the Scandinavian countries and the Netherlands. As to French and German, the 2006 survey revealed that, in comparison with the situation in 2001, the eastern enlargement had changed the balance between the two languages in the EU: while a relatively high number of citizens in the new member states (23 percent)

('Lammert wants German as official language in the Constitution'); (http://www. spiegel.de/politik/Deutschland/0,1518,440156,00.html).

[14] The Education and Culture Directorate-General. General Unit 'Centre for the citizen – Analysis of public opinion', 2001: Europeans and languages (*Eurobarometer 54 special*).

[15] Directorate General Press and Communication, 2006: Europeans and their Languages, *Special Eurobarometer 243*.

[16] Spanish and Russian stand at 6 percent; compare *Special Eurobarometer* 243 (2006: 12).

[17] Compare *Special Eurobarometer* 243 (2006: 16).

stated that they master German, the knowledge of French within this group of countries was scarce (3 percent).[18] The 2001 and 2006 Eurobarometer studies do not provide a breakdown of lack of knowledge of foreign languages according to member country. But from other Eurobarometer reports covering approximately the same period, one can infer that the United Kingdom exhibits the highest levels in this regard; there a mere 25 percent of citizens questioned claim that they can speak another language well enough to be able to hold a conversation in it.[19]

The results of such surveys must certainly be very carefully qualified, because they do not reflect an objective evaluation by third parties but only express individuals' subjective self-assessments of their levels of knowledge of foreign languages. Such self-evaluations are apparently culturally filtered. To give one example: Do the different percentages of interviewees who claim that their English is 'very good' in Denmark (46 percent) and in Finland (23 percent) point at real differences in levels of linguistic competence or rather at differences in the self-perception of this competence?[20] In any case, we should keep in mind that the data on the prevalence of knowledge of foreign languages must be supplemented by an assessment of the functional scope of this knowledge. In the EU25, 38 percent of citizens declare that they have knowledge of English. Yet just 22 percent within this group consider their level of English to be 'very good'.[21] Apparently, however, only such a level means that a person can successfully employ the foreign language in all ordinary situations, for example, that she is able to understand the contents of a newspaper completely or to write a formal letter.[22] Basically, a realistic assessment of knowledge of foreign languages would require conducting standardized language tests throughout Europe. Although the figures presented in the Eurobarometer reports coincide more or less with other tentative findings,[23] they do not offer more than a very rough approximation of the actual level of knowledge of foreign languages in the EU.

For a better assessment of the survey results, it makes sense to contrast them with data on instruction in foreign languages in European schools. At levels I and II of general secondary education, English is clearly the dominant foreign language in Western Europe. In Denmark, Germany,

---

[18] Compare *Special Eurobarometer* 243 (2006: 12).

[19] According to *Eurobarometer* 52, the proportion is 19 percent, whereas *Eurobarometer* 55 sets the figure at 27 percent; compare European Commission (2000, 2001b).

[20] Compare *Special Eurobarometer* 243 (2006), Annexes (Table D48f.2).

[21] Compare *Special Eurobarometer* 243 (2006: 14).

[22] This specification of what a level of 'very good' knowledge of a language actually means is taken from the appendix to the *Eurobarometer 54 special report* (2001), as it is not given in *Special Eurobarometer* 243 (2006).

[23] See, for example, the data presented by de Swaan (1993: 151–66).

Finland, France, Austria, Sweden and Spain the proportion of students who receive some English instruction is between 90 and 100 percent. Only in Dutch-speaking Belgium and in Luxembourg does French as a foreign language achieve comparably high levels. Also interesting in this regard is an examination of the situation in the new member states and candidate countries in Eastern Europe. Here the leading role of English is less pronounced than in the West. In the Czech Republic, Slovakia, Poland and Hungary, German and English are equally prevalent as the most frequently taught foreign languages with totals of around 50 percent. French, by contrast, plays a subordinate role among the group of Eastern European new member and candidate countries, with the exception of Romania, where it features as the principal foreign language even ahead of English.[24] In the old EU15, on average, at secondary school levels I and II, the Luxembourgers learned the most foreign languages with 2.9. The Finns reached 2.4, the French 1.7 languages; the Germans with a figure of 1.2 ranked in the bottom third, just ahead of the Spanish and the Italians (with 1.1 each).[25]

In sum, data such as these leave no room for doubt concerning the leading position of English as a foreign language in Europe. Nevertheless, the picture is more nuanced than this might suggest. The actual potential of English as a lingua franca is diminished for the present by the fact that only about one-fifth of the 38 percent of EU citizens who claim to have knowledge of English as a foreign language describe their ability as 'very good'. To put it bluntly, English may be a reliable medium for asking directions for many Europeans when they are abroad, but that does not make it the linguistic cement of a transnational political community. Moreover, knowledge of English is not uniformly distributed throughout the European continent. In the Scandinavian countries, the German-speaking area and the Netherlands, competence in English as a foreign language is on average higher than in other parts of the EU. In spite of the dominance of English, French and German as foreign languages can claim some regional bastions. The relative strength of German in comparison with French has increased significantly after the enlargement of the EU to the east. Finally, it is generally true that competence in foreign languages is an indicator of social status throughout the EU. The higher a person's level of education, the more likely she is to speak one or more foreign languages.[26] If one wanted to summarize the situation

---

[24] All figures are for the school year 1996–1997 (Eurydice 2001: 96–9).

[25] Figures for the school year 1995–1996 or, in the case of Luxembourg, the school year 1994–1995, from the *iwd-Informationsdienst* of the *Institut der deutschen Wirtschaft*, 24, 15 June 2001, 'Deutsche Schulen wenig polyglott' ('German schools not very polyglot').

[26] Compare *Eurobarometer 54 special report* (2001: 4), *Special Eurobarometer* 243 (2006: 17).

in an incisive formula, one could say that English has clearly established itself as the 'first second language' of Europeans, but it is still far from being a 'second first language' (Habermas 1998: 161; cf. Section 6.1 in this chapter).

We also get a rather nuanced picture when we examine the spectrum of opinions among EU citizens on the issue of language diversity and its practical implications. The Eurobarometer special studies quoted earlier also contain a range of information on this question. The table *Europeans and Foreign Languages* presents a summary of the responses to a series of questions concerning the problem of communication in the EU. Generally speaking, when we compare the 2001 and 2006 surveys, it seems that the eastern enlargement has implied a greater acceptance of multilingualism. A possible explanation for this development is that all new accession countries comprise small- to medium-sized language communities whose members have traditionally been expected to learn additional languages for enhancing their communicative repertoire. Thus, the findings for 2006 indicate that there is a high predisposition towards overcoming communicative barriers by acquiring one or even two foreign languages. However, an overview of the results brings some revealing tensions to light as well. If we focus on the 2001 report, the first striking fact is the high level of acceptance of a foreign language curriculum focused on the EU, with English clearly emerging as the preferred standard option. The hegemony of English in the opinions of Europeans is much more pronounced than the socio-linguistic basis actually enjoyed by English as a foreign language in Europe. But the openness to acquiring a foreign language, in general, and English, in particular, goes along with an almost equally strong impulse to defend one's own native language with a view to the next round of expansion. The idea that the increase in the number of EU member states will lead to the introduction of a common language is not shared by a majority of respondents.[27] The 2006 report shows an increased support for a common language, which the survey, this time, leaves unspecified. Yet, remarkably, the support goes hand in hand with the widely shared view that all languages spoken within the Union should be treated equally (see Table 6.1).

We find a complex spectrum of foreign language competence and of attitudes relevant for language politics and policies among EU citizens.

---

[27] On this point, see also the study of the *Institut für Deutsche Sprache*, according to which only 8 percent of Germans support a single language for Europe. In addition, support for the idea of a common lingua franca coupled with the preservation of the individual languages does not go beyond 30.8 percent, whereas 41.1 percent are in favour of the complete preservation of language diversity. Compare *Süddeutsche Zeitung*, 14 April 2001 ('Wettbewerbsnachteil Muttersprache' ['Native language a competitive disadvantage']).

Table 6.1. *Europeans and Foreign Languages*

Questions put to all respondents in the EU15 (*Eurobarometer 54 special report, 2001*)	Agree %	Disagree %	Don't know %
Everyone in the European Union should be able to speak one European Union language in addition to their mother tongue	71.1	20.2	8.7
Everyone in the European Union should be able to speak English	69.4	22.5	8.1
The enlargement of the Union to include new member countries means that we must protect our own languages more	63.4	22.6	14.0
The enlargement of the European Union to include new member countries means that we all have to start speaking a common language	38	46.8	15.2
In my region, people are good at speaking foreign languages	34.3	39.0	26.7
Everyone in the European Union should be able to speak two European Union languages in addition to their mother tongue	32.4	53.4	14.1
I prefer to watch foreign films with subtitles, rather than dubbed	29.8	59.6	10.6

Questions put to all respondents in the EU25 (*Special Eurobarometer 243, 2006*)			
Everyone in the European Union should be able to speak one European Union language in addition to their mother tongue	84	12	4
All languages within the European Union should be treated equally	72	21	7
Everyone in the European Union should be able to speak a common language	70	25	5
The European institutions should adopt one single language to communicate with European citizens	55	40	5
In my country, people are good at speaking other languages	44	45	11
I prefer to watch foreign films and programmes with subtitles, rather than dubbed	37	56	6

Sources: The Education and Culture Directorate-General. General Unit 'Centre for the citizen – Analysis of public opinion', 2001: Europeans and languages (*Eurobarometer 54 special*); Directorate General Press and Communication, 2006: Europeans and their Languages, *Special Eurobarometer 243.*

What approach do the European institutions adopt given the situation described? The EU does not have any powers which would allow it to exercise direct influence on language policy within the member states. Yet the Union does exert a strong indirect influence on the European language constellation. It begins with the fact that language regulations within European institutions function as a signal concerning the international status of languages. Linguists argue that the future of German as a foreign language, for example, depends crucially on whether the German government succeeds in making German a regular working language within institutions and governing bodies of the EU (Ammon 2004). Moreover, it is clear that the increasing frequency and intensity of transnational communication implied by the process of integration have consequences for language policies within the European states.

As we saw in Chapter 3, the political architecture of European unification is based on the premise that a sharp separation must be made between the sphere of economic integration and the sphere of cultural identity in the member states. According to the prevailing view, the creation of a Common Market and a European 'government' need not and ought not be taken as an excuse for political measures aimed at cultural homogeneity. However, it is not always possible to make a clear distinction in practice between culture and the economy (De Witte 1993: 164). In the first place, there are unavoidable spillover effects from market integration into the cultural sphere. Moreover, such effects lead to efforts on the part of member states and regions to immunize market segments from the pressures of transnational competition by appealing to the primacy of culture.

Europe's single market rests on four pillars: the free movement of capital, the free movement of services, the free movement of goods and the free movement of persons. In realizing the four freedoms, language diversity gives rise to transaction costs that would not occur in a linguistically homogeneous environment. The essential goal of the four market freedoms is to facilitate the unhindered cross-border exercise of economic activities. Because language is a medium of such transactions, the market freedoms also implicitly include freedom in the use of language in transnational economic activities. The result is a potential conflict with language policy, especially in multilingual member states, and with the requirement to protect cultural diversity.

I would like to illustrate this point briefly with the example of the free movement of persons and the associated freedom to conduct business and freedom of employment for EU citizens. The principle of freedom of movement of labour in the internal market forbids a member state from restricting access to its labour market through regulations which disadvantage workers from another member state. According to Community law, the transnational freedom to conduct business and freedom of employment can indeed be restricted if a job calls for specific language knowledge. But as long as it cannot be proven that such knowledge is professionally necessary, the presumption is that a member state indirectly discriminates against foreign workers if it links the granting of a post to a particular linguistic competence. In a series of decisions since 1968, the European Court of Justice (ECJ) has taken the view that the principle of freedom of movement also holds for employment in the civil service sector, with the exception of those areas which play a key role in the exercise of a state's sovereign powers, such as the administration of justice and the police. Language criteria often feature in job announcements and recruitment for positions in the public sector in particular (De Witte 1991: 165–8). This raises the question of the implications of these criteria for the free movement of persons.

The question became the subject of a legal dispute in the *Groener* case on which the ECJ made a finding in 1989.[28] Anita Groener, a Dutch citizen, was employed on a part-time basis as an instructor in painting at the College of Marketing and Design in Dublin. In order to transform the job into a permanent full-time position, she had to take an examination in Irish – according to the Irish Constitution, the national language and the first official language of Ireland – which she failed. The Irish Ministry of Education duly declined to appoint her to the post. Ms Groener contested this, basing her case primarily on the fact that instruction was conducted in English, as is the norm in Irish educational institutions such as her College. In her field, she alleged, knowledge of Irish is not actually required. Therefore, the refusal of the Ministry to grant her the position constituted indirect discrimination. The case was referred by the Irish side to the ECJ, which found in favour of the Irish State. It granted that, in practice, knowledge of Irish was not strictly necessary for instruction in Anita Groener's area of expertise. Nevertheless, it recognized the right of the Republic of Ireland to protect and promote the national language in public domains beyond the immediate requirements of a context of instruction. The ECJ accorded greater weight to this right than to the principle of freedom of movement for employees. At the same time, it qualified its judgment with the remark that this did not entail a general presumption in favour of the priority of regulations governing language in the member states over the freedoms of the Common Market, and it reserved the right to decide individual cases on a contextual basis.

---

[28] My account of the case follows De Witte (1993: 159–60) and Usher (1998: 228–9).

The potential for conflict between the functional imperatives of the internal market and European language diversity has not diminished since 1989. On the contrary, following the transition to the Monetary Union, the ambivalences in the relation between the goals of market integration and respect for linguistic-cultural pluralism have become even more apparent. The balancing act between protecting diversity and indirect standardization seems to be a persistent feature of the EU. When the EU institutions present citizens with initiatives in the domain of language policy they do so under the banner of multilingualism. A good example of this is the LINGUA programme initiated by the Commission in 1990.[29] The primary goal of LINGUA is to enhance knowledge of foreign languages in the member states, with the qualification that the foreign languages in question are those of other member states. LINGUA is dedicated to the promotion of all official EU languages and is specifically designed to encourage Europeans to learn the smaller official languages of the Union. The means employed include, among other things, student exchanges, continuing education of teachers and the development of new methods of language instruction. At the insistence of France and Germany, the conceptualization and implementation of the programme were deliberately designed to promote the acquisition of foreign languages 'in general'; this should ensure that the programme would not contribute to further consolidating the supremacy of English.

Under the auspices of the EU and the Council of Europe, 2001 was declared the 'European Year of Languages'. The focus of institutional activities during the year was a pan-European information campaign. It aimed at celebrating linguistic diversity as a central aspect of the European cultural heritage. At the same time, it sought to encourage Europeans to learn new languages. Here, too, the express goal was to take account of the full spectrum of European languages. In the course of the formal act of presentation of the Year of Languages in Barcelona, the then EU Commissioner for Education and Culture, Viviane Reding of Luxembourg, declared with great emphasis: 'There are no major and minor languages. There are no more or less important languages. All languages are important. I do not find the concept of a minority language particularly appealing'.[30]

Still it would be an illusion to think that Europe is on the brink of transforming itself into a quasi-Babylonian utopia. The indirect effects on

---

[29] For a detailed description of this programme, see Siguan (1995: 172–80).

[30] Quoted from *Avui*, 24 April 2001 ('La comissària d'Educació defensa que no hi ha llengües minoritàries' ['The Education Commissioner argues that there are no minority languages']).

language policy of EU activities in important areas of transnational social communication carry more weight than the institutional discourse on the language question. The dilemma of the EU is one which inevitably arises out of the coexistence of the expressive and the instrumental dimensions of language in multilingual contexts. The EU is forced to acknowledge that languages have an important identity-constituting moment. However, the technical game rules of market-driven integration often leave little room for the political articulation of expressive motifs. For example, when the Commission works on promoting the construction of transnational networks for research and development, it also contributes willy-nilly to solidifying the hegemony of English in the European research field. The framework programmes of the EU to promote research officially respect multilingualism; however, as a general rule, the participants assume that the operative language for the selection procedure is in fact English (Wright 2000: 218). Particularly symptomatic of the general situation seem to be the tendencies in the area of the development and implementation of new information technology, to which the Commission accords great importance for constructing a European space of communication. I will turn to the associated problems in the next section.

6.4 Vanishing Point Internet?

There seems to be a widespread consensus among political analysts concerning the central role which communication and information will have to play if the opportunities for democratic participation within the complex system of European governance are to be enhanced. Implicitly or explicitly, the use of new communication technologies is expected to play a crucial role in this context. In the 'White Paper on European Governance', published by the European Commission in Brussels in 2001, there is a section outlining proposals for reforming Europe's institutional framework in which we find, among other things, the following statements (European Commission 2001: 11–12):

Democracy depends on people being able to take part in public debate. To do this, they must have access to reliable information on European issues and be able to scrutinize the policy process in its various stages . . .

Information and communication technologies have an important role. Accordingly, the EU's EUROPA Website . . . is set to evolve into an inter-active platform for information, feedback and debate, linking parallel networks across the Union.

Providing more information and more effective communication are a precondition for generating a sense of belonging to Europe. The aim should be to create a trans-national 'space' where citizens from different countries can discuss what they perceive as being the important challenges for the Union. This should help policy makers to stay in touch with European public opinion, and could guide them in identifying European projects which mobilize public support.

The document stresses throughout the importance of the dissemination of information, especially in connection with communication technologies. Since the launching of the Information Society Project in the 1990s, the EU, and especially the Commission, has indeed presented several important policy initiatives to promote the idea of e-government (Chadwick and May 2003: 272). After the presentation of the Bangemann Report (European Union 1994), with its recommendations concerning 'Europe and the global information society', EU institutions have consistently played a prominent role as supporters of the infrastructural changes associated with the diffusion of new information and communication technologies.

To judge from the approach adopted in the 'White Paper on European Governance', it would seem that the experts working on behalf of the Commission drew inspiration from the much-acclaimed trilogy of Manuel Castells (1996, 1997, 1998) devoted to a thorough analysis of the 'Information Age'. According to Castells (1998: 318–32), the EU represents the most advanced political response to the globalization process, including the challenges it poses in the field of communication technology. The Union is interpreted as the primary manifestation of a new kind of polity – the 'network state' – which is in the process of emerging. Not only does it represent an original way of linking an integrated economic zone to variable and decentralized 'nodes' of political authority; it also constitutes an autonomous communicative space in which information flows bypass the control of nation-states and in which cultural identities are transformed (Castells 1998: 324). However, Castells' approach leaves open to what extent and in what specific ways information technology could be used to confer the shape of a democratic transnational public sphere on the communicative space of the European 'network state'.

For a treatment of the communication theme that intends to offer a response to the pressing challenges of polity-building in the EU, we may turn to the perspective adopted by Joseph Weiler, one of the main experts in matters of European constitutionalism. Weiler (1999: 349) focuses on the Internet with the stated goal of 'discussing some proposals concerning the technology of transnational democracy'. The plan, which is presented under the evocative title *Lexcalibur*, envisages creating a virtual 'European Public Square'. This should be an Internet web site covering 'the entire decision-making process of the Community, especially, but not only comitology' (Weiler 1999: 351). By facilitating access to important information and enhancing the transparency of the policy process,

Lexcalibur is designed to enrich trans-European public debates and to serve as a *virtual* resource for strengthening participation in the world of *real* politics. The goal is to use the Internet to create more opportunities for both individual citizens and collective actors to become involved in EU politics, thereby enhancing the Union's legitimacy and increasing its democratic potential. As Weiler (1999: 353) puts it, in such a scenario the Internet 'is to serve as the true starting point for the emergence of a functioning deliberative political community, in other words, a European polity-cum-civic-society'.

One can hardly object to plans to put the Internet to democratic use. In the current discussions concerning transnational democracy in Europe, however, there is a strong tendency to blur the line between the normative and the empirical analysis of the potential contribution of communication technology to restructuring the democratic public space. Quite often, it is taken for granted that what the Internet *could* and *should* do *is already* becoming an empirical reality. But, unfortunately, noble political intentions are not always immediately reflected in actual trends.

This observation is confirmed by some basic facts which should be taken into account in a provisional assessment of the impact of the infrastructural changes in the sphere of information on the constitution of a democratic public sphere in the EU. Eurobarometer surveys containing data on media use and access to modern information tools in the EU report that there has been a tremendous increase in access to new forms of information technology in Europe in recent years. Thus, the household access rate to the Internet across the European Union, which had been 28 percent in October 2000, reached 43 percent in November 2002 (*Flash Eurobarometer* 135: 5). The number of Internet connections across Europe is expanding rapidly. Nevertheless, it should also be noted that, for the time being, the distribution of Internet resources remains strikingly uneven across the EU member states. Whereas the rate of access in 2002 was above 60 percent in Sweden, Denmark and the Netherlands, it was as low as 14 percent in Greece, with Portugal and Spain at 31 percent, Italy 35 percent, France 36 percent, Germany 46 percent and the UK 50 percent (*Flash Eurobarometer* 135: 4).

Moreover, the evidence provided by Eurobarometer data sheds some light on an aspect of Internet use that seems particularly relevant for the present discussion: namely, the formation of a *virtual* European public sphere. It seems that up to now the Internet has not developed a high profile as a source of information concerning the EU. When European citizens want to find out about what the EU is doing, 59 percent watch television, 35 percent read the daily newspapers, 23 percent turn on the radio and 19 percent consult information brochures. Only 15 percent of the respondents use the Internet as a source of information on European issues, in spite of the considerable efforts EU institutions have invested to develop attractive and highly accessible web sites.[31] At the same time, the sharp increase in the use of new information technology in 'e-Europe' has not been accompanied by a parallel development in the public's own assessment of its knowledge of EU affairs. Whereas the proportion of people who considered that they knew 'quite a lot to a great deal' about the EU was 24 percent in spring 1999 (*Eurobarometer* 51); the corresponding value for 2001 decreased to 21 percent (*Eurobarometer* 55) and increased again to 27 percent in spring 2003 (*Eurobaromètre* 59). Although based on a short time interval, the trend shows that there is no automatic correspondence between the technological infrastructure and the transnational consciousness of European citizens.

Thus far, therefore, the Internet's transformative effects on European public space have to be judged as having been relatively modest, at least with regard to the domain of political mass communication. Apparently, in the empire of new information and communication technologies, the TV is still king. Thus, according to data presented by the European Commission's DG Press in 2003, almost all Europeans (98 percent) watch television, with news and current affairs being the most watched kind of program (89 percent). In contrast, a majority of Europeans (53 percent) still do not use a computer, and only one-third (35 percent) surf the Internet (DG Press 2003: 4–6). The example of the Internet shows that the use of new information technology does not necessarily widen the communicative scope of Europe's political space; rather, it highlights a more general, elitist tendency that has haunted the formation of a European public sphere since political integration began to intensify in the 1990s. As Philip Schlesinger (1999) shows, there *is* evidence of the emergence of new communicative spaces in Europe. However, the scope of these spaces is rather restricted. The data collected in Eurobarometer surveys reveal that the groups who allegedly have the highest levels of knowledge on the EU are managers and the most highly educated, with women and the unemployed at the opposite end of the scale. Thus, Schlesinger (1999: 271) points out that business surveys increasingly take the use of the World Wide Web and of e-mail as an indicator of elite status.

Against this background, one has to keep in mind that, as Mansell and Steinmueller (2000: 39–45) argue, the formation of a European cyberspace is closely linked to changes in citizenship status and to the emergence of new forms of social inequality. Internet access and use are

---

[31] For an exhaustive listing of sources of information on the EU, see Table 4.2 in *Eurobaromètre Standard* 59 (2003).

not unrelated to issues of inclusion and exclusion. Accordingly, advanced information and communication technologies, while offering a potential instrument against exclusion, can also contribute to creating new kinds of disadvantages. The extent to which new technologies can be used to overcome exclusion does not depend on technology per se; it is a matter of institutional provisions which may contribute to reducing the cognitive barriers to the use of new information assets by socially excluded groups. In fact, costs and lack of skills turn out to be among the main reasons Europeans cite for not using the Internet, according to a survey prepared for the European Commission.[32]

As long as a suitable 'virtual citizenship' regime has not been established by political means, the Internet might even be contributing to reinforcing the top-heaviness of the structures of transnational communication in Europe. Both inside and outside the domain of new information technologies, the emerging sphere of interrelated European publics is basically a communicative space occupied by elites (Schlesinger 1999: 276). Public communication flows in this space are channelled through specific print media; the *Financial Times Europe* can be considered the authoritative transnational press organ for political and economic elites with a strong interest in European affairs. It is in the very context of elite communication where English has been most clearly consolidating its position as a nascent lingua franca in Europe (de Swaan 1993).

When it comes to cognitive barriers to broader access to the emerging European cyberspace, the question of language must not be neglected. However virtual it may be, political communication in cyberspace still requires a linguistic medium. Regardless of the communication technology utilized, this medium will be related to language communities with palpable cultural identities in the real world. Hence, the issue of relying on the Internet for the sake of transnational democracy should not be addressed without taking into account its linguistic aspects. The politics of language has often remained a secondary topic in the discourse on transnational democracy. At the same time, EU institutions have been making remarkable efforts to prevent language from becoming the subject of a potentially explosive public debate in Europe (Kraus 2000). It is symptomatic that, in the whole White Paper on European Governance, the language question receives scant attention, aside from a short note on the relevance of guaranteeing the linguistic accessibility of information on the EU for a broad European public. According to the document, this implies delivering information in all of the official European languages (i.e. 23, at present) 'if the Union is not to

---

[32] See *Eurobaromètre* 55.2, 2001 ('Les Européens et la E-INCLUSION'): 5.

exclude a vast proportion of its population' (Commission of the European Communities 2001: 11).

Nevertheless, the practice adopted by European institutions when using the Internet for informational purposes does not always match this noble objective. On the Commission's web site, many documents are available only in English or French, with German being the most likely third option. The limited resources of the EU's translation services are obviously a constraining factor in this respect. However, things become somewhat bizarre when information about a regional development project financed with European funds and located on a North Frisian island (belonging to Germany) is only given in French on the EU's web site. Similarly, it is not easy to understand why an EU project carried out to help homeless children in Palermo only gets Internet coverage in English.[33]

Communication problems of this kind are not limited to the anecdotal level. Linguistic barriers in Europe's emerging ensemble of communicative spaces remain fairly high. Foreign language skills are distributed unevenly, both socially and geographically, displaying a pattern similar to the use of the Internet. The linguistically and informationally versatile citizen, who is willing to get actively involved in European public debates, belongs to the upper strata of society and lives disproportionally in Northern or Central Europe rather than on the Union's Latin rim. In sum, the democratic potential of transnational Internet use will remain restricted as long as 'user resource issues, such as ability to receive and interpret information' (Chadwick and May 2003: 272) are not taken into account.

According to a well-known argument, the invention and dissemination of print technologies initiated fundamental changes in the patterns of human communication and played a decisive role in the formation of the modern nation-state as a historically new form of political organization (Anderson 1991, Deutsch 1966, Warner 1990). At the present stage, it would be premature to try to assess the real effect of the Internet in fostering the birth of large-scale political communities which transcend national borders. Thus far, however, the European situation does not offer much evidence that new information technology per se will swiftly lead to more extensive forms of political integration at the transnational level. The Internet may well foster the emergence and spread of new patterns of political membership. The anti-globalization movement is invariably offered as an example of such a trend. But the Internet can just as well

---

[33] The examples are taken from an article 'Englisch bevorzugt' ('English preferred') published in the *Frankfurter Rundschau* on 6 July 2001.

serve as an instrument for accommodating 'old' identities to new conditions and for maintaining them across time and geographical space. For example, the World Wide Web and digital technologies provide diaspora groups with new possibilities for maintaining ties with their homeland. To the extent that modern means of communication offer a wide array of options for preserving collective identities on a non-territorial basis, one can speculate on the growing importance of 'virtual ethnic communities' (Elkins 1997) in global politics. With the new information technologies, the figure of the 'long-distance nationalist' (Anderson 1992: 12), be it a Kurd who supports the Kurdish cause from Germany or a Tamil who promotes the goals of the Sri Lankan Tamil movement from Australia, potentially acquires a new and more dynamic significance.

As regards the European situation, in the first place it is likely that the ambivalence characteristic of processes of public communication in the Internet already discernable at the national level[34] will, if anything, increase in the transnational domain. An undoubtedly positive trend is the decentralization of expertise and the construction of cross-border issue-specific networks. On the negative side, by contrast, are tendencies towards a progressive fragmentation of the public, with the associated decrease in interest in relating political discourse to the 'common good'. In addition, there is an imminent danger that the top-heaviness of modern government (which is, after all, government by elites) will continue to increase if far-reaching institutional measures are not taken to construct a framework for the public use of information technologies that can satisfy democratic standards of legitimacy.

6.5   Which Language for a European Civil Society?

Even if we assume that linguistic integration does not have to mean integration in just one language, the EU is still far from being able to rely on the structures of a linguistically integrated civil society. In an effort to circumvent conflicts, European institutions have thus far avoided openly addressing the language question. But it remains to be seen to what extent the strategy of avoidance has ultimately contributed to reducing the political contentiousness of the language problem. From the perspective of a constitutionalization – not to speak of a thoroughgoing democratization – of the Union the current situation can hardly be judged satisfactory. As we saw in the previous chapters, the political diffidence in confronting the language question has led to a series of normatively highly questionable results. Particularly problematic is the globally weak,

---

[34] For a case study of the USA, see Sunstein (2001).

and in many ways inequitable, connection between European political institutions and a European civil society.

It is no exaggeration to regard citizens as the key element of a democratic order (Schmitter 2000: 5). By comparison with other regimes, only democracies can do full justice to the civil, political and social dimensions of the status of citizenship. This status is not exhausted by its legal components. The exercise of civil rights always has, in addition, an irreducible cognitive dimension. In the context of modern representative democracies, the idea of self-government implies, for example, mature and articulate citizens who are able to make competent assessments of the decisions of their representatives. Consequently, the citizenship status in practice always also reflects the results of deep political and cultural socialization processes in which educational institutions play a decisive role.[35] The education system fulfils the important task of transmitting to all members of society a minimum of cognitive competence which turns them into autonomous political subjects. In Western democracies this minimum involves as a general rule the acquisition of reading and writing skills and of 'general knowledge' in areas such as geography and history, which is also supposed to be a knowledge of those layers of one's 'own' identity which one has in common with other fellow citizens. Where the cognitive dimensions of the citizenship status are neglected, the prospects of placing processes of public communication on a broad democratic footing also suffer. It is precisely at this point that the political deficits of European integration have until now been most glaring; here too the inability of the institutions to address the language question directly seems particularly revealing. As long as a significant portion of the population in the member states lacks the communicative means to participate in trans-European political discourses, the status of citizenship of the Union will necessarily remain on shaky ground.

What possibilities exist to meet the challenges of language policy in the EU in a constructive manner? Without doubt, when considering transnational communication at the level of the European citizenry, we must begin from different premises than in the institutional domain. For employees and officials in the administration, the ability and willingness to work in a polyglot environment are a taken-for-granted part of the required professional qualifications. Also in the case of political office-holders whose main area of activity lies in the European institutions, one may expect a minimum of competence in foreign languages, however acquired. By contrast, one cannot reasonably demand that the

---

[35] On the role of schools and political education in the formation of democratic civic communities, see Callan (1997) as well as March and Olsen (2000).

44 percent of EU citizens who – according to the 2006 survey data – do not have any knowledge of foreign languages should quickly acquire such knowledge in order to become equally qualified members of a transnational polity based upon communication and participation. The priority for the present must be to develop a long-term strategy for dealing with the language question. Its primary goals would be, on the one hand, to extend and reinforce the communicative foundations of the project of European integration and, on the other, to preserve the language diversity which for normative reasons cannot be placed in question. To fall back on a pair of concepts introduced by Fritz Scharpf (1994: 131), language policy programmes for Europe will have to be compatible with the communicative needs of a transnational community while respecting the autonomy of the various language groups within this community. Beyond that, reactions to such programmes will crucially depend on the extent to which the details of the programme prove to be both pragmatic *and* just.

From the standpoint of fairness, the most elegant solution to the language problem might be to find a maximally neutral common vehicle of communication. The requirement of impartiality is in theory consistent with a number of alternatives. One possibility would be to agree on one of the 'minor' or 'marginal' European languages, one which does not even belong to one of the large language families.[36] Acquiring this language, therefore, would involve the same costs for the bulk of European citizens. A further option that is sometimes mooted is Latin. Although its neutrality is questionable, as it stands at the origin of one of the Continent's more important language groups, this might be compensated by the fact that it served as the European lingua franca in learned circles over a long historical period. In a query to the Commission in 1974, the members of the European Parliament, Patijn and Van der Hek, did indeed propose re-establishing the traditional bridging function of the Latin language by reviving it on a broader basis. The Commission responded that such an initiative was not within its sphere of competence (Coulmas 1991b: 31). Aside from 'dead' languages, artificial languages such as Volapük and Esperanto are also occasionally the focus of speculation on how a unified European linguistic space could be created in a just manner. Supporters of Esperanto see the EU as an ideal context for realizing their utopia of linguistic internationalism, though their vision has not generated much enthusiasm within European institutions (Phillipson 2003: 171–4). There are also more ironic proposals. Thus, the Finnish columnist Jukka Ukkola (1997) took the idea of an artificial language as the basis for a commentary in which he mockingly advocates the creation

---

[36] Basque or Estonian come to mind as candidates which meet such criteria.

of a genuinely EU-based idiom. He describes how a 'European Language Union' would come into being by applying the principles that had already been adopted in the making of the European Monetary Union. Hence, its medium of communication, which Ukkola calls *Das Linguaque*, is proportionally composed of all official languages of the Union.[37] In a similar vein, Diego Marani – a translator for the Council of Ministers in Brussels who is also a novelist – has made a more systematic attempt at creating an 'integrative' European language, which he has given the name *Europanto*.[38] Irrespective of such humorous contributions to dealing with the language issue in Europe, it is hard to deny that the advocates of linguistic and cultural neutrality have a point. At the same time, however, judged by criteria of realism and pragmatism, it also seems that neither a time-honoured language like Latin nor more modern, artificial languages such as Esperanto represent viable candidates for a European lingua franca.

Hence, those who wish to accord priority to criteria of pragmatism and communicative efficiency will be inclined to advocate making English the official lingua franca of the European public space. The advantages of English are well known. The communication potential already possessed by the English language outstrips that of all other European languages. If the trends of the past decades continue, it will further consolidate this position within the EU (de Swaan 2001: 162–5). When young people from different European language groups come together these days, as a general rule English serves as virtually the 'natural' medium of dialogue. A comparison of job advertisements in several European countries reveals that English is by far the most frequently required language on the European labour market (Ammon 1994: 7). Admittedly, one should not be too hasty in overestimating the actual diffusion of English on the European continent. Nor should we overlook the fact that other languages continue to fulfil lingua franca functions in Europe, though on a much lower level. But this in no way diminishes the inexorably increasing dominance of English.

---

[37] How would this sound? According to Ukkola, the sentence 'My good fellow, could you please give me a packet of Holokki–Saima cigarettes [a traditional Finnish brand]?' would be translated to *Das Linguaque* as follows: 'Könnten you, bona monsieur, procurarmi huis een aket Hålåk–Saimaa, por favor?'

[38] A collection of documents written in this language can be found on the Europanto web site (www.europanto.be). As a text included in that sample informs: Europanto ist uno melangio van de meer importantes Europese linguas mit also eine poquito van andere europese linguas, sommige Latinus, sommige old grec. Qui know ten moins zwei europese linguas kan Europanto undergrepen. From nu avanti, Du need keine mas foreignas linguas studie und Du kan mit el entiero mundo communicare danke al Europanto (http://www.europanto.be/G7_pilotaprojecto.html).

The advantages of the English option from the point of view of efficiency derive primarily from the fact that European language policy would ultimately only have to give its blessing to facts already created by the European language market. Demand for English instruction is everywhere apparent. More and more parents want their children to begin learning English early at school and preschool. Adults who did not learn English, or enough English, at school attend courses to improve their knowledge of the language. In the new Eastern European democracies in particular, English is often seen as a direct link to Western affluence, technological progress and a world of consumption tinged with glamour (Phillipson and Skutnabb-Kangas 1994). That a good level of English is an advantage that opens up additional career opportunities is a widely held view in the non-English-speaking member states of the EU. In the final analysis, the high level of acceptance of English as a foreign language, as expressed in the Eurobarometer language surveys (cf. Section 6.3), is not really surprising. Nor is the fact that EFL – *English as a Foreign Language* – has become an important source of economic revenue for the United Kingdom.

Giving institutional sanction to the de facto role of English would at any rate contribute to keeping the necessary investments for the regulation and enhancement of the transmission of foreign languages in the EU relatively low. That English has established itself as the European lingua franca actually has less to do with European developments than with developments at the global level. The triumphal procession of *European English* is in reality just one aspect of the triumphal procession of *global English*. In fact, the position of English as a global language has reached dimensions without historical precedent.[39] English is the language of the global finance markets. In the domain of research, it sets the proverbial tone. In the natural sciences, it has an almost complete monopoly. Even in the humanities, other traditional European languages of learning, such as French, German and Russian, can often maintain only niche positions (Ammon 1994: 5–6). But outside of specialized domains of communication as well, (American) English has permeated the everyday lives of people all over the world. This is presumably less a consequence of the direct exercise of political power under the banner of the *pax Americana* than an expression of the cultural hegemony of a lifestyle represented by Hollywood, Coca-Cola and McDonald's. However one views these developments, it cannot be disputed that no other language can match the advantages of English as a lingua franca that can be used

[39] For an analysis of this phenomenon from the perspective of linguistics, see Crystal (1997).

in a multiplicity of communicative contexts both inside and outside Europe.

6.6   The Political Option of a Converging Multilingualism

Why then, notwithstanding the situation just described, is *English only* not recommendable as a political strategy for dealing with the communication problems facing European civil society? I would like to present my answer in four steps which focus successively on different aspects of the language problem. In each case, I will pay particular attention to the political character of the problem.

First, granting English official status as the exclusive European lingua franca would not obviously be consistent with the requirements of justice. For the great majority of EU citizens, English is a foreign language. By contrast, in the member states United Kingdom, Ireland and Malta, which together constitute around 14 percent of the population of the EU25, it is an official language and also for most people their mother tongue. *European English* thereby reveals the same normative Achilles heel as does *global English* on a larger scale: its neutrality is contestable. English serves as the linguistic medium of comprehensive transnational communication communities. All those who are able to participate in the relevant communication processes, whether they are native speakers or not, benefit from the existence of such communities. However, the costs created by the emergence of an integrated English-language communicative space are not equally distributed. Knowledge of English as the requisite medium of communication is the birthright of a minority of participants; for the others, by contrast, it is the product of substantial educational efforts.[40] Recent psycholinguistic studies estimate the average time investment required by non-native speakers in the research domain to acquire a knowledge of English sufficient for participation in conferences and for publication at 10,000 learning hours (Ammon 2001b). One might speculate on how much less effort would be required if the educational goal were 'merely' to achieve a level of English sufficient for regular participation in transnational processes of political communication in the EU. But this is the decisive point: it may seem obvious to view good English knowledge as an important individual career advantage, or as an indispensable precondition for gaining access to circles of academically trained experts; but that does not make English automatically a broadly based legitimate foundation for a European political public sphere.

---

[40] For an interesting analysis of the indirect additional costs incurred by non-Anglophone states due to trends towards linguistic globalization, see Van Parijs (2000b).

Second, opting for *European English* has obvious political connotations which cannot be overlooked. It would be absurd to regard the hegemony of English as the product of a global conspiracy at the level of language policy. Nevertheless, English undoubtedly owes its dominant position more to political and economic power relations than to its inherent characteristics. The rich, multifaceted character of the 'European cultural heritage' frequently invoked in official declarations would inevitably be severely compromised by a one-sided privileging of English at the linguistic level. For some, this *cultural* narrowing may seem an acceptable price to be paid for optimizing possibilities of communication in transnational space. But it is likely to have serious implications for the reproduction of the *political* identities which are constitutive of political communities as well. This can be shown by an example from 'isolationist' Switzerland, which has until now been subject to a comparatively weak pressure to Europeanize. The introduction of English as the first foreign language ahead of French by German-speaking cantons such as Zurich led to disputes because it broke with the traditional rule that the first foreign language for all Swiss schoolchildren should be one of the national languages (generally, either German or French). This transgression was seen especially by the French side as a renunciation of a shared understanding of Swiss identity. The political sponsors of the measure countered that children from well-to-do families would get instruction in English anyway, and thereby enjoy advantages later in their careers, and that it is the task of state agencies to promote equality of opportunity through the public school system.[41] This example reveals a genuine dilemma which arises in different forms in many parts of Europe and cannot be simply dismissed as the expression of an outdated cultural sentimentalism. Moreover, that a narrowed cultural horizon as a general rule has consequences when it comes to perceiving political problems is shown – to take just one example – by the Oxford social scientist Larry Siedentop. In his book, *Democracy in Europe*, in which he commends the historical model of federalism in the USA as a suitable model for the EU, he declares that English is the only adequate lingua franca for the project of integration (Siedentop 2000: 12, 132–4). The book contains extended discussions of how counterproductive the French approach to questions of political integration is and on how to assess the German attitude towards Brussels. However, non-British sources on the European political debates are scarcely mentioned.[42]

---

[41] Compare *The Economist*, 18 November 2001 ('Switzerland: Fifth tongue, fifth column?') and the *New York Times*, 16 April 2001 ('Languages in Peril, Some in Europe Fear').

[42] I owe this reference to Paul Nemitz (personal communication, February 2001).

Third, precisely the successful diffusion of English may reduce its potential to serve as the standard medium of transnational public communication in the EU. This might seem paradoxical at first sight. However, the success story of English as a global lingua franca is in large part the result of millions of primarily instrumental calculations. People learn English to advance their careers, because they seek selective access to certain sources of information, or because they want to be able to use an efficient means of communication for travel or to maintain a network of foreign contacts. Of course, there is nothing objectionable about such motivations. Nevertheless, the extent to which they provide a stable basis for the communicative integration of a political community remains questionable. In his sceptical remarks on the ideological binding force of cultural globalization, Michael Mann (2001: 65) has the following to say about the role of English: 'English is advancing as the medium of public communication in the most modern sectors; but while many use the language to do business, they do not tell jokes or make love in it. Nor do their social movements mobilize in English, either peacefully or in battle'. Mann is clearly alluding to the difference between the instrumental and the expressive aspects of language when he underlines the limited functional scope of *global English*. This distinction was discussed in detail earlier (cf. Chapter 4, Section 4.1) and provided the point of departure for the analysis of politically significant patterns of linguistic identity. Mann's point is that the 'naked' instrumentalism of English as a global medium of communication makes it difficult to foster the expressive bonds of linguistic communication. In an ironic commentary, the poet Enric Casasses, an *enfant terrible* of the contemporary Catalan literary scene, takes up the point forcefully:

An idiom such as English, for example, is so widely diffused that it no longer expresses anything at all; it is merely a tool. And the fact that a Mongolian learns English does not indicate that any cultural barriers have been overcome – it is no different than if he were to study electronics. A cultural relation between a Kurd and a Slovenian, by contrast, could constitute a genuine enrichment for these two cultures . . .[43]

Such opinions may seem exaggerated. But, applied to the process of European polity-building, they nevertheless reflect a concrete underlying

---

[43] Enric Casasses, 'Pollastre' ('Chicken'), in *Avui*, 2 Nov 2000. In the Catalan original, the quotation reads: 'Un idioma per exemple com l'anglès està tan difós per tot arreu que ja no vol dir res, és una pura eina; i el fet que un mongol aprengui anglès no té cap transcendència cultural, és com si estudiés electrònica, mentre que una relació cultural entre un kurd i un eslovè pot ser una autèntica relació d'enriquiment d'aquestes dues cultures . . .'

problem. Insofar as *European English* as a regional variant of *global English* becomes a generalized form of *Eurospeak*, it is indeed to be feared that the transnational component of identity will lack the solid foundation of a communicatively generated common political culture in the consciousness of EU citizens. With the instrumental narrowing of transnational structures of communication, an important moment of political identification would also be lost. But expressive motives would not disappear from politics simply because they were banned from the European stage. Instead, they would be channelled with even greater intensity into national and local public discourses, thereby further promoting tendencies towards the renationalization of Europe.

Fourth, a politics for which *English only* represents the royal road to the communicative integration of the European citizenry will have to face the objection that it does not take the potential for linguistic and cultural conflict seriously enough. The political consecration of English would imply, first of all, the banishing of the other European languages from key contexts of transnational communication. A tendency which has long been in the offing in the economic and scientific realms would thereby be confirmed at the level of European politics. Clearly, such a step would have implications for the constellations of language policies in the members states themselves beyond its impact at the European level. It would be unrealistic to think that the role of *European English* as a medium of 'high' communication could be indefinitely confined to the transnational level. Instead, the likelihood is that English would become a genuine competitor for the national languages in key areas of administration and education. Some originally non-Anglophone European states seem to be approaching such a situation rather quickly. In Denmark, for instance, in 2006 the parliamentary group of the *Radikale Venstre* (Progressive Liberals) produced a strategy paper on how to tackle globalization which included the recommendation to declare English the second official language of the country.[44]

A scenario of this kind raises the prospect a thoroughgoing Europeanization of diglossia. As already outlined (cf. Chapter 4, Section 4.4), in many cases the concept of diglossia makes an important contribution to understanding conflicts at the level of language policy. Among members of language groups who feel that they are not receiving due recognition, diglossia inspires feelings of resentment, which in turn fuel political mobilizations. The dominance of *European English* in all key areas of elevated everyday communication would lead to formerly strongly institutionalized official languages finding themselves in a situation not unlike that of

---

[44] *Neue Zürcher Zeitung*, 24 August 2006 ('Der globalisierte Däne' ['The globalized Dane'].

minority languages and *patois* in nation-states. They would be used in the family, among friends and acquaintances and in everyday local interactions, but more and more rarely in universities, in prestigious professional fields or in high politics. It would be astounding if such a development were not to lead to conflicts. Thus, the aforementioned proposal to assign English an official status in Denmark gave immediately rise to massive concerns about the disappearing of Danish from the public space. And indeed: Why should Europeans behave completely differently from those Quebeckers who, in spite of being perfectly fluent in English and notwithstanding the overwhelming communication potential of English in North America, insist on securing a prominent place for French in all functionally important social contexts of communication in their province? Against this it might be objected, not without justification, that English in the EU, in contrast with Canada, is not an essential component of a historically charged relation between a majority and a minority. But whereas it is true that an equivalent of the traditional Anglophone dominance is absent in the European case, it cannot be ruled out that the representatives of those cultural segments who are associated with the hegemony of *European English* would ultimately become the focus of resentment on account of language policy.[45]

If the objections outlined are correct, it remains to inquire what alternative strategies to *English only* are available as the basis for the communicative integration of a European citizenry. Harmonizing communicative efficiency with the postulate that cultural diversity should be politically recognized must seem a hopeless undertaking in light of the arguments presented thus far. However, the EU is well known for consistently coming up with ingenious compromises through protracted negotiations. From this perspective, an effective approach to the language question might be a 'piecemeal' one which opened it up to compromises. This requires, on the one hand, specifying a comprehensive framework for a solution and, on the other hand, seeking the most flexible answers possible to the language question within this framework.

Converging multilingualism may represent a viable framework for the EU's language policy. By 'converging multilingualism' I mean a model which, in creating shared contexts of communication, attempts to find a necessarily precarious balance between pragmatism and respect for diversity. In view of the continuing importance of those layers of political identity which are intimately bound up with particular cultural and linguistic life-worlds, the EU has at present no alternative to showing its

---

[45] Fishman (1998) expresses scepticism concerning the prospects of long-term political acceptance of *global English* for analogous reasons.

citizens a high level of multilingual sensitivity. In the long run, a European language curriculum must be devised which is designed to break down barriers to understanding by creating overlapping communicative repertoires. Expectations concerning the anchoring or anchorability of multilingual competences in civil society will have to be less maximalist than in the domain of institutions. Hence, it would be foolish to demonize English and its potential as a lingua franca in Europe. At the same time, however, it would be misleading to regard the continental variant of *global English* a priori as expressing the shared will of the community of European peoples on questions of language policy.

Accordingly, the 'canonical' European repertoire of languages should include English without reservation, but it should also cover other languages wherever possible. To expect the EU to play Don Quixote tilting at the windmills of *global English* doesn't make much sense. On the other hand, the systematic promotion of English as a lingua franca by the European institutions would be like giving Microsoft a public subvention to develop software. Hence, the Union should set itself the goal of promoting a multilingualism which – while certainly more selective than the good-will approach of the LINGUA programme – goes beyond English. The combination of languages to be promoted would ultimately depend on socio-cultural contextual factors. These factors would include, for instance, the specific regulatory needs of multilingual states. Of particular importance, in my view, is the *political* component of the systematic attempt to promote multilingualism on a European scale. According to this, an essential motive for spreading foreign languages must be to foster the kind of intercultural ethos Wilhelm von Humboldt had in mind when he made a connection between learning a new language and 'gaining a new standpoint in how we view the world' (cf. Chapter 4, Section 4.1). From this angle, foreign language instruction should be considered an important element of political education in Europe. The development of the EU into a polity constituted in such a way that it allows for innovative responses to identity conflicts calls for nothing more than the generalization of intercultural competence. Intercultural competence will also help the Union to win the respect at the global level which is garnered by those who have learnt to respect others.

Moreover, a converging multilingualism based on varying sets of two to three languages offers the prospect of alleviating the problem of diglossia through a functional and regional diversification of European publics. Taking its orientation from the subsidiarity principle, the European political map could be divided into clusters of countries, regions and groups with linguistic-cultural affinities. For example, in the EU25 one could envisage the emergence of a Latin, a Scandinavian, a Teutonic and an

Atlantic network.[46] Within the various clusters, existing communicative proximity would in many cases make it possible to take advantage of a passive bilingualism in which A and B mutually understand each other even though each employs a different language. As regards the pragmatic side, we should not underestimate the communicative efficiency of multilingual systems built on this kind of logic. Thus, Colomer (1996: 134–6) uses probabilistic models to demonstrate that in a domain in which four languages are spoken and each individual is bilingual, the probability that two randomly chosen individuals with different mother tongues can communicate in a shared language is 78 percent. In a domain with 10 languages, the 'communicative probability' is 89 percent, provided that all individuals speak three languages (including their mother tongue). Such calculations show that inner-European communication potentials could be sharply increased through greater coordination of the foreign languages curriculum. The EU cannot square the language circle. However, defusing identity conflicts based on language should prove to be a manageable task through a combination of multilingualism and recognition in the structuring of European politics. Let us keep in mind here that a politically appropriate representation of diversity will not necessarily have to imply a mirror representation of diversity (cf. Chapter 5, Section 5.4).

One point should be re-emphasized to close this chapter. The first and fundamental step towards clarifying the problem of communication in the multinational European community must be to thematize the language question openly at the level of *politics*. The hitherto prevailing strategy of EU institutions, in general, and of the Commission, in particular, of not putting the question on the agenda in an attempt to avoid conflicts means that the domain of political culture is in danger of succumbing to the logic of negative integration. Barriers to communication in transnational space are indeed being torn down; but because the overarching institutional regulatory framework remains diffuse, the market – in the present case, the language market – ultimately replaces politics. However, market mechanisms alone are unlikely to foster a collective European identity that is more than the sum of purely instrumental calculations. As Jürgen Habermas observes, the '*systemic* dynamic' driving the Economic and Monetary Union 'by itself would not be enough to allow a form of mutual, transnational trust to emerge behind the back, so to speak, of the *cultural* substrate'.[47] This points to a problem to which European language

---

[46] In the case of the Nordic countries, such a network has long since acquired a stable institutional profile in the shape of the Nordic Council (cf. Berg 1988).

[47] Habermas (2001: 102, emphasis in original).

policy must not shut its eyes. Ultimately, the political constitutionaliza-tion of Europe as a multinational union must involve preventing precisely such 'behind the back' effects. In view of the obvious reluctance among EU leaders to confront the language issue seriously, it is difficult to avoid the impression that the powers that be in Brussels expect that the neces-sary impulses for the construction of a communicatively integrated civil society will arise 'spontaneously' and ultimately elevate *European English* into a comfortable and politically unchallenged monopoly position. The argument developed here should make clear that the expectation of a more or less 'spontaneous', market-based solution to the language prob-lem[48] rests on questionable assumptions. Language is a major European political issue and it should be treated as such. *Which* specific commu-nication rules hold within European civil society may ultimately be less important than *how* these rules are formulated and implemented. Noth-ing would be more regrettable than to deny the citizens and peoples of Europe the opportunity to participate actively in politically shaping the transnational communicative space in which their concerns are supposed to find expression.

---

[48] This expectation also occasionally shines through dimly in discussions of the language issue by social scientists (see, for example, Laitin 1997 or de Swaan 2001).

Recognition, self-determination and
     integration in a union of diversity

The line of argument developed in the previous chapters sought to demonstrate the central importance of the language question for the construction of a legitimate political order in Europe. In the course of the development of modern European democracies, language emerged as a crucial link between the cultural and political identities of citizens. Nowhere in Europe does membership in linguistic groups reflect a 'primordial' natural condition; it is rather the result of politics and of complex processes of social institutionalization. As an expression of cultural diversity, the phenomenon of European multilingualism must be accorded huge political importance in addition to its linguistic and anthropological significance. Hence, linguistic differentiation is a striking feature of political culture in the European Union (EU) and consequently also deserves close attention in debates over the future of integration. No European constitutional project can be successfully politically anchored without integrating into its normative architecture the socio-cultural resources on which a transnational order must be founded.

A key aspect of the argument presented here is the warning against allowing the 'inevitable' instrumentalism of market integration to spill over into the domain of political culture. The identity of a European civil society must take account of the diversity of cultural patterns of identification that centrally shape the self-understanding of the various political communities discernable within the EU. This normative task can be deduced from the essential European treaty texts. It is, at the same time, a de facto political imperative, for the project of integration will not be able to assume a durable form if it does not do justice to claims to distinctiveness within the European multinational constellation. To bring system integration and social integration at the transnational level into a balance, though necessarily a precarious one, is one of the greatest challenges currently facing European politics.[1] The EU has a duty to

---

[1] Here I am drawing on the classical distinction introduced by Lockwood (1964). Other well-known conceptual pairs in contemporary social theory, such as 'options' and

protect the diversity of cultures. To achieve this in the context of creating a unified institutional framework for regulating the economic and political domains is a strikingly novel historical task. The issue of language shows that it is, in addition, a very difficult and potentially conflictual task. In what follows, I will examine two perspectives designed to meet this challenge in a constructive manner. First, I will assess the potential of the principle of subsidiarity for a politics of recognition in Europe. Then, I will turn to the question of what consequences the development of a transnational political space has for the concept of democratic self-determination. In conclusion, I will argue that a reflexive 'processing' of diversity in the context of building Europe requires tackling the politics of language in the Union with the language of politics.

7.1   Recognition and Subsidiarity

In the course of its development, the European polity has increasingly assumed the shape of a polycentric multinational community. This community lacks a hegemonic power that could integrate it territorially. Similarly, the process of supranational integration has deeply transformed the sovereign character of the member states of the Union. In a significant number of institutional fields, go-it-alone policies by nation-states have become impossible due to the growing Europeanization of decision-making. The dynamic of Europeanization is also loosening the traditional bond between cultural and political identities which is a characteristic feature of sovereign statehood. Whereas the nation-states increasingly refrain from interpreting old prerogatives in the institutionalization of collective identity in a rigid manner, the EU is not seeking to acquire new prerogatives. Hence, the Union can indeed be regarded as a postsovereign order that makes a clear break with the model of nation-state rule. It not only refrains from exercising power of cultural definition but it is also disposed to respect plurality of politically relevant cultural memberships within its sphere of influence.[2] With the process of integration, a politics of recognition on a European scale has also undergone an often more than merely implicit normative enhancement. However, mutual cultural recognition also gets embroiled in striking contradictions within the institutional framework of the EU. On the one hand, the practice of recognition is consistently distorted by its fixation on pre-established nation-state

'ligatures' in Dahrendorf (1979) or 'system' and 'life-world' in Habermas (1981), operate with a similar contrast.
[2] For a stimulating proposal on how to conceive of the EU as a postsovereign political community, see MacCormick (1999: 123–36).

identities. Subnational, transnational and intercultural or 'hybrid' patterns of membership have a clearly subordinate status in the mix of official European identity strategies. The 'thin' nationalism that is inscribed in the structures of the EU often turns the articulation of cultural identity into an instrument for the pursuit of national interests by the member states. On the other hand, the dominance of nation-state discourses of legitimation in the intergovernmental negotiation system makes it impossible to reach decisions when it comes to defining common ground in dealing with the challenges of diversity. Language policy provides a good example of such blockages. The field of de facto regulatory power is surrendered to the market by trends that favour the depoliticization of the problem of European identity at the institutional level.

What course should a politics of recognition pursue in order to avoid the contradictions described? Here it is a question of showing due political regard to the diversity of cultures while reflecting universally valid principles of equality, such as those contained in the 'Charter of Rights of the European Union', for example, and bringing them to bear in the formation of transnational institutions. In pursuing this endeavour, neither should diversity be reduced to the particular identities of homogeneous nation-states nor should it be abandoned to 'benign neglect' in the name of an abstract cosmopolitan identity. The principle of subsidiarity potentially offers a point of reference for the institutional anchoring of a corresponding politics of recognition in the EU.

It may seem surprising that I should fall back on the principle of subsidiarity at this point. Very few concepts have been subjected to such an extent to a purely tactical use in recent years as the concept of subsidiarity. After the concept found its way into the text of the Maastricht Treaty, it initially acquired an almost magical attractive power throughout Europe at the beginning of the 1990s. The expectation was frequently voiced that subsidiarity would make the European institutions capable of reacting to the multiplicity of identities and the divergences of interests in transnational politics in a flexible manner. However, from the beginning the concept lacked a more precise substantive meaning. First, the Maastricht debates exhibited two very different basic positions on the use of the concept of subsidiarity in the political context of the EU (Voigt 1996: 279). On the one hand, some member states, in particular the United Kingdom, saw the contractual emphasis on the principle of subsidiarity as a guarantee for the preservation of nation-state sovereignty rights over the European level of decision-making. On the other hand, federal states, such as Germany and Belgium, as well as regions with a strong institutional profile, such as Catalonia, understood subsidiarity as a mechanism that should counteract centralizing tendencies at all territorial political levels. Ultimately, the concept formed the basis of a typical intergovernmental compromise formula. In the negotiations which led to the Treaty on European Union, it gave expression to a vague minimal consensus to take account of the different degrees to which the individual member states favoured integration in the context of the political unification of Europe.[3] Following Maastricht, subsidiarity also appeared to some European governments as in fact a useful guiding principle for proceeding with the European process of unification on the basis of a differentiated dynamic of integration.

In the meantime, the initially abrupt revival of the venerable concept of subsidiarity on the European political scene has clearly petered out. The appropriation of the concept by the EU must be seen in hindsight as an evasive tactical manoeuvre designed to circumvent irresoluble conflicts concerning the division of competences between Brussels and the member states and the 'finality' of the process of European unification. This in fact already provided the background for prompt obituaries to subsidiarity (Freiburghaus 1997). The concept seems to have lost a good deal of the attractiveness which it had during the period of ferment following Maastricht. Its sudden popularity now seems almost like a trivial anecdote of European politics. Why, then, should it be worthwhile drawing a connection between recognition and the principle of subsidiarity?

In my view, on one specific reading at least, subsidiarity remains important for founding a European political discourse. It is relevant above all if one is not willing to regard the sovereign territorial state as the only legitimate form of political community (MacCormick 1999: 156). For, notwithstanding its often-arbitrary use in the European debate, the principle of subsidiarity can be understood as a major rival to the idea of an indivisible sovereignty in modern political thought, though one which for the most part has led a shadowy existence. Subsidiarity is doubtlessly a shifting concept that has widely ramified roots in the history of ideas. One strand of tradition leads back to the medieval scholasticism of Thomas Aquinas. This strand was later taken up by Catholic social teaching in the industrial age. The concordance doctrine formulated by the Calvinistically influenced Johannes Althusius at the beginning of the seventeenth century must count as a second major source for the development of the concept of subsidiarity. A third major influence, albeit often implicit, on the principle of subsidiarity were liberal conceptions of the autonomy of civil society in relation to state institutions. As is well known, such notions

---

[3] For different interpretations of subsidiarity in the context of Maastricht, see the contributions of Cass (1992), Cox (1994) and van Kersbergen and Verbeek (1994).

played a particularly prominent role in the genesis of the Anglo-Saxon democracies.[4]

In the early modern period, city-states and city leagues attested to the existence of institutional alternatives to the sovereign territorial state in Europe (Spruyt 1994, Tilly 1990). These alternatives were not able to prevail in the course of the historically contingent process of political modernization. However, residues of the model of order they embodied continued to exercise influence where spheres of government were divided up functionally and territorially in accordance with criteria of subsidiarity during the formation of the modern state. Within the network of European cities which stretched from the German Hanseatic League to the contemporary Benelux region and from Northern Italy to Catalonia, attempts to impose the hegemony of a single ruling centre on a clearly defined sovereign territory, which marked the age of absolutism, met with massive resistance. It is not a coincidence that federalism traditionally played a prominent role in the Europe of city-states.

In culturally differentiated communities, in particular, a division of competences in accordance with the idea of subsidiarity was motivated by the goal of combining the preservation of group-specific patterns of identity with the duty of the state to foster group-transcending solidarity. According to the principle of subsidiarity, the legitimacy of the state should be recognized. At the same time, however, state competences must be restricted in favour of substate and non-state institutions. On the one hand, the superordinate political unit has the duty to provide aid, where necessary; on the other hand, the smaller, subordinate units are assigned a key role within a hierarchy of political communities when jurisdictions are defined (Höffe 2002: 129, 131). As democratization progressed, it seemed impermissible in contexts of pronounced cultural heterogeneity to ignore the concerns of significant structural minorities and to legitimate democratic decisions primarily as the deliverance of the majority will. The result was the functional diversification and decentralization of political decision-making especially in 'consociational' democracies (cf. Chapter 3, Section 3.4), with the application of the majority rule remaining restricted in general to the smaller and more homogeneous communities within the state federation. Thus, a relation of tension existed between the principle of subsidiarity and the concept of sovereignty not only in the history of ideas but also in political reality. In unitary nation-states, the undivided decision-making power of the demos

---

[4] For an account of the various sources of the idea of subsidiarity from the perspective of the history of ideas, see Waschkuhn (1995); for a concise overview of the concept's multiple normative meanings, see Føllesdal (1998).

understood in majoritarian terms was concentrated at the centre. Culturally segmented societies, by contrast, often divided political power on the
federal model or bound the social groups as comprehensively as possible
into institutional decision-making processes governed by the imperative
of consensus (Ebbinghaus and Kraus 1997: 339–44).

In view of the major importance attached to socio-cultural differentiation in the construction of the European institutional order, the political
potential of the principle of subsidiarity for the EU should be obvious.
In this connection, one of the reasons why the concept of subsidiarity
could achieve such popularity in European political discourse – namely,
its ambiguity – may even prove to some extent to be an advantage. As
I have emphasized, on the continental European understanding of subsidiarity, it is essentially a principle governing how institutions should
be structured, one which seeks to divide political responsibilities in a
heterogeneous community in a context-sensitive manner. Heterogeneity
can be more or less salient and can overlap to a greater or lesser extent
with territorially circumscribed units. This open and flexible character of
subsidiarity is what allows jurisdictions to be differentiated according to
different criteria and 'to treat different things differently'.

Hence, one can see subsidiarity as a mechanism for regulating differentiated integration within a shared political domain. 'Differentiated
integration' has become a grab-bag category in the European debate for
strategies of integration that seek a modus vivendi with the various modes
of articulation of heterogeneity in the Union without permanently under-
mining its capacity for institutional action.[5] In all probability, the sharp
increase in heterogeneity due to the eastern enlargement of the EU will
lead, at least temporarily, to an increasingly steep gradient among levels
of integration in Europe. However, quite apart from its use as a formula
that is supposed to facilitate a precarious balance between the challenges
posed by the enlargement and deepening of the Union, the category of
differentiated integration can also be invoked to show due regard for the
criterion of recognition of diversity in institutional domains that are especially relevant for the reproduction of cultural identity.

If one views it as a principle of territorial order that links cultural heterogeneity with differentiated forms of political integration, subsidiarity
provides the basis for an asymmetrical federalism. In practice, all federal
systems exhibit some elements of asymmetry. It is generally fuelled by
the patterns of diversity discernable in the relations between the member
states and the federation, as well as in the relations among the component

---

[5] On this understanding, the category encompasses such terms as a 'variable geometry',
'concentric circles', 'Europe à la carte', 'core Europe', etc.; see Stubb (1996).

states themselves. The differences among the various forms of political interrelations do not necessarily have to be laid down by the constitution. On the other hand, asymmetrical modes of federalism that are explicitly prescribed by the constitution seem to be particularly relevant in multinational contexts in which it is important to be able to regulate the forms and degrees of integration in accordance with the specific policy field in question.[6] Their potential for a politics of recognition of the diversity of cultural identities within the framework of a common Union citizenship is obvious. In this context, one should be wary of restricting legitimate forms of subsidiary asymmetry to the level of member states. A brief consideration of the status of regions in the EU should help to clarify this argument.

The establishment of the Committee of the Regions is widely regarded as one of the main results of the application of the principle of subsidiarity within the European institutions. The Committee provided the 'third level' of the EU with an official representative organ. Granted, the Committee is a politically weak body with purely consultative functions. Thus, the most important point of access for the articulation of regional interests within the EU is in fact structural policy. Through the structural funds for overcoming geographical disparities, considerable financial resources are transferred from Brussels to regional and local organizations. With its structural programmes, the Commission has created institutional incentives throughout the EU for regional self-organization specifically designed to take maximum advantage of subventions. However, self-organization at the regional level often merely leads to the creation of administrative façades located below the level of the central state. Hence, the political spectrum which the 'Europe of the Regions' encompasses extends from semi-sovereign subnational units to regional authorities conceived on the drawing boards of central state bureaucracies and lacking independent political powers to any significant extent. The institutional impulses for constructing regional organizational channels emanating from the EU did not take account of this heterogeneity. Yet, the example of structural policy shows that the influence of the regions on the launching and the implementation of development plans is especially pronounced when, as in Germany and Spain, the subnational actors already possess a significant degree of institutional autonomy from the central government. In countries, such as France, in which the territorial division of powers is only weakly developed, by contrast, the centralized state remains the authority which sets the tone in decisions over the

---

[6] On this, see Requejo (1999: 269–71), who adopts the concept of federal asymmetry from Tarlton (1965) and extends it to multinational political structures.

specific contents of structural policies (Marks 1996). From the perspective of subnational units with legislative competences, the application of the principle of subsidiarity in the Committe of the Regions does not do justice to the complexity of the cultural and territorial patterns of diversity within the EU (Requejo 2001: 130). In fact, the residual character of the Committee is a symptom of the failure to achieve a uniform, context-independent standard model of regional representation in the Union.

To repeat, the advantage of the principle of subsidiarity over rigid federal models of order for intermeshing cultural and political identities in Europe is its openness. With the help of this principle, cultural diversity in the EU could be institutionalized in different degrees and with different implications on different political levels. The rigid coupling of the legitimation of political authority with uniform patterns of collective belonging, which is characteristic of the process of European nation-state formation, would in this way be loosened. This not only concerns the postulate underlying, for example, the European Charter of Regional or Minority Languages that cultural identities beneath the level of the nation-state should also be recognized. As explained earlier (cf. Chapter 5, Section 5.4), the transnational hinge function of particular European languages could serve as a selection criterion in reforming the institutional language regime of the EU. By a similar logic, cross-border linguistic-cultural clusters could form in the process of constructing public spaces of communication in the EU, on the model of converging multilingualism (cf. Chapter 6, Section 6.6). An understanding of democratic integration inspired by the idea of subsidiarity in a way which is appropriate to the times recognizes the value and the political relevance of cultural diversity without qualification. It accords particular consideration to territoriality and the historical continuity of collective membership, without however wishing to freeze or 'essentialize' the corresponding patterns of identity. Thus, it is worth recalling in this context that the available political mechanisms for realizing notions of subsidiarity in social domains of key significance for the recognition of cultural identities – for example, education, schools and the media – are by no means restricted to the division of competences in accordance with the territorial principle. Linguistic-cultural diversity can also be protected based on functional group autonomy.[7]

---

[7] On this, see, for example, Otto Bauer's (1924 [1907]) proposals for regulating the problem of nationalities in the territories of the Habsburg Empire, which were not put into practice in the Austro-Hungarian polity but are still revived to this day in other multinational contexts.

Finally, we should draw attention to a factor that seems essential for an adequate understanding of the interplay between subsidiarity and recognition in a European multinational community. Subsidiarity does not aim at the mutual exclusion or insulation of groups. It establishes a relation between the right to the preservation and promotion of cultural distinctiveness and the definition of a group-transcending common good. The protection of 'sovereignty in one's own circle' entails an obligation to give a fair hearing to the concerns of others – *audi alteram partem* – and to respect the overarching institutional framework of an open intercultural dialogue. Subsidiarity is not a mechanism of cultural segregation but, rather, a *mode of integration*. Distributing political competences to protect plurality is supposed to make it easier for groups who are taking part in the construction of a multilevel order to demonstrate mutual loyalty.[8] In the first place, recognition on the interpretation of the principle of subsidiarity proposed here presupposes the readiness to take a reflexive attitude towards one's own identity. On the other hand, mutual loyalty implies that the moral resource of solidarity can be activated in a group-transcending manner, whether in the form of 'federal loyalty' (*Bundestreue*) or in the form of voluntary obligations that materialize in social policy programs. Hence, the relative weakness of structures for developing broad-based processes of transnational political communication in the EU, due to its negative impact on the horizontal integration of a European civil society, is closely related to the problematic of subsidiarity.

7.2   Self-Determination

As a mechanism for diversifying institutional power and for 'parcelling' domains of sovereignty, subsidiarity in the EU should counteract possible political alienation effects in local contexts due to a Europeanization of governance that is necessarily uncoupled from particular realms of social interaction. However, as we have seen, subsidiarity not only serves the purpose of guaranteeing high levels of political and administrative decentralization. The principle also implies an overarching level of political integration. Regardless of how comprehensive it may be, the decentralization of decision-making competences does not render the creation of an overarching framework for legitimating European policy superfluous. Accordingly, things that are decided collectively continue to require collective representation and interpretation. The attempt to circumvent the problematic of political communication as well as the associated questions of a European language regime and the recognition of linguistic

---

[8] Compare Bellamy (1999: 203–9); for similar arguments, see Frankenberg (2001: 534–8).

identities, by dividing them in accordance with criteria of subsidiarity, no longer works in cases where European law annuls local legal norms or if the Commission is supposed to foster a European 'common good' over the member states. In such a context, the ultimate normative point of reference for justifying the outcomes of European decision-making remains the European citizenry as a whole. Thus, the question of the foundations of a European civil society leads back to the demos problematic and the paradox of sovereignty (cf. Chapter 2, Section 2.4). Here it is not at all a question of projecting collective patterns of membership in a rigid manner onto the reified identities of nation-states following in a 'Westphalian' vein. However, in light of all that we know about the intimate interrelation between politics and culture in modern societies, it would be equally dubious to postulate that a European civil society could be bound together solely by reinforcing the political institutions of the EU in the spirit of a cosmopolitan voluntarism. Given this background, what are the prospects of a political integration of Europe that could satisfy democratic standards?

Modern democracies rest on the connection between the concepts of self-government and popular sovereignty. The democratic exercise of political authority implies in essence that the sovereign people rules itself. Self-government presupposes, in turn, that the collective 'self' which serves as a source of legitimation for the institutional decision processes exhibits a politically sustainable identity as the foundation of democracy. However, according to Rousseau's paradox, the democratic collective subject cannot itself be constituted in a democratic manner. The determination of the 'self' which exercises its right to political self-determination occurs prior to the 'hour zero' of democracy in a context external to democracy itself.[9] In the ideal-typical model of the development of modern nation-states, the identity of citizens who make the transition to self-government found a prior fixed anchoring point inself the existing structures of statehood. But the political integration of Europe differs importantly from the processes of nation-state formation by the fact that it must dispense with a 'strong' attribution of identity in the sense of a fusion of political and cultural patterns of affiliation. Hence, as a modality of political membership, European identity is highly self-reflexive.

---

[9] See also Jennings (1956: 56), for whom the paradox of sovereignty became a quite concrete practical challenge in view of the difficulties of providing the new states which arose during the decolonization following the Second World War with maximally legitimate borders. He expressed this challenge in the succinct formula: 'the people cannot decide until somebody decides who are the people'.

This reflexivity is connected, in the first place, with the institutional profile of the Union, though sometimes in contradictory ways. Building blocks of European 'belonging' such as EU citizenship have a derivative character resulting from the fact that each individual belongs to a member state. Hence, the EU does certainly not place the significance of nation-state identities in question. On the other hand, precisely the 'derivative' and 'constructed' character of EU citizenship underscores the fact that the European citizen status is a status of members of a multinational community. In affirming their 'own' identities, Swedish, French and Polish people, as Europeans, cannot avoid also acknowledging the right to affirm 'other' identities. The political institutionalization of a transnational level of identity thereby creates new conditions for a reflexive approach to 'established' patterns of identity. In the political-cultural web of identities of the EU, the state cultures continue to enjoy a clearly privileged position. The recognition of diversity seems to be correspondingly distorted by a statist bias. However, one must still grant that official efforts to institutionalize cultural diversity within the transnational domain of the EU have achieved an extraordinarily high level, especially when one takes the European nation-state as the historical point of comparison. The political impact of the dynamics of recognition within Europe can be clearly seen from the example of language. Integral multilingualism, which holds de jure in the EU, reflects the reciprocal obligation to respect the cultures of the member states embodied in their national languages. To the extent that such a practice of recognition expresses the 'intrinsic' value of a culture without, for example, first inquiring into the political 'strength' or the communicative 'utility' of its language in the overall constellation of the Union, it is very difficult to draw a clear normative dividing line between the status of state cultures and the status of cultures that must get by the without the support of the state. The successive Europeanization of language rights, which also includes regional and minority linguistic communities, demonstrates that it is hard to prevent a 'spilling over' of recognition beyond the sanctioning of nation-state identities.

In a sense, in this way the EU has taken some, if only hesitant and ultimately implicit, steps in the direction of a 'deep' understanding of diversity. For Charles Taylor (1994: 183), 'deep diversity' in the Canadian context means not only that the federation, as is already the case, recognizes the plurality of cultural memberships in principle as one of its constitutional features. In order to arrive at a second level of institutional regulation of diversity, in Taylor's view it would, in addition, have to recognize that such a plurality entails different forms of political attachment to the federation. For Canadians of Italian origin in Toronto, identification with Canada has a different political significance than for a member of the Cree or for a Quebecker. Whereas the one group embraces the offer of assimilation to a Canadian 'mosaic identity' as a desirable integration option, for the other groups the identities of the 'substate' communities may retain precedence. From Taylor's perspective, diversity means that all involved learn to accept their different degrees of identification with the superordinate federation.

Following a similar line of argumentation, one could say that the integration process within the EU at least presents an opportunity to extend considerably the potential for a reflexive treatment of cultural diversity. 'European identity', in this view, would be the product of attachment to a transnational context that would enable a Belgian of Moroccan descent as well as a Scot or an Italian to regard themselves as political equals in a community that has no wish to level the differences between the specific cultural identifications of its members. Whereas EU citizenship would confer a universal and effective transnational character on central aspects of citizen status, the consolidation of a common European identity would not call for much more than respect for difference and a willingness to tolerate the 'other'.[10] Looking towards Canada also means, of course, not shutting one's eyes to the irreducible moment of tension which cultural diversity entails under democratic conditions. This tension can give rise to severe political challenges. Consequently, a European civil society founded on diversity must not be confused with an illusory multicultural paradise. A reflexive relation to the problem of identity is not a magical tool for generating consent; all it can accomplish is to foster an intercultural willingness to learn. However, this willingness to learn turns out to be at the same time an essential presupposition for the institutional channelling of intercultural conflict.

The discussion of the language question has shown that in culturally differentiated political communities recognition is of primary importance for anchoring the moment of reflexivity in relations between groups. The exercise of political liberty rights is always socially embedded. Multilingual democracies pay tribute to this embedding by recognizing specific linguistic identities. In contrast with earlier historical phases of community formation, the creation of the EU transnational order forces all participants to a greater extent to conceive of the socio-cultural dimensions of political integration as an essential aspect of institutional change. More than ever before, therefore, we in Europe also need models of democratic

---

[10] On the derivation of a normatively ambitious model of transnational citizenship that takes account of the significance of cultural diversity, see Bader (1997); compare also Benhabib (2002).

politics that do not regard individual citizens as abstract and isolated monads, but as actors in a socially constituted field. Political action is not presuppositionless but is tied to prior social achievements. Among the most important of these prior achievements is the communicative competence which is indissolubly linked to the medium of language.

As a social good, language shows how important the implications of membership in a group can be for our development as individuals. The collective bond of language situates us in the social world before we become fully autonomous persons. We are only able to transcend in part the patterns of identity which are transmitted to us by language through free acts of will. In the course of our socialization, we initially have no other choice but to 'accept' a linguistic identity. Without the development of a linguistic faculty that reflects the influence of specific cultural and environmental factors, we would not be able to announce our ability and our desire to assume responsibility. The example of language demonstrates how much our freedom, precisely as political freedom, remains a situated freedom.[11] Freedom in a social context is both a linguistically articulated and a linguistically mediated freedom. A politics of recognition of linguistic identities is oriented to this very aspect of mediation. To this extent, the recognition of linguistic rights always at the same time acknowledges an interconnection between individual possibilities of development and a feature of group membership. If a specific element of belonging to a group constitutes a relevant aspect of my identity as a person and the corresponding group suffers injustice or is subject to status disadvantages, then my individual self-respect and self-esteem also suffer.[12] Hence, depending on the specific multilingual situation, only a politics of recognition will often create the necessary preconditions for the emergence of comparable spaces of freedom across the boundaries of language communities. If it is to approach an 'ever-closer union' of its peoples, Europe must develop a political ethos founded on intercultural empathy in which respect for linguistic diversity plays an important role. If the Union is to be capable of opening up new paths of democratic integration 'united in diversity' without being torn apart as a political community by identity conflicts, a high level of intercultural competence must exist in European civil society.

---

[11] On the concept of a situated, socially 'framed' freedom that can only be experienced intersubjectively, see Merleau-Ponty (1966: 493–520). I am indebted to James Tully for this reference to Merleau-Ponty's classical contribution to a contextual theory of freedom.

[12] On the importance of self-respect and self-esteem in the structure of social relations of recognition, see Honneth (1994).

The politics of recognition ultimately expresses the fact that the citizens themselves should not be regarded as a 'given', exogenous factor even in democratic processes. Rather, 'citizenization'[13] and its institutional regulation are elementary features of democratic politics. Against this background, the concept of self-determination can also be extended in a way that makes the principle particularly interesting for delimiting the problem of European integration. As I have argued, recognition is an important presupposition for a reflexive treatment of identity that includes other identities. Viewed in this light, recognition turns out to be a resource for self-determination in a quite literal sense. Here recognition need not imply the institutional determination of a specific set of identity patterns, as in the case of nation-states and certain variants of the consociational model. On the contrary, viewed from the perspective defended here, recognition is not a mechanism for institutionalizing a static politics of 'being'; rather, recognition should serve as a guide for forming a reflexively grounded politics of 'becoming'. The reflexivity at which recognition aims also facilitates 'identity work' and change of identity.[14] Hence, democratic self-determination can be interpreted on the basis of recognition as a dynamic circuit in which the identity of the collective 'self' which functions as the demos becomes an object of democratic politics: the collective 'self' transpires as the first and highest political decision-making authority; the exercise of this very decision-making authority, however, also allows that the 'self' can transform itself. Democracy and the demos emerge in tandem.[15]

From such a perspective, therefore, one can view recognition under contemporary conditions of cultural diversity ultimately as a factor that produces the 'Münchhausen effect' through which a democratic collective subject can be constituted in a legitimate manner notwithstanding the paradox of sovereignty. In the stories recorded by Bürger (1997 [1788]: 35–6), the Baron von Münchhausen relates the following occurrence:

Another time I wanted to set myself over a swamp that did not seem so wide at first sight as I found it to be once I had taken my leap. Hence as I hovered in the air I turned back in the direction I had come to take a longer run at it. Alas my second leap was still too short and I fell not far from the edge up to my neck into the swamp. I would have unfailingly drowned had the strength of my own arm

---

[13] Here I am adopting a concept of Tully (2001: 25).
[14] Honneth (2003) highlights the normative status of the concept of recognition for the foundation for an emancipatory understanding of politics.
[15] On this 'tandem', see the reflections in Cederman and Kraus (2005: 285–93).

not sufficed to pull me out again by my own hair along with my horse which I clasped tightly between my knees.[16]

If one applies this story to the situation in the EU, it is tempting to see the morass as the problem of democracy in which the project of erecting a legitimate transnational order is in danger of sinking. The 'strong arm' which would lend support to Europe as a political community is, I am tempted to say, the strong arm of recognition. A constitution for Europe would have to satisfy the requirements of a new kind of multinational community. The moment of cultural diversity so thoroughly pervades this community that the foundations for the production of political unity can indeed appear precarious at times. But in this the EU merely exhibits in a particularly immediate way a problem that was traditionally 'solved' – in the context of the emergence of modern statehood – by the 'course of history' as determined by the facticity of political power relations. Europe as a multiform and differentiated political order will have to live with a diffuse, heterogeneous and processual demos. Today political self-determination in Europe can no longer mean 'self-fixation'. Consequently, the dilemmas of European identity politics which I have dealt with in detail here can hardly be conjured out of existence by the mechanisms of constitutional engineering, however ingenious. In such a constellation, the threat that questions of identity can arise constantly hovers over everyday political decision-making processes for resolving conflicts of interest. The authority of a superordinate collective 'self' to define the common good in multinational democracies is often secured only through long drawn-out negotiations. Due to the plurality of sources of legitimation, conflicts of interest can flare up into identity conflicts that affect the foundations of the political community itself.

If the Union is to develop in the long run into something more than an intergovernmental forum for harmonizing market regulations and domesticating nation-state power politics, it will have to seek institutional models that are adequate to the European multinational constellation in all of its manifestations. In this, it can take heart from the fact that it is a polity composed of established democracies. Crises in the 'communal foundations' of the EU would, as a consequence, not necessarily be synonymous with a crisis of European democracy. In addition, Europe as a

---

[16] 'Ein andres Mal wollte ich über einen Morast setzen, der mir anfänglich nicht so breit vorkam, als ich ihn fand, da ich mitten im Sprunge war. Schwebend in der Luft wendete ich daher wieder um, wo ich hergekommen war, um einen größeren Anlauf zu nehmen. Gleichwohl sprang ich auch zum zweiten Male noch zu kurz und fiel nicht weit vom andern Ufer bis an den Hals in den Morast. Hier hätte ich unfehlbar umkommen müssen, wenn nicht die Stärke meines eigenen Armes mich an meinem eigenen Haarzopfe, samt dem Pferde, welches ich fest zwischen meine Knie schloß, wieder herausgezogen hätte.'

political project will acquire greater normative drawing power only when the Union succeeds in communicating in a convincing manner that it is especially concerned to make the imperatives of system integration at the transnational level compatible with preserving the diversity of cultures, languages and forms of life. The promise of linking equality in an overarching civil society with respect for plurality and protection of the particular is a normatively demanding project. If the political potential to promote this undertaking exists anywhere, then it exists in Europe. However, the signs of the times do not augur well for the fact that the EU together with its citizens, peoples and states are already on a sure course to fulfil this great normative potential.

7.3   Diversity as a Political Challenge

The route to the EU was initiated with the establishment of the European Economic Community in the 1950s. Up to present times, the Common Market continues to be one of the key aspects shaping the view we as Europeans have of Europe. The functional primacy granted to market integration in the process of building Europe may have contributed to fostering a semi-institutional approach towards European identity in which citizens are largely perceived as consumers of political products, and thus 'relieved' of being active participants in the process of polity-building. We may thus indeed speculate to what extent notions of legitimacy that were based upon great technocratic success stories rather than upon the contingent course of the democratic process has been for a long while one of the main characteristics of the politics of European integration (Weiler 2004: 142–3). At any rate, it does not seem too exaggerated to argue that relying on a market-oriented view of integration has offered an easy way to avoid entering a more substantial debate on what it means to be a citizen in a diverse polity. The all but ritualistic insistence on the crucial role diversity is supposed to play in the making of a common transnational space can hardly compensate for the rather limited progress Europe has made in developing a proper language of diversity for articulating its politics.

European institutions are officially committed to making sure that such a language of diversity will not be just subsumed under the language of the market in an unbounded economy. The 'sense of diversity' inherent to the market view would hardly go beyond the perspective of the *United Colors of Benetton* ads which some years ago showed us nice pictures of little children representing different parts of the world, joining in a good-hearted commercial campaign. In contrast with this kind of approach, our exploration of the language issue in the EU has shown that coming to grips with diversity may well involve tough normative dilemmas. The adequate response to the dilemmas, however, can hardly consist in abandoning politics to the effects of the market. Rather, language policy should be considered as a genuine vehicle for articulating diversity in the emerging European polity. Instead of trying to work out a new political grammar for the language of diversity, the EU has thus far opted for holding on to the pledge that emphasizes the crucial importance of respecting linguistic diversity in the process of integration. Notwithstanding its recurrent declarations of good intent, the Union has been reluctant to tackle the language issue by political means. Ultimately, the lack of institutional intervention in the European 'language market' has important political implications.

If building Europe also means constructing a shared civic identity, we cannot refrain from discussing how this identity should be interwoven with diversity and its language, or, rather, its languages. The question bears substantially on the cognitive dimensions of the citizenship status in a transnational polity. If the language question remains subject to strategies of depoliticization, the EU will end up celebrating only a permissive diversity, in which many things may be represented as long as they do not bear political weight. Recognition would thereby become a largely symbolic act, which would not require much effort at perceiving and dealing with difference. In contrast, a more ambitious recognition of the other would require us to develop an empathic perspective for understanding each other in ways that are meaningful and hence involve going through the experience of collective learning. To try to circumvent the difficult decisions that would set the framework for an active and unambiguous European language policy might in the long run entail that diversity is undermined: a commitment to diversity that remains a facile lip service lacking an effective political basis is likely to end up paving the way toward uniformity.

The question ultimately to be addressed in this context is how to achieve 'integration in diversity' in conjunction with forms of a collective experience based upon large-scale horizontal communication and interaction among Union citizens. Such an endeavour may require defining mechanisms that could contribute to generate a dynamic at the European level which, at the surface, might appear to have some similarity with the waves of social mobilization that characterized the high time of nation-state formation on the continent (Deutsch 1966). Nevertheless, there is one crucial difference between former historical periods and the present, namely that such a dynamic nowadays cannot rely on the equally static as rigid identity attributions which lie at the core of many currents of nationalism over the past 200 years.

To the extent that the analysis put forward here is correct, 'grand' constitution-making, whose spectacular failure Europe experienced in 2005, might not be the all-decisive factor when it comes to determining the political future of the Union. An even more important role might be played by a constitutional politics whose focus is on the micro-level of integration and on offering citizens new ground for self-determination. At any rate, a 'constitutional politics' of this kind seems to be needed if a transformation of the permissive consensus into a more reflexive collective involvement in the process of European polity-building is to take place. Such a 'second-order' constitutionalism must be considered as a key for linking the integration of Europe to new forms of citizenship and, thus, for giving the Union a legitimacy basis it will hardly obtain by relying primarily on institutional engineering. As one of the great pioneers of integration studies has argued (Deutsch 1976: 14), historical evidence shows us that a praxis-driven dynamic of collective learning is the decisive element in any process of political integration. Viewed from this angle, a web of socio-cultural relations serves as the proper cement of integration. As long as there is not such a web, the institutions created in the integration process will stand on shaky ground.[17]

Solidifying the structures of a citizens' Europe requires finding an approach towards political integration which offers an equivalent to the processes of mobilization characteristic of the age of nationalism, but which at the same time, to be normatively sound, has to be immune to all quasi-nationalist pretensions. The Union's 'grand' constitutional master plan has not really tackled the question of how to set the bases for large-scale transnational communication in Europe. This, however, is one of the most pressing questions the EU unavoidably faces from the perspective of the 'second-order' constitutionalism that is advocated here.

At closer scrutiny, the initial image of a political community of Europeans united by diversity and in diversity has vanished considerably. To the extent that it remains an abstract and rather vague principle, diversity is doomed to be displaced by the pressures to achieve communicative efficiency and by the functional imperatives of market integration. In the process of building Europe, the order of the day should therefore be to give diversity a more graspable meaning. This will definitely require bringing the issue of diversity into the realm of politics and confronting it by political means. A politics which is eager to embrace the language of diversity will start from the premise that a 'naïve', one-dimensional diversity is hardly a cause which is worth struggling for. It will rather aim

---

[17] For an elaboration of this argument against the background of democratic theory see Kraus (2006: 217–22).

at developing the perspective of a 'complex' diversity, to put it in terms that may sound slightly pleonastic, but nevertheless make sense. An understanding of diversity as the simple addition of different elements may well lead to both a normative and an empirical impasse, as we have seen in the case of the European language regime. The European cause hinges upon the generalization of an intercultural competence that can become politically effective. To attain such a competence, we need rules that help us to reflexively 'process' diversity. This reflexivity does not imply that we construct a mirror replica of diversity. If it is to communicate in a language of diversity, Europe will have to employ more than *one* language. However, if Europe does not want to end up paving the way for uniformity, it will certainly not be enough to stick to the all-too-comforting official litany in which one member state language is simply added to the next.

European polity-building thus faces the task of 'translating' diversity – of bringing its manifold layers into a form that, instead of simply reproducing it, transforms it reflexively. A Europe constituted as a diverse political community must make for an overlapping of public spheres and increase the connectivity of discourses related to a variegated repertoire of identities and interests. At the same time, it has to link transnational will-formation to communicative structures which still offer sufficient leeway for the articulation of linguistic and cultural difference. Put in other words: as European citizens, we may ultimately have to communicate with each other in *one* language; yet we should then communicate in ways that continue to make Europe's other languages audible, too, and contribute to keeping them present. In the end, this could be a politics of language that substantially enhances our understanding of the language of diversity.

References

Aarnio, Eero J., 1995: 'Minority Rights in the Council of Europe: Current Developments', in: Alan Phillips and Allan Rosas, eds., *Universal Minority Rights*, Turku: Åbo Akademis tryckeri, 123–33

Abelès, Marc, and Bellier, Irène, 1996: 'La Commission européenne: du compromis culturel à la culture politique du compromis', in: *Revue Française de Science Politique*, 46 (3), 431–55

Abromeit, Heidrun, 1998: *Democracy in Europe*, New York: Berghahn

Abromeit, Heidrun, 2002: *Wozu braucht man Demokratie? Die postnationale Herausforderung der Demokratietheorie*, Opladen: Leske + Budrich

Acton, Lord John, 1922 [1862]: *The History of Freedom and Other Essays*, London: Macmillan

Allardt, Erik, 1979: *Implications of the Ethnic Revival in Modern, Industrialized Society. A Comparative Study of the Linguistic Minorities in Western Europe*, Helsinki: Societas Scientiarum Fennica (*Commentationes Scientiarum Socialium* 12, 1979)

Amato, Giuliano, and Batt, Judy, 1999: *The Long-Term Implications of EU Enlargement: The Nature of the New Border. Final Report of the Reflection Group*, Florence: Robert Schuman Centre for Advanced Studies

Ammon, Ulrich, 1994: 'The Present Dominance of English in Europe. With an Outlook on Possible Solutions to the European Language Problems', in: *Sociolinguistica*, 8, 1–14

Ammon, Ulrich, 2001a: 'Deutsch als Lingua franca in Europa', in: *Sociolinguistica*, 15, 32–41

Ammon, Ulrich, 2001b: 'Gesetzmäßigkeiten der Standardisierung', in: *Frankfurter Rundschau*, 19 June 2001

Ammon, Ulrich, 2004: 'Sprachenpolitik in Europa – Unter dem vorrangigen Aspekt von Deutsch als Fremdsprache (II)', in: *DaF*, 1, 3–9

Anderson, Benedict, 1991: *Imagined Communities*, London: Verso (revised edition)

Anderson, Benedict, 1992: 'The New World Disorder', in: *New Left Review*, 192, 3–13

Archibugi, Daniele, 1995: 'From the United Nations to Cosmopolitan Democracy', in: Daniele Archibugi and David Held, eds., *Cosmopolitan Democracy*, Cambridge: Polity Press, 121–62

Arel, Dominique, 2001: 'Political Stability in Multinational Democracies: Comparing Language Dynamics in Brussels, Montreal and Barcelona', in: Alain-G. Gagnon and James Tully, eds., *Multinational Democracies*, Cambridge University Press, 65–89

Bader, Veit, 1997: 'The Cultural Conditions of Transnational Citizenship. On the Interpenetration of Political and Ethnic Cultures', in: *Political Theory*, 25, 771–813

Balcells, Albert, 1991: *El nacionalismo catalán*, Madrid: historia 16

Barry, Brian, 2001: *Culture and Equality. An Egalitarian Critique of Multiculturalism*, Cambridge: Polity Press

Bauer, Otto, 1924 [1907]: *Die Nationalitätenfrage und die Sozialdemokratie*, Vienna: Verlag der Wiener Volksbuchhandlung

Beauftragte der Bundesregierung für Ausländerfragen, ed., 2002: *Daten und Fakten zur Ausländersituation*, 20. Auflage, February 2002 [www.bundesauslaenderbeauftragte.de/daten/infos.htm]

Beck, Ulrich 1998: 'Wie wird Demokratie im Zeitalter der Globalisierung möglich? – Eine Einleitung', in: Ulrich Beck, ed., *Politik der Globalisierung*, Frankfurt: Suhrkamp, 7–66

Bellamy, Richard, 1999: *Liberalism and Pluralism. Towards a Politics of Compromise*, London: Routledge

Bellamy, Richard, 2005: 'Which Constitution for What Kind of Europe? Three Models of European Constitutionalism', in: François Cheneval, ed., *Legitimationsgrundlagen der Europäischen Union*, Münster: LIT, 97–112

Benhabib, Seyla, 2002: *The Claims of Culture. Equality and Diversity in the Global Era*, Princeton University Press

Berg, Axel, 1988: *Der Nordische Rat und der Nordische Ministerrat. Organe für die Zusammenarbeit der nordischen Staaten. Eine Darstellung aus rechtlicher Sicht*, Frankfurt: Peter Lang

Berting, Jan, 1997: 'European Social Transformations and European Culture', in: Martin Doornbos and Sudipta Kaviraj, eds., *Dynamics of State Formation. India and Europe Compared*, New Delhi: Sage, 411–37

Billig, Michael, 1995: *Banal Nationalism*, London: Sage

Birnbaum, Pierre, 1998: *La France imaginée*, Paris: Fayard

Blumenwitz, Dieter, 1996: 'Das Recht auf Gebrauch der Minderheitensprache. Gegenwärtiger Stand und Entwicklungstendenzen im europäischen Völkerrecht', in: Karin Bott-Bodenhausen, ed., *Unterdrückte Sprachen: Sprachverbote und das Recht auf Gebrauch der Minderheitensprachen*, Frankfurt: Peter Lang, 159–202

Bobbio, Norberto, 1988: *Die Zukunft der Demokratie*, Berlin: Rotbuch

Böckenförde, Ernst-Wolfgang, 1999: *Staat, Nation, Europa. Studien zur Staatslehre, Verfassungstheorie und Rechtsphilosophie*, Frankfurt: Suhrkamp

Bourdieu, Pierre, 1991: *Language and Symbolic Power*, Cambridge, MA: Harvard University Press

Brubaker, Rogers, and Cooper, Frederick, 2000: 'Beyond ≫identity≪', in: *Theory and Society*, 29, 1–47

Bueno, Jesús, 1999: *Babilonia y Babel: el Parlamento Europeo desde dentro*, Barcelona: Ediciones B

Bürger, Gottfried August, 1997 [1788]: *Wunderbare Reisen des Freiherrn von Münchhausen*, Frankfurt: Insel

Burgess, Michael, 2000: *Federalism and European Union: The Building of Europe, 1950–2000*, London: Routledge

Burke, Peter, 2004: *Languages and Communities in Early Modern Europe*, Cambridge University Press

Callan, Eamonn, 1997: *Creating Citizens. Political Education and Liberal Democracy*, Oxford University Press

Carens, Joseph H., 2000: *Culture, Citizenship and Community. A Contextual Exploration of Justice as Evenhandedness*, Oxford University Press

Casasses, Enric, 2000: 'Pollastre', in: *Avui*, 2 November 2000

Cass, Deborah Z., 1992: 'The Word That Saves Maastricht? The Principle of Subsidiarity and the Division of Powers within the European Community', in: *Common Market Law Review*, 29, 1107–36

Castells, Manuel, 1996: *The Rise of the Network Society*, Oxford: Blackwell

Castells, Manuel, 1997: *The Power of Identity*, Oxford: Blackwell

Castells, Manuel, 1998: *End of Millenium*, Oxford: Blackwell

Castiglione, Dario, 2004: 'Reflections on Europe's Constitutional Future', in: *Constellations*, 11 (3), 393–411

Cederman, Lars-Erik, and Kraus, Peter A., 2005: 'Transnational Communication and the European Demos', in: Robert Latham and Saskia Sassen, eds., *Digital Formations: Information Technology and New Architectures in the Global Realm*, Princeton University Press, 283–311

Cerutti, Furio, and Rudolph, Enno, eds., 2001: *A Soul for Europe. On the Political and Cultural Identity of the Europeans. Vol. 1, A Reader*, Leuven: Peeters

Chadwick, Andrew, and May, Christopher, 2003: 'Interaction between States and Citizens in the Age of the Internet: "e-Government" in the United States, Britain, and the European Union', in: *Governance*, 16, 271–300

Chryssochoou, Dimitris N., 1998: *Democracy in the European Union*, London: Tauris

Colomer, Josep M., 1996: *La utilitat del bilingüisme*, Barcelona: edicions 62

Commission européenne, 2001: *L'Opinion Publique Européenne Face à l'Elargissement de l'U. E., à la Monnaie Unique et au Futur de l'Europe. Présentation de quelques faits marquants* (résultats de l'Eurobaromètre 55, »spécial bureaux de représentation«) Brussels, 2 July 2001

Connolly, William E., 1993: 'Democracy and Territoriality', in: Marjorie Ringrose and Adam J. Lerner, eds., *Reimagining the Nation*, Buckingham: Open University Press, 49–75

Consolidated Version of the Treaty Establishing the European Community (Official Journal of the European Communities, C 325, 24 December 2002)

Coulmas, Florian, 1991a: 'European Integration and the Idea of the National Language. Ideological Roots and Economic Consequences', in: Florian Coulmas, ed., *A Language Policy for the European Community. Prospects and Quandaries*, Berlin: Mouton de Gruyter, 1–43

Coulmas, Florian, 1991b: 'Die Sprachenregelung in den Organen der EG als Teil einer europäischen Sprachenpolitik', in: *Sociolinguistica*, 5, 24–36

Coulmas, Florian, 1992: *Die Wirtschaft mit der Sprache. Eine sprachsoziologische Studie*, Frankfurt: Suhrkamp

Cox, Andrew, 1994: 'Derogation, Subsidiarity and the Single Market', in: *Journal of Common Market Studies*, 32, 127–48

Crouch, Colin, 1999: *Social Change in Western Europe*, Oxford University Press

Crystal, David, 1997: *English as a Global Language*, Cambridge University Press

Crystal, David, 2000: *Language Death*, Cambridge University Press

Dahl, Robert A., 1971: *Polyarchy. Participation and Opposition*, New Haven, CT: Yale University Press

Dahl, Robert A., 1989: *Democracy and Its Critics*, New Haven, CT: Yale University Press

Dahl, Robert A., 1994: 'A Democratic Dilemma: System Effectiveness versus Citizen Participation', in: *Political Science Quarterly*, 109 (1), 23–34

Dahrendorf, Ralf, 1979: *Lebenschancen. Anläufe zur sozialen und politischen Theorie*, Frankfurt: Suhrkamp

de Saussure, Ferdinand, 1972 [1916]: *Cours de linguistique générale*, Paris: Payot

de Swaan, Abram, 1993: 'The Evolving European Language System: A Theory of Communication Potential and Language Competition', in: *International Political Science Review*, 14 (3), 241–55

de Swaan, Abram, 2001: *Words of the World. The Global Language System*, Cambridge: Polity Press

De Witte, Bruno, 1991: 'The Impact of European Community Rules on Linguistic Policies of the Member States', in: Florian Coulmas, ed., *A Language Policy for the European Community. Prospects and Quandaries*, Berlin: Mouton de Gruyter, 163–77

De Witte, Bruno, 1993: 'Cultural Legitimation: Back to the Language Question', in: Soledad García, ed., *European Identity and the Search for Legitimacy*, London: Pinter, 154–71

De Witte, Bruno, ed., 2003: *Ten Reflections on the Constitutional Treaty for Europe*, Florence: Robert Schuman Centre for Advanced Studies

Dedman, Martin J., 1996: *The Origins and Development of the European Union 1945–95. A History of European Integration*, London: Routledge

Delanty, Gerard, 1995: *Inventing Europe. Idea, Identity, Reality*, Houndmills: Macmillan

Delors, Jacques, 2000: 'Europa, el continente de la duda', in: *El País*, 21 September 2000

Deubner, Christian, 2003: 'Differenzierte Integration: Übergangserscheinung oder Strukturmerkmal der künftigen Europäischen Union?', in: *APuZ*, 1–2, 24–32

Deutsch, Karl W., 1966: *Nationalism and Social Communication*, Cambridge, MA: MIT Press

Deutsch, Karl W., 1976: *Die Schweiz als ein paradigmatischer Fall politischer Integration*, Bern: Haupt

Deutsch, Karl W., Burrell, Sidney A., Kann, Robert A., Lee, Jr., Maurice, Lichterman, Martin, Lindgren, Raymond E., Loewenheim, Francis L., and Van Wagenem, Richard W., 1957: *Political Community in the North Atlantic Area*, Princeton University Press

Dewandre, Nicole, and Lenoble, Jacques, eds., 1994: *Projekt Europa. Postnationale Identität: Grundlage für eine europäische Demokratie?*, Berlin: Schelzky & Jeep

DG Press, 2003: 'European Citizens and the Media'. National Reports. Public Opinion in the European Union, Directorate General Press, Brussels, May 2003

Dobson, Lynn, and Follesdal, Andreas, eds., 2004: Political Theory and the European Constitution, London: Routledge

Dumont, Hugues, 1994: 'Die Zuständigkeiten der Europäischen Gemeinschaft auf dem Gebiet der Kultur', in: Nicole Dewandre and Jacques Lenoble, eds, Projekt Europa. Postnationale Identität: Grundlage für eine europäische Demokratie?, Berlin: Schelzky & Jeep, 119–42

Easton, David, 1965: A Systems Analysis of Political Life, New York: Wiley

Ebbinghaus, Bernhard, and Kraus, Peter A., 1997: 'Die variable Geometrie der Subsidiarität: Zur Problematik territorialer und funktionaler Integration in Europa', in: Thomas König, Elmar Rieger and Hermann Schmitt, eds., Europäische Institutionenpolitik, Frankfurt: Campus, 335–57

Eder, Klaus, 1999: 'Integration durch Kultur? Das Paradox der Suche nach einer europäischen Identität', in: Reinhold Viehoff and Rien T. Segers, eds., Kultur. Identität. Europa. Über die Schwierigkeiten und Möglichkeiten einer Konstruktion, Frankfurt: Suhrkamp, 147–79

Eder, Klaus, 2000: 'Zur Transformation nationalstaatlicher Öffentlichkeit in Europa. Von der Sprachgemeinschaft zur issuespezifischen Kommunikationsgemeinschaft', in: Berliner Journal für Soziologie, 2, 167–84

Eder, Klaus, 2004: 'Europäische Öffentlichkeit und multiple Identitäten – das Ende des Volksbegriffs', in: Claudio Franzius and Ulrich K. Preuß, eds., Europäische Öffentlichkeit, Baden-Baden: Nomos, 61–80

Elkins, David J., 1997: 'Globalization, Telecommunication, and Virtual Ethnic Communities', in: International Political Science Review, 18, 139–52

Enzensberger, Hans Magnus, 1992: Büchnerpreis-Rede 1963. Mit einem Essay von Friedrich Diekmann, Hamburg: Europäische Verlagsanstalt

Eriksen, Erik Oddvar, and Fossum, John Erik, 2000: 'Conclusion: Legitimation through Deliberation', in: Erik Oddvar Eriksen and John Erik Fossum, eds., Democracy in the European Union. Integration through deliberation?, London: Routledge, 256–69

Eriksen, Thomas Hylland, 1997: 'In Search of Brussels: Creolization, Insularity and Identity Dilemmas in Post-National Europe', in: J. Peter Burgess, ed., Cultural Politics and Political Culture in Postmodern Europe, Amsterdam: Rodopi, 245–73

Ernst, Andreas, 1998: 'Vielsprachigkeit, Öffentlichkeit und politische Integration: schweizerische Erfahrungen und europäische Perspektiven', in: Schweizerische Zeitschrift für Politische Wissenschaft, 4 (4), 225–40

Eurobarometer 42, 1995

Eurobarometer 50, 1999

Eurobarometer 52, 2000

Eurobarometer 54 Special Report, 2001: Europeans and languages

Eurobarometer 60, 2004

Eurobarometer 62, 2005

Eurobarometer 63, 2005

European Union, 1994: Recommendations to the European Council: Europe and the Global Information Society (Bangemann Report), Brussels

European Union, 1999: *Selected instruments taken from the Treaties. Book I. Volume I*, Luxembourg: Office for Official Publications of the European Communities

Eurydice, 2001: *Foreign Language Teaching in Schools in Europe*, Brussels: Eurydice. The Information Network on Education in Europe

Featherstone, Kevin, 1994: 'Jean Monnet and the "Democratic Deficit" in the European Union', *Journal of Common Market Studies*, 32, 149–70

Ferguson, Charles A., 1959: 'Diglossia', in: *Word*, 15, 325–40

Ferry, Jean-Marc, 1994: 'Die Relevanz des Postnationalen', in: Nicole Dewandre and Jacques Lenoble, eds., *Projekt Europa. Postnationale Identität: Grundlage für eine europäische Demokratie?*, Berlin: Schelzky & Jeep, 30–41

Fischer, Joschka, 2000: 'Vom Staatenverbund zur Föderation: Gedanken über die Finalität der europäischen Integration (Rede in der Humboldt-Universität in Berlin am 12. Mai 2000)', in: Christian Joerges, Yves Mény and J. H. H. Weiler, eds., *What Kind of Constitution for What Kind of Polity? Responses to Joschka Fischer*, Florence: Robert Schuman Centre for Advanced Studies/European University Institute, 5–17

Fishman, Joshua A., 1967: 'Bilingualism with and without Diglossia; Diglossia with and without Bilingualism', in: *Journal of Social Issues*, 23 (2), 29–38

Fishman, Joshua A., 1971: 'The Sociology of Language: An Interdisciplinary Social Science Approach to Language in Society', in: Joshua A. Fishman, ed., *Advances in the Sociology of Language, Vol. I*, The Hague: Mouton, 217–404

Fishman, Joshua A., 1973: *Language and Nationalism*, Rowley, MA: Newbury House

Fishman, Joshua A., 1998: 'The New Linguistic Order', in: *Foreign Policy*, 113 (Winter 1998–1999), 26–40

Flash Eurobarometer, 2002: *Flash Eurobarometer* 135. Internet and the Public at Large. Realised by EOS Gallup Europe upon request of the European Commission (Directorate General Information Society), November 2002

Flash Eurobarometer, 2004: *Flash Eurobarometer* 162. Post European elections 2004 survey

Føllesdal, Andreas, 1998: 'Subsidiarity', in: *Journal of Political Philosophy*, 6, 231–59

Frankenberg, Günter, 2001: 'Die Rückkehr des Vertrages. Überlegungen zur Verfassung der Europäischen Union', in: Lutz Wingert and Klaus Günther, eds., *Die Öffentlichkeit der Vernunft und die Vernunft der Öffentlichkeit. Festschrift für Jürgen Habermas*, Frankfurt: Suhrkamp, 507–38

Fraser, Nancy, and Honneth, Axel, 2003: *Umverteilung oder Anerkennung*, Frankfurt: Suhrkamp

Freiburghaus, Dieter, 1997: 'Subsidiarität – ein Nachruf. Überlegung zur Bedeutung von "Zauberworten" im europäischen politischen Diskurs', in: *Schweizerische Zeitschrift für Politische Wissenschaft*, 3 (3), 197–227

Fukuyama, Francis, 2004: *State-Building. Governance and World Order in the 21st Century*, Ithaca, NY: Cornell University Press

Gagnon, Alain G., ed., 1984: *Quebec. State and Society*, Toronto: Methuen

Galántai, József, 1992: *Trianon and the Protection of Minorities*, Budapest: Corvina

García, Soledad, ed., 1993: *European Identity and the Search for Legitimacy*, London: Pinter

Geertz, Clifford, 1980: *Negara. The Theatre State in Nineteenth-Century Bali*, Princeton University Press

Gehnen, Marianne, 1991: 'Die Arbeitssprachen in der Kommission der Europäischen Gemeinschaften unter besonderer Berücksichtigung des Französischen', in: *Sociolinguistica*, 5, 51–63

Gellner, Ernest, 1983: *Nations and Nationalism*, London: Blackwell

Gellner, Ernest, 1997: *Nationalism*, London: Weidenfeld & Nicolson

Gerhards, Jürgen, 1993: 'Westeuropäische Integration und die Schwierigkeiten der Entstehung einer europäischen Öffentlichkeit', in: *Zeitschrift für Soziologie*, 22, 96–110

Gerhards, Jürgen, 2000: 'Europäisierung von Ökonomie und Politik und die Trägheit der Entstehung einer europäischen Öffentlichkeit', in: Maurizio Bach, ed., *Die Europäisierung nationaler Gesellschaften (Kölner Zeitschrift für Soziologie und Sozialpsychologie, Sonderheft 40)*, 11–35

Giddens, Anthony, 1984: *The Constitution of Society*, Cambridge: Polity Press

Giddens, Anthony, 1985: *The Nation-State and Violence*, Cambridge: Polity Press

Glotz, Peter, 1995: 'Integration und Eigensinn: Kommunikationsraum Europa – eine Chimäre?', in: Lutz Erbring, ed., *Kommunikationsraum Europa*, Konstanz: UVK Medien/Ölschläger, 17–26

Goebl, Hans, 1997: 'Le rappel de l'histoire: le plurilinguisme dans la vieille monarchie habsbourgeoise', in: *Sociolinguistica*, 11, 109–22

Goodin, Robert E., 2004: 'Representing Diversity', in: *British Journal of Political Science*, 34, 453–68

Görlach, Willi, Leinen, Jo, and Linkohr, Rolf, 2000: 'Die Europäische Union ist längst ein Staat', in: *Frankfurter Rundschau*, 27 November 2000

Grande, Edgar, 2000a: 'Post-National Democracy in Europe', in: Michael Th. Greven and Louis W. Pauly, eds., *Democracy beyond the State?*, Lanham, MD: Rowman & Littlefield, 115–38

Grande, Edgar, 2000b: 'Multi-Level Governance: Institutionelle Besonderheiten und Funktionsbedingungen des europäischen Mehrebenensystems', in: Edgar Grande and Markus Jachtenfuchs, eds., *Wie problemlösungsfähig ist die EU?*, Baden-Baden: Nomos, 11–30

Greven, Michael Th., 1997: 'Der politische Raum als Maß des Politischen – Europa als Beispiel', in: Thomas König, Elmar Rieger and Hermann Schmitt, eds., *Europäische Institutionenpolitik*, Frankfurt: Campus, 45–65

Greven, Michael Th., 2000: 'Can the European Union Finally Become a Democracy?', in: Michael Th. Greven and Louis W. Pauly, eds., *Democracy beyond the State?*, Lanham, MD: Rowman & Littlefield, 35–61

Grimm, Dieter, 1995: 'Does Europe Need a Constitution?', in: *European Law Journal*, 1 (3), 282–302

Grin, François, 2000: *Evaluating Policy-Measures for Minority Languages in Europe: Towards Effective, Cost-Effective and Democratic Implementation* (ECMI Report No. 6), Flensburg: European Centre for Minority Issues

Haarmann, Harald, 1991: 'Monolingualism versus Selective Multilingualism –
On the Future Alternatives for Europe as It Integrates in the 1990s', in: *Sociolinguistica*, 5, 7–23

Haarmann, Harald, 1993: *Die Sprachenwelt Europas*, Frankfurt: Campus

Haas, Ernst B., 1958: *The Uniting of Europe. Political, Social and Economical Forces 1950–1957*, London: Stevens & Sons

Häberle, Peter, 2000: *Gibt es eine europäische Öffentlichkeit?*, Berlin: de Gruyter

Habermas, Jürgen, 1981: *Theorie des kommunikativen Handelns*, 2 vols., Frankfurt: Suhrkamp

Habermas, Jürgen, 1990 [1962]: *Strukturwandel der Öffentlichkeit: Untersuchungen zu einer Kategorie der bürgerlichen Gesellschaft*, Frankfurt: Suhrkamp (new edition)

Habermas, Jürgen, 1998: *The Inclusion of the Other*, Cambridge, MA: MIT Press

Habermas, Jürgen, 2001: *The Postnational Constellation*, Cambridge, MA: MIT Press

Habermas, Jürgen, 2006: *Time of Transitions*, Cambridge, MA: MIT Press

Hagège, Claude, 1996: *Welche Sprache für Europa? Verständigung in der Vielfalt*, Frankfurt: Campus

Hagège, Claude, 2000: *Halte à la mort des langues*, Paris: Odile Jacob

Hallstein, Walter, 1973: *Die Europäische Gemeinschaft*, Düsseldorf: Econ

Haselhuber, Jakob, 1991: 'Erste Ergebnisse einer empirischen Untersuchung zur Sprachensituation in der EG-Kommission (Februar 1990)', in: *Sociolinguistica*, 5, 37–50

Held, David, 1995: *Democracy and the Global Order. From the Modern State to Cosmopolitan Governance*, Cambridge: Polity Press

Herder, Johann Gottfried, 2001 [1772]: *Abhandlung über den Ursprung der Sprache*, Stuttgart: Philipp Reclam jun.

Hilpold, Peter, 1996: 'La protecció de les minories lingüístiques a Àustria', in: *Els drets lingüístics a la nova Europa. Actes del Simposi Internacional de Llengües Europees i Legislacions*, Gandia (País Valencià), 2, 3 i 4 de març de 1995, Barcelona: Editorial Mediterrània, 128–53

Hix, Simon, 1999: *The Political System of the European Union*, New York: St. Martin's Press

Hobsbawm, Eric J., 1990: *Nations and Nationalism since 1780*, Cambridge University Press

Höffe, Ottfried, 2002: *Demokratie im Zeitalter der Globalisierung*, Munich: Beck

Holenstein, Elmar, 1998: *Kulturphilosophische Perspektiven: Schulbeispiel Schweiz; europäische Identität auf dem Prüfstand; globale Verständigungsmöglichkeiten*, Frankfurt: Suhrkamp

Honneth, Axel, 1994: *Kampf um Anerkennung. Zur moralischen Grammatik sozialer Konflikte*, Frankfurt: Suhrkamp

Honneth, Axel, 2003: 'Umverteilung als Anerkennung. Eine Erwiderung auf Nancy Fraser', in: Nancy Fraser and Axel Honneth: *Umverteilung oder Anerkennung?*, Frankfurt: Suhrkamp, 129–224

Hooghe, Liesbet, and Marks, Gary, 2001: *Multi-Level Governance and European Integration*, Lanham, MD: Rowman & Littlefield

Howe, Paul, 1995: 'A Community of Europeans: The Requisite Underpinnings', in: *Journal of Common Market Studies*, 33, 27–46

Ignatieff, Michael, 2000: *The Rights Revolution*, Toronto: Anansi

Ignatieff, Michael, 2003: *Empire Lite. Nation-Building in Bosnia, Kosovo, Afghanistan*, Toronto: Penguin

Jachtenfuchs, Markus, and Kohler-Koch, Beate, eds., 1996: *Europäische Integration*, Opladen: Leske + Budrich

Jacob, James E., and Gordon, David C., 1985: 'Language Policy in France', in: William R. Beer and James E. Jacob, eds., *Language Policy and National Unity*, Totowa, NJ: Rowman & Allanheld, 106–33

Jászi, Oscar, 1961 [1929]: *The Dissolution of the Habsburg Monarchy*, University of Chicago Press

Jennings, Ivor, 1956: *The Approach to Self-Government*, Cambridge University Press

Joerges, Christian, 1996: 'Das Recht im Prozeß der europäischen Integration', in: Markus Jachtenfuchs and Beate Kohler-Koch, eds., *Europäische Integration*, Opladen: Leske + Budrich, 73–108

Joerges, Christian, and Everson, Michelle, 2000: 'Challenging the Bureaucratic Challenge', in: Erik Oddvar Eriksen and John Erik Fossum, eds., *Democracy in the European Union. Integration through deliberation?*, London: Routledge, 164–88

Joerges, Christian, and Neyer, Jürgen, 1998: 'Von intergouvernementalem Verhandeln zur deliberativen Politik: Gründe und Chancen für eine Konstitutionalisierung der europäischen Komitologie', in: Beate Kohler-Koch, ed., *Regieren in entgrenzten Räumen*, Opladen: Westdeutscher Verlag (Politische Vierteljahresschrift, Sonderheft 29), 207–33

Jospin, Lionel, 2001: *L'avenir de l'Europe* [www.lemonde.fr/imprimer_article/0,6063,189921,00.html]

Judt, Tony, 1996: *A Grand Illusion? An Essay on Europe*, New York: Hill and Wang

Kaelble, Hartmut, 2001: *Wege zur Demokratie. Von der Französischen Revolution zur Europäischen Union*, Stuttgart: DVA

Keohane, Robert O., and Hoffmann, Stanley, eds., 1991: *The New European Community. Decisionmaking and Institutional Change*, Boulder, CO: Westview Press

Kielmansegg, Peter Graf, 1996: 'Integration und Demokratie', in: Markus Jachtenfuchs and Beate Kohler-Koch, eds., *Europäische Integration*, Opladen: Leske + Budrich, 47–71

Kohler-Koch, Beate, 1998: 'Die Europäisierung nationaler Demokratien: Verschleiß eines europäischen Kulturerbes?', in: Michael Th. Greven, ed., *Demokratie – eine Kultur des Westens?*, Opladen: Leske + Budrich, 263–88

Koslowski, Rey, 1999: 'A Constructivist Approach to Understanding the European Union as a Federal Polity', in: *Journal of European Public Policy*, 6, 561–78

Krasner, Stephen D. and Pascual, Carlos, 2005: 'Adressing State Failure', in: *Foreign Affairs*, 84 (4), 153–63

Kraus, Peter A., 1996: *Nationalismus und Demokratie. Politik im spanischen Staat der Autonomen Gemeinschaften*, Wiesbaden: Deutscher Universitäts-Verlag

Kraus, Peter A., 2000: 'Political Unity and Linguistic Diversity in Europe', in: *Archives Européennes de Sociologie*, XLI (1), 138–63

Kraus, Peter A., 2003: 'Cultural Pluralism and European Polity-Building: Neither Westphalia nor Cosmopolis', in: *Journal of Common Market Studies*, 41, 665–86

Kraus, Peter A., 2004: 'A Union of Peoples? Diversity and the Predicaments of a Multinational Polity', in: Lynn Dobson and Andreas Follesdal, eds.: *Political Theory and the European Constitution*, London: Routledge, 40–55

Kraus, Peter A., 2006: 'Legitimation, Democracy and Diversity in the European Union', in: *International Journal on Multicultural Societies*, 8 (2), 203–24

Kraus, Peter A., 2007: 'Katalonien im demokratischen Spanien', in: Walther L. Bernecker, Torsten Eßer and Peter A. Kraus: *Eine kleine Geschichte Kataloniens*, Frankfurt: Suhrkamp, 149–247

Kreile, Michael, ed., 1992: *Die Integration Europas*, Opladen: Westdeutscher Verlag (*Politische Vierteljahresschrift*, Sonderheft 23)

Krivine, Alain, 2000: 'Cosas vistas en el Parlamento Europeo', in: *El País*, 16 January 2000

Kymlicka, Will, 1995: *Multicultural Citizenship*, Oxford University Press

Kymlicka, Will, 1998: *Finding Our Way: Rethinking Ethnocultural Relations in Canada*, Toronto University Press

Laborde, Cécile, 2001: 'The Culture(s) of the Republic. Nationalism and Multiculturalism in French Republican Thought', in: *Political Theory*, 29, 716–35

Labrie, Normand, 1993: *La construction linguistique de la Communauté européenne*, Paris: Honoré Champion

Laffan, Brigid, 1996: 'The Politics of Identity and Political Order in Europe', in: *Journal of Common Market Studies*, 34, 81–102

Lafont, Robert, 1967: *La Révolution Régionaliste*, Paris: Gallimard

Laitin, David D., 1997: 'The Cultural Identities of a European State', in: *Politics and Society*, 25 (3), 277–302

Laitin, David D., 2000: 'Language Conflict and Violence: The Straw That Strengthens the Camel's Back', in: *Archives Européennes de Sociologie*, XLI (1), 97–137

Laponce, J.A., 1987: *Languages and Their Territories*, University of Toronto Press

Laurens, Olivier, 1994: 'Le projet européen de traduction automatique Eurotra', in: Claude Truchot, ed., *Le plurilinguisme européen. Théories et pratiques en théorie linguistique*, Paris: Champion, 389–408

Le Pourhiet, Anne-Marie, 2001: 'Langue(s) et Constitution(s)', in: *Raisons Politiques*, 2, 207–15

Leclerc, Jacques 2004: *Finlande* [http://www.tlfq.ulaval.ca/axl/europe/finlande.htm] (last update: 9 December 2004)

Leclerc, Jacques, 2005a: *Les langues par continent* [http://www.tlfq.ulaval.ca/axl/Langues/1div_continent.htm] (last update: 16 February 2005)

Leclerc, Jacques 2005b: *Belgique. Constitution coordonnée du 17 février 1994* [http://www.tlfq.ulaval.ca/axl/europe/belgiqueconst.htm] (last update: 26 April 2005)

Leclerc, Jacques 2005c: *Suisse fédérale* [http://www.tlfq.ulaval.ca/axl/europe/suissefed.htm] (last update: 21 August 2005)

Leclerc, Jacques 2005d: *France. Situation géopolitique et démolinguistique* [http://www.tlfq.ulaval.ca/axl/europe/france-1demo.htm] (last update: 14 December 2005)

Lehmbruch, Gerhard, 1983: 'Konkordanzdemokratie', in: Manfred G. Schmidt, ed., *Westliche Industriegesellschaften. Wirtschaft-Gesellschaft-Politik. Pipers Wörterbuch zur Politik, Vol. 2*, Munich: Piper, 198–203

Lepsius, M. Rainer, 1990: *Interessen, Ideen und Institutionen*, Opladen: Westdeutscher Verlag

Lepsius, M. Rainer, 1993: *Demokratie in Deutschland*, Göttingen: Vandenhoeck & Ruprecht

Lepsius, M. Rainer, 1999: 'Die Europäische Union. Ökonomisch-politische Integration und kulturelle Pluralität', in: Reinhold Viehoff and Rien T. Segers, eds., *Kultur. Identität. Europa. Über die Schwierigkeiten und Möglichkeiten einer Konstruktion*, Frankfurt: Suhrkamp, 201–22

Leton, André and Miroir, André, 1999: *Les conflits communautaires en Belgique*, Paris: PUF

Lijphart, Arend, 1977: *Democracy in Plural Societies*, New Haven: Yale University Press

Lindberg, Leon N., and Scheingold, Stuart A., 1970: *Europe's Would-Be Polity. Patterns of Change in the European Community*, Englewood Cliffs, NJ: Prentice-Hall

Linz, Juan J., and Stepan, Alfred, 1996: *Problems of Democratic Transition and Consolidation: Southern Europe, South America, and Post-Communist Europe*, Baltimore: Johns Hopkins University Press

Lockwood, David, 1964: 'Social Integration and System Integration', in: George K. Zollschan and Walter Hirsch, eds., *Explorations in Social Change*, Boston: Houghton Mifflin, 244–57

Loth, Wilfried, 1996: *Der Weg nach Europa*, Göttingen: Vandenhoeck & Ruprecht (3rd edition)

Maas, Utz, 1989: *Sprachpolitik und politische Sprachwissenschaft*, Frankfurt: Suhrkamp

Maas, Utz, Mehlem, Ulrich, and Schroeder, Christoph, 2004: 'Mehrsprachigkeit und Mehrschriftigkeit bei Migranten in Deutschland', in: Klaus J. Bade, Michael Bommes and Rainer Münz, eds., *Migrationsreport 2004. Fakten – Analysen – Perspektiven*, Frankfurt: Campus, 117–49

MacCormick, Neil, 1995: 'The *Maastricht-Urteil*: Sovereignty Now', in: *European Law Journal*, 1 (3), 259–66

MacCormick, Neil, 1999: *Questioning Sovereignty. Law, State, and Nation in the European Commonwealth*, Oxford University Press

Manent, Pierre, 1997: 'Democracy without Nations?', in: *Journal of Democracy*, 8 (2), 92–102

Mann, Michael, 2001: 'Globalization and September 11', in: *New Left Review*, 12, 51–72

Mann, Michael, 2005: *The Dark Side of Democracy. Explaining Ethnic Cleansing*, Cambridge University Press

Mansell, Robin and Steinmueller, W. Edward, 2000: *Mobilizing the Information Society*, Oxford University Press

March, James G., and Olsen, Johan P., 2000: 'Democracy and Schooling: An Institutional Perspective', in: Lorraine M. McDonnell, P. Michael Timpane and Roger Benjamin, eds., *Rediscovering the Democratic Purposes of Education*, Lawrence: University Press of Kansas

Marks, Gary, 1996: 'Politikmuster und Einflußlogik in der Strukturpolitik', in: Markus Jachtenfuchs and Beate Kohler-Koch, eds., *Europäische Integration*, Opladen: Leske + Budrich, 313–43

Marks, Gary, 1997: 'A Third Lens: Comparing European Integration and State Building', in: Jytte Klausen and Louise Tilly, eds., *European Integration in Social and Historical Perspective*, Lanham, MD: Rowman & Littlefield, 23–43

Marks, Gary, Scharpf, Fritz W., Schmitter, Philippe C., and Streeck, Wolfgang, 1996: *Governance in the European Union*, London: Sage

Marshall, T.H., 1950: *Citizenship and Social Class and Other Essays*, Cambridge University Press

McRae, Kenneth D., 1983: *Conflict and Compromise in Multilingual Societies, Vol. 1: Switzerland*, Waterloo, Ontario: Wilfrid Laurier University Press

McRae, Kenneth D., 1986: *Conflict and Compromise in Multilingual Societies, Vol. 2: Belgium*, Waterloo, Ontario: Wilfrid Laurier University Press

McRae, Kenneth D., 1997: *Conflict and Compromise in Multilingual Societies, Vol. 3: Finland*, Waterloo, Ontario: Wilfrid Laurier University Press

Meckel, Miriam, 1994: *Fernsehen ohne Grenzen? Europas Fernsehen zwischen Integration und Segmentierung*, Opladen: Westdeutscher Verlag

Meehan, Elizabeth, 1993: *Citizenship and the European Community*, London: Sage

Merleau-Ponty, Maurice, 1966: *Phänomenologie der Wahrnehmung*, Berlin: de Gruyter

Mill, John Stuart, 1972 [1861]: 'Considerations on Representative Government', in: John Stuart Mill: *Utilitarianism. Liberty. Representative Government* (ed. H. C. Acton), London: Dent, 187–428

Miller, David, 1995: *On Nationality*, Oxford: Clarendon Press

Milward, Alan S., 1992: *The European Rescue of the Nation-State*, London: Routledge

Moravcsik, Andrew, 1998: *The Choice for Europe. Social Purpose and State Power from Messina to Maastricht*, Ithaca, NY: Cornell University Press

Muschg, Adolf, 1998: 'Ein Land kommt sich abhanden', in: *Die Zeit*, 26 March 1998

Nemitz, Paul F., 2000: '10 Jahre Gericht Erster Instanz der Europäischen Gemeinschaften. Zur verfassungsgerichtsähnlichen Verantwortung des Gerichts im Beihilfenrecht', in: *Die öffentliche Verwaltung*, 53 (11), 437–49

Neunreither, Karlheinz, 1998: 'Governance without Opposition: The Case of the European Union', in: *Government and Opposition*, 33 (4), 419–41

Neunreither, Karlheinz, 2001: 'The European Union in Nice: A Minimalist Approach to a Historic Challenge', in: *Government and Opposition*, 36 (2), 184–208

Niess, Frank, 2001: *Die europäische Idee – aus dem Geist des Widerstands*, Frankfurt: Suhrkamp

Nissen, Silke, 2004: 'Europäische Identität und die Zukunft Europas', in: *APuZ*, 38, 21–9

Offe, Claus, 1998a: 'Demokratie und Wohlfahrtsstaat: Eine europäische Regimeform unter dem Streß der europäischen Integration', in: Wolfgang Streeck, ed., *Internationale Wirtschaft, nationale Demokratie. Herausforderungen für die Demokratietheorie*, Frankfurt: Campus, 99–136

Offe, Claus, 1998b: 'Designing Institutions in East European Transitions', in: Robert Goodin, ed., *The Theory of Institutional Design*, Cambridge University Press, 199–226

O'Neill, Michael, 1996: *The Politics of European Integration*, London: Routledge

Pakulski, Jan, 1997: 'Cultural Citizenship', in: *Citizenship Studies*, 1 (1), 73–86

Parekh, Bhikhu, 1997: 'Cultural Diversity and the Modern State', in: Martin Doornbos and Sudipta Kaviraj, eds., *Dynamics of State Formation. India and Europe Compared*, New Delhi: Sage, 177–203

Phillipson, Robert, 2003: *English-Only Europe? Challenging Language Policy*, London: Routledge

Phillipson, Robert, and Skutnabb-Kangas, Tove , 1994: 'English, Panacea or Pandemic', in: *Sociolinguistica*, 8, 73–87

Preuß, Ulrich K., 1999: 'Auf der Suche nach Europas Verfassung', in: *Transit*, 17, 154–74

Przeworski, Adam et al., 1995: *Sustainable Democracy*, Cambridge University Press

Puhle, Hans-Jürgen, 1995: *Staaten, Nationen und Regionen in Europa*, Vienna: Picus

Raeithel, Gert, 2000: 'Wir wollen viel Wow', in: *Der Spiegel*, 44 (30 Oct 2000), 240–4

Réaume, Denise, 1991: 'The Constitutional Protection of Language: Survival or Security?', in: David Schneiderman, ed., *Language and the State. The Law and Politics of Identity*, Cowansville: Les Éditions Yvon Blais, 37–57

Reese-Schäfer, Walter, 1999: 'Supranationale oder transnationale Identität. Zwei Modelle kultureller Integration in Europa', in: Reinhold Viehoff and Rien T. Segers, eds., *Kultur. Identität. Europa. Über die Schwierigkeiten und Möglichkeiten einer Konstruktion*, Frankfurt: Suhrkamp, 253–66

Reif, Karlheinz, 1993: 'Cultural Convergence and Cultural Diversity as Factors in European Identity', in: Soledad García, ed., *European Identity and the Search for Legitimacy*, London: Pinter, 131–53

Requejo, Ferran, 1999: 'Cultural Pluralism, Nationalism and Federalism: A Revision of Democratic Citizenship in Plurinational States', in: *European Journal of Political Research*, 35, 255–86

Requejo, Ferran, 2001: 'Political Liberalism in Multinational States: The Legitimacy of Plural and Asymmetrical Federalism', in: Alain-G. Gagnon and James Tully, eds., *Multinational Democracies*, Cambridge University Press, 110–32

Ricento, Thomas, 1998: 'National Language Policy in the United States', in: Thomas Ricento and Barbara Brunaby, eds., *Language and Politics in the United States and Canada. Myths and Realities*, Mahwah, NJ: Lawrence Erlbaum Associates, 85–112

Rifkin, Jeremy, 2004: *The European Dream*, New York: Tarcher/Penguin

Rokkan, Stein, 1975: 'Dimensions of State-Formation and Nation-Building: A Possible Paradigm for Research on Variations within Europe', in: Charles Tilly, ed., *The Formation of National States in Western Europe*, Princeton University Press, 562–600

Rokkan, Stein, 1999: *State Formation, Nation-Building, and Mass Politics in Europe*, Oxford University Press

Rokkan, Stein, and Urwin, Derek W., 1983: *Economy, Territory, Identity. Politics of West European Peripheries*, London: Sage

Ross, George, 1995: *Jacques Delors and European Integration*, Cambridge: Polity Press

Rousseau, Jean-Jacques, 1998 [1762]: *Du contrat social. Édition originale commentée par Voltaire*, Paris: Le Serpent à Plumes

Rustow, Dankwart A., 1975: 'Language, Nations, and Democracy', in: Jean-Guy Savard and Richard Vigneault, eds., *Les États multilingues: problèmes et solutions*, Québec: Les Presses de l'Université Laval, 43–60

Sbragia, Alberta M., ed., 1992: *Euro-Politics. Institutions and Policymaking in the "New" European Community*, Washington, DC: The Brookings Institution

Scharpf, Fritz W., 1994: *Optionen des Föderalismus in Deutschland und Europa*, Frankfurt: Campus

Scharpf, Fritz W., 1996: 'Politische Optionen im vollendeten Binnenmarkt', in: Markus Jachtenfuchs and Beate Kohler-Koch, eds., *Europäische Integration*, Opladen: Leske + Budrich, 109–40

Scharpf, Fritz W., 1997: 'Economic Integration, Democracy and the Welfare State', in: *Journal of European Public Policy*, 4, 18–36

Scharpf, Fritz W., 1999: *Governing in Europe: Effective and Democratic?*, Oxford University Press

Schlesinger, Philip, 1999: 'Changing Spaces of Political Communication: The Case of the European Union', in: *Political Communication*, 16, 263–79

Schlesinger, Philip, and Kevin, Deirdre, 2000: 'Can the European Union Become a Sphere of Publics?', in: Erik Oddvar Eriksen and John Erik Fossum, eds., *Democracy in the European Union. Integration through Deliberation?*, London: Routledge, 207–29

Schloßmacher, Michael, 1994: 'Die Arbeitssprachen in den Organen der Europäischen Gemeinschaft. Methoden und Ergebnisse einer empirischen Untersuchung', in: *Sociolinguistica*, 8, 101–22

Schmidt, Manfred G., 2000: 'Der konsoziative Staat. Hypothesen zur politischen Struktur und zum politischen Leistungsprofil der Europäischen Union', in: Edgar Grande and Markus Jachtenfuchs, eds., *Wie problemlösungsfähig ist die EU?*, Baden-Baden: Nomos, 33–57

Schmitter, Philippe C., 1996a: 'Examining the Present Euro-Polity with the Help of Past Theories', in: Gary Marks, Fritz W. Scharpf, Philippe C. Schmitter and Wolfgang Streeck: *Governance in the European Union*, London: Sage, 1–14

Schmitter, Philippe C., 1996b: 'Imagining the Future of the Euro-Polity with the Help of New Concepts', in: Gary Marks, Fritz W. Scharpf, Philippe C. Schmitter and Wolfgang Streeck: *Governance in the European Union*, London: Sage, 121–50

Schmitter, Philippe C., 2000: *How to Democratize the European Union . . . And Why Bother?*, Lanham, MD: Rowman & Littlefield

Schneider, Heinrich, 1977: *Leitbilder der Europapolitik 1. Der Weg zur Integration*, Bonn: Europa Union Verlag

Schöpflin, George, 1999: 'Globalisierung und Identität. Gehört die Zukunft dem Ethnischen?', in: *Transit*, 17, 46–54

Schulze, Hagen, 1999: *Staat und Nation in der europäischen Geschichte*, Munich: Beck

Shore, Chris, 2000: *Building Europe. The Cultural Politics of European Integration*, London: Routledge

Siedentop, Larry, 2000: *Democracy in Europe*, London: Penguin

Siguan, Miquel, 1995: *L'Europa de les llengües*, Barcelona: edicions 62

Special Eurobarometer 243, 2006: Europeans and Their Languages

Spruyt, Hendrik, 1994: *The Sovereign State and Its Competitors*, Princeton University Press

Stråth, Bo, 2000a: 'Europe as a Discourse', in: Bo Stråth, ed., *Europe and the Other and Europe as the Other*, Brussels: P. I. E.-Peter Lang, 13–44

Stråth, Bo, 2000b: 'Multiple Europes: Integration, Identity and Demarcation to the Other', in: Bo Stråth, ed., *Europe and the Other and Europe as the Other*, Brussels: P.I.E.-Peter Lang, 385–420

Streeck, Wolfgang, 1996: 'Neo-Voluntarism: A New European Social Policy Regime?', in: Gary Marks, Fritz W. Scharpf, Philippe C. Schmitter and Wolfgang Streeck: *Governance in the European Union*, London: Sage, 64–94

Streeck, Wolfgang, 1998: 'Einleitung: Internationale Wirtschaft, nationale Demokratie?', in: Wolfgang Streeck, ed., *Internationale Wirtschaft, nationale Demokratie. Herausforderungen für die Demokratietheorie*, Frankfurt: Campus, 11–58

Streeck, Wolfgang, 1999: 'Vom Binnenmarkt zum Bundesstaat? Überlegungen zur politischen Ökonomie der europäischen Sozialpolitik', in: Wolfgang Streeck: *Korporatismus in Deutschland. Zwischen Nationalstaat und Europäischer Union*, Frankfurt: Campus, 67–111

Stubb, Alexander C.-G., 1996: 'A Categorization of Differentiated Integration', in: *Journal of Common Market Studies*, 34, 283–95

Sunstein, Cass, 2001: *republic.com*, Princeton University Press

Symonides, Janusz, 1998: 'Cultural Rights: A Neglected Category of Human Rights', in: *International Social Science Journal*, 156, 559–72

Tamir, Yael, 1993: *Liberal Nationalism*, Princeton University Press

Tarlton, Charles, 1965: 'Symmetry and Asymmetry as Elements of Federalism: A Theoretical Speculation', in: *Journal of Politics*, 27 (4), 861–74

Tarrow, Sidney, 2001: 'Contentious Politics in a Composite Polity', in: Doug Imig and Sidney Tarrow, eds., *Contentious Europeans: Protest and Politics in an Emerging Polity*, Oxford: Rowman & Littlefield, 233–251

Taylor, Charles, 1985: *Human Agency and Language. Philosophical Papers I*, Cambridge University Press

Taylor, Charles, 1989: *Sources of the Self*, Cambridge, MA: Harvard University Press

Taylor, Charles, 1992: *Multiculturalism and "The Politics of Recognition"*, Princeton University Press

Taylor, Charles, 1994: *Reconciling the Solitudes. Essays on Canadian Federalism and Nationalism*, Montreal & Kingston: McGill–Queen's University Press

Taylor, Charles, 1995: *Philosophical Arguments*, Cambridge, MA: Harvard University Press

Taylor, Charles 2003: 'No Community, No Democracy, Part I', in: *The Responsive Community*, 13 (4), 17–27

Taylor, Charles 2004: 'No Community, No Democracy, Part II', in: *The Responsive Community*, 14 (1), 15–23

Taylor, Paul, 1990: 'Consociationalism and Federalism as Approaches to International Integration', in: A. J. R. Groom and Paul Taylor, eds., *Frameworks for International Cooperation*, London: Pinter, 172–84

Teasdale, Anthony L., 1999: 'The Politics of the 1999 European Elections', in: *Government and Opposition*, 34 (4), 435–55

Therborn, Göran, 1977: 'The Rule of Capital and the Rise of Democracy', in: *New Left Review*, 103, 3–41

Thiel, Elke, 1998: *Die Europäische Union. Von der Integration der Märkte zu gemeinsamen Politiken*, Opladen: Leske + Budrich

Tilly, Charles, 1990: *Coercion, Capital, and European States, AD 990–1990*, Oxford: Blackwell

Tilly, Charles, 1992: 'Futures of European States', in: *Social Research*, 59, 705–17

Tiryakian, Edward A., and Rogowski, Ronald, eds., 1985: *New Nationalisms of the Developed West*, Boston: Allen & Unwin

Toivanen, Reetta, 2000: *Minderheitenrechte als Identitätsressource. Die Sorben in Deutschland und die Saamen in Finnland*, Hamburg: LIT

Toivanen, Reetta, 2005: 'Das Paradox der Minderheitenrechte in Europa', in: *SWS-Rundschau*, 45 (2), 185–207

Tomuschat, Christian, 1996: 'Menschenrechte und Minderheitenschutz', in: Hanspeter Neuhold and Bruno Simma, eds., *Neues europäisches Völkerrecht nach dem Ende des Ost-West-Konfliktes?*, Baden-Baden: Nomos, 89–110

'Treaty establishing a Constitution for Europe', 2004: *Official Journal of the European Union*, C 310, 47, 16 December 2004

Tully, James, 1995: *Strange Multiplicity. Constitutionalism in an Age of Diversity*, Cambridge University Press

Tully, James, 2000: 'Struggles over Recognition and Distribution', in: *Constellations*, 7 (4), 469–82

Tully, James, 2001: 'Introduction', in: Alain-G. Gagnon and James Tully, eds., *Multinational Democracies*, Cambridge University Press, 1–33

Turner, Bryan S., 1994: 'Postmodern Culture/Modern Citizens', in: Bart van Steenbergen, ed., *The Condition of Citizenship*, London: Sage, 153–68

Ukkola, Jukka, 1997: 'Emusta Eluun', in: *Suomen Kuvalehti*, 25–26, 19 June 1997

Usher, John A., 1998: 'Languages and the European Union', in: Malcolm Anderson and Eberhard Bort, eds., *The Frontiers of Europe*, London: Pinter, 222–34

van Hoof-Haferkamp, Renée, 1991: 'L'interprétation de conférence à la Communauté européenne', in: *Sociolinguistica*, 5, 64–9

van Kersbergen, Kees and Verbeek, Bertjan, 1994: 'The Politics of Subsidiarity in the European Union', in: *Journal of Common Market Studies*, 32, 215–36

Van Parijs, Philippe, 2000a: 'Should Europe be Belgian? On the Institutional Design of Multilingual Polities', in: Karl Hinrichs, Herbert Kitschelt and Helmut Wiesenthal, eds., *Kontingenz und Krise. Institutionenpolitik in kapitalistischen und postsozialistischen Gesellschaften*, Frankfurt: Campus, 59–78

Van Parijs, Philippe, 2000b: 'The Ground Floor of the World: On the Socio-economic Consequences of Linguistic Globalization', in: *International Political Science Review*, 21 (2), 217–33

Van Parijs, Philippe, 2004: 'Europe's Linguistic Challenge', in: *Archives Européennes de Sociologie*, XLV (1), 113–54

Vandamme, Jacques, 1994: 'La citoyenneté européenne comme élement d'identité européenne', in: Robert Picht, ed., *L'Identité Européenne. Analyses et propositions pour le renforcement d'une Europe pluraliste*, Brussels: Presses Interuniversitaires Européennes, 253–70

Voigt, Rüdiger, 1996: *Des Staates neue Kleider. Entwicklungslinien moderner Staatlichkeit*, Baden-Baden: Nomos

Volz, Walter, 1994: 'Englisch als einzige Arbeitssprache der Institutionen der Europäischen Gemeinschaft? Vorzüge und Nachteile aus der Sicht eines Insiders', in: *Sociolinguistica*, 8, 88–100

von Beyme, Klaus, 1999: *Die parlamentarische Demokratie*, Opladen: Westdeutscher Verlag (3rd edition)

von Busekist, Astrid, 1998: *La Belgique. Politique des langues et construction de l'État*, Paris: Duculot

von Humboldt, Wilhelm, 1963 [1830–1835]: *Ueber die Verschiedenheit des menschlichen Sprachbaues und ihren Einfluss auf die geistige Entwicklung des Menschengeschlechts*, in: ders.: *Werke in fünf Bänden, III, Schriften zur Sprachphilosophie*, Berlin: Rütten & Loening, 368–756

Walker, Neil, 2004: 'The Legacy of Europe's Constitutional Moment', in: *Constellations*, 11 (3), 368–92

Wallace, Helen, 1997: 'Pan-European Integration: A Real or Imagined Community?', in: *Government and Opposition*, 32 (2), 215–33

Wallace, Helen, 1999: 'Whose Europe Is It Anyway? The 1998 Stein Rokkan Lecture', in: *European Journal of Political Research*, 35, 287–306

Warner, Michael, 1990: *The Letters of the Republic: Publication and the Public Sphere in Eighteenth-Century America*, Cambridge, MA: Harvard University Press

Waschkuhn, Arno, 1995: *Was ist Subsidiarität? Ein sozialphilosophisches Ordnungsprinzip: Von Thomas von Aquin bis zur "Civil Society"*, Opladen: Westdeutscher Verlag

Weber, Eugen, 1976: *Peasants into Frenchmen*, Stanford University Press

Weiler, J.H.H., 1991: 'The Transformation of Europe', in: *Yale Law Journal*, 100, 2403–83

Weiler, J.H.H., 1995: 'Does Europe Need a Constitution? Reflections on Demos, Telos and the German Maastricht Decision', in: *European Law Journal*, 1 (3), 219–58

Weiler, J.H.H., 1999: *The Constitution of Europe*, Cambridge University Press

Weiler, J.H.H., 2001: 'Federalism without Constitutionalism: Europe's *Sonderweg*', in: Kalypso Nicolaidis and Robert Howse, eds., *The Federal Vision. Legitimacy and Levels of Governance in the United States and the European Union*, Oxford University Press, 54–70

Weiler, J.H.H., 2004: *Ein christliches Europa. Erkundungsgänge*, Salzburg: Pustet

Weinstein, Brian, 1990: 'Language Policy and Political Development: An Overview', in: Brian Weinstein, ed., *Language Policy and Political Development*, Norwood, NJ: Ablex, 1–21

Wessels, Wolfgang, 1997: 'An Ever Closer Fusion? A Dynamic Macropolitical View on Integration Processes', in: *Journal of Common Market Studies*, 35, 267–99

Wildenmann, Rudolf, ed., 1991: *Staatswerdung Europas? Optionen für eine Europäische Union*, Baden-Baden: Nomos

Wright, Sue, 2000: *Community and Communication. The Role of Language in Nation State Building and European Integration*, Clevedon: Multilingual Matters

Wuorinen, John, 1931: *Nationalism in Modern Finland*, New York: Columbia University Press

Zetterholm, Staffan, 1994: 'Why Is Cultural Diversity a Political Problem? A Discussion of Cultural Barriers to Political Integration', in: Staffan Zetterholm, ed., *National Cultures and European Integration. Explanatory Essays on Cultural Diversity and Common Policies*, Oxford: Berg, 65–82

Zolberg, Aristide R., 1977: 'Splitting the Difference: Federalization without Federalism in Belgium', in: Milton J. Esman, ed., *Ethnic Conflict in the Western World*, Ithaca, NY: Cornell University Press, 103–42

Zolo, Danilo, 1992: *Democracy and Complexity*, Cambridge: Polity Press

Zürn, Michael, 2000: 'Democratic Governance beyond the Nation-State', in: Michael Th. Greven and Louis W. Pauly, eds., *Democracy beyond the State?*, Lanham, MD: Rowman & Littlefield, 91–114

Index

Other books in the series (*continued from page iii*)

Jonas Tallberg   *Leadership and Negotiation in the European Union*
Rachel A. Cichowski   *The European Court and Civil Society: Litigation, Mobilization and Governance*
Simon Hix, Abdul G. Noury and Gérard Roland   *Democratic Politics in the European Parliament*